# Stirring the Head, Heart, AND Soul

Third Edition

Third Edition

# Stirring the Head, Heart, AND Soul

*Redefining Curriculum, Instruction, and Concept-Based Learning*

# H. LYNN ERICKSON

**CORWIN PRESS**
A SAGE Company
Thousand Oaks, CA 91320

*For information*:

Corwin Press
A SAGE Company
2455 Teller Road
Thousand Oaks, California 91320
www.corwinpress.com

SAGE Ltd.
1 Oliver's Yard
55 City Road
London EC1Y 1SP
United Kingdom

SAGE India Pvt. Ltd.
B 1/I 1 Mohan Cooperative
   Industrial Area
Mathura Road, New Delhi 110 044
India

SAGE Asia-Pacific Pte. Ltd.
33 Pekin Street #02–01
Far East Square
Singapore 048763

Printed in the United States of America

*Library of Congress Cataloging-in-Publication Data*

Erickson, H. Lynn.
Stirring the head, heart, and soul: Redefining curriculum, instruction, and concept-based learning/H. Lynn Erickson.—3rd ed.
        p. cm.
Includes bibliographical references and index.
ISBN 978-1-4129-2521-1 (cloth)
ISBN 978-1-4129-2522-8 (pbk.)
    1. Curriculum change—United States.  2.  Curriculum-based assessment—United States.
3. Educational change—United States.  4.  Educational tests and measurements—United States.
I. Title.

LB1570.E74 2008
375.000973—dc22                                    2007029951

This book is printed on acid-free paper.

07  08  09  10  11    10  9  8  7  6  5  4  3  2  1

| | |
|---|---|
| *Acquisitions Editor:* | Cathy Hernandez |
| *Editorial Assistants:* | Megan Bedell and Cathleen Mortensen |
| *Production Editor:* | Melanie Birdsall |
| *Copy Editor:* | Alison Hope |
| *Typesetter:* | C&M Digitals (P) Ltd. |
| *Proofreader:* | Gail Fay |
| *Indexer:* | Sylvia Coates |
| *Cover Designer:* | Lisa Miller |

# Contents

# Preface

Innovations launch in schools like fireworks in July. Some explode with a bang, like the "whole language" movement, and whiz back and forth trying to find their philosophical resting place. Some, like the 1970s "new math," shoot straight up and then nose-dive, leaving a trail of fading light. Some give a little "pop," hoping for attention, and some, like the National Standards and No Child Left Behind legislation, implode with a sonic boom as we run for cover from the fallout.

As an educator over the past four decades, I helped to detonate some of the dazzling displays. Through these experiences, I gained a sense of when to tuck and when to toss from Innovation's door. Eager to aid learning, educators embrace innovation and fad with wholesale zealousness. We buy the program dogma with nary a question, disregarding the research that doesn't fit into the popular paradigm instead of asking, "What is reasonable, and what is not?"

This book will discuss what is reasonable and workable in contemporary curriculum design and provide educators with a practical structure for deciding whether to tuck or toss from the dizzying display of the day. The overriding message throughout this book will be the need to design curriculum and instruction that will guide thinking and learning from the factual level to the conceptual level of understanding—the level where knowledge transfers and thinking become integrated.

The standards movement, so prominent today, defines student standards as "what we want our students to know and be able to do by the time they graduate from high school." In districts across the United States, these standards deal with processes and skills, factual content knowledge, and conceptual understanding. Standards provide an anchor for aligning district curricula, but standards vary in their expectations and design. In some states, the design raises the intellectual bar for district curricula; in others, the state design actually impedes quality curricular programming and instruction.

National and state policy makers call for performance-based assessments using benchmark indicators of progress, at various grade levels, to ensure that students are attaining the identified process and content abilities. Benchmark indicators are examples of developmental performance related to the student standards that have been identified for various grade levels or grade groupings.

This book will examine the current state of curriculum and instruction and propose a curricular plan for achieving higher standards without sacrificing intellectual integrity. The proposed plan will focus on the following premises:

- Thinking teachers inspire thinking students. We need curriculum frameworks that encourage teachers to use facts and skills to develop a deeper understanding of key concepts and principles of disciplines.
- When curriculum and instruction engage the personal intellect of students (and teachers), students are more motivated and interested in the study, and exhibit a greater degree of retention and understanding.
- Self-assessment is a powerful learning tool for both students and teachers.
- Curriculum that is relevant to issues surrounding the human condition and our world challenges the intellect and engages the spirit.
- Concept-based curricula are more effective than topic-based curricula, for the world of today and tomorrow, because they take teaching and learning to a higher level as students analyze, synthesize, and generalize from facts to deeper understanding.

As you read the following chapters, you will evaluate the elements and impediments of the change process in learning organizations, and you will look at the factors of time, training, and funding. You will design a vision for learning that links desired student outcomes with sound schooling practice. You will learn new approaches to the development of subject area and interdisciplinary curricula, and explore the changing character of student assessment. Finally, you will consider what it takes to stir the head, heart, and soul and form a vision of loving to learn. Students and teachers who love to learn create positive tension and energy that ripples through a room with enthusiasm, curiosity, and creativity. It is my hope that you will leave this book with that same creative tension and energy—loving to learn and eager to stir the head, heart, and soul.

# Acknowledgments

S pecial thanks to critical friends who provided suggestions and reviews for different portions of this book:

- Paulett Ellis, CTE Professional Development and Curriculum Specialist, Department of Education on the Arizona Career and Technical Education Program, Arizona
- Dr. Lois Lanning, Assistant Superintendent, Pomperaug Regional School District 15, Middlebury/Southbury, Connecticut
- Del Whitmire, English and Drama Instructor, Green Bay Public Schools, Green Bay, Wisconsin

Corwin Press gratefully acknowledges the contributions of the following reviewers:

Janet Crews
Instructional Coach
Clayton School District
Clayton, MO

Raymond A. Lowery
Principal
Alief Kerr High School
Houston, TX

Beverly Ellen Schoonmaker Alfeld
Educational Consultant
Crystal Lake, IL

Ann P. Monroe-Baillargeon
Associate Professor and Chair
Division of Education, Alfred
    University
Alfred, NY

# About the Author

**H. Lynn Erickson** is an independent consultant assisting schools and districts around the country and internationally with curriculum design. From 1987 to 1994, she was Director of Curriculum for the Federal Way Public Schools in Federal Way, Washington. She is a recognized presenter at national conferences and is featured in the video *Creating Concept-Based Curriculum for Deep Understanding* (produced by The Video Journal), as well as in videos for the Association for Supervision and Curriculum Development. She is the author of *Concept-Based Curriculum and Instruction for the Thinking Classroom* (2007).

She was born and raised in Fairbanks, Alaska, the daughter of a pioneering gold miner and a first-grade teacher. She graduated from the University of Alaska in 1968 and taught different levels for 12 years. She also served as a reading specialist before moving with her family to Missoula, Montana. At the University of Montana, she earned master's and doctorate degrees in Curriculum and Instruction and Advanced School Administration. She worked as the Curriculum Coordinator for Missoula's Public Schools before becoming a school principal for six years in Libby, Montana.

She and Ken Erickson have two grown children, Kelly Cameron and Kenneth Erickson; a daughter-in-law, Jodie Erickson; and two grandsons, Trevor and Conner Cameron. They stir her heart and soul. When she isn't traveling to school districts, she and Ken enjoy rollerblading, motorcycle riding, and flying.

Lynn Erickson's e-mail address is lynn.erickson@comcast.net if you would like to share thoughts on this book.

# Making Change in a Changing World

## THE STATE OF EDUCATIONAL CHANGE

### Innovations and Restructuring

Everybody is doing it. Ask an elementary grade teacher anywhere in the country, "What are the innovations in your school?" and the litany ensues: "differentiation, curriculum mapping, **cooperative learning**, interdisciplinary curriculum, inclusion, professional learning communities," and so on. Secondary schools are joining many of the elementary grade movements and adding innovations of their own, from creative block scheduling to theme-based high schools and academies.

The national impetus to restructure schools and improve education has brought us into the best and worst of times. The best of times:

- Encouraging alternative approaches to school structures such as academies, and programs such as the International Baccalaureate diploma program
- Articulating clearly in **curriculum** documents what students should know and be able to do in an increasingly complex world
- Helping students develop greater self-efficacy and self-esteem as they take more responsibility for learning
- Encouraging teachers to design learning experiences for students instead of relying solely on textbooks as the controller of what and how to teach
- Critically examining education at all levels in light of changing paradigms for teaching and learning

But the current pressure to raise test scores at all costs yields troubling practices in too many schools, reflecting the worst of times:

- A narrowing of the curriculum to "test-item" teaching, or the sacrifice of science and social studies in the earlier grades to make more time for reading and mathematics skill drill. The photocopier gasps for air.

- "Frill" programs such as art, music, and physical education are cut to make more time for "real" academics. Oh—and let's cut that real time waster in the elementary grade levels: recess.
- Less teacher-designed instruction and a heavy, increased reliance on textbook or scripted programs. New programs are purchased with abandon, each one purported to be the silver bullet to achieve success. The plethora of programs leads to teacher confusion as they try to sort everything out and plan a coherent program of instruction in the limited school day.
- Secondary schools cut back—or cut out—**career and technical education** because of their cost, or implement a laser-like emphasis on core academic **standards** and college preparation for all students.
- And finally, there is the issue of student and teacher drop-out:
  o Too often, students who feel they cannot make the grade drop out in middle school or high school rather than be tagged a no-diploma failure.
  o Teachers and administrators leave the profession because they feel that the narrow focus on test scores has changed the institution—the tried and true philosophy of nurturing the "whole child" in American education is being replaced by a narrow numbers perspective, and the art and joy of teaching is being drained away.

One can understand the panic felt by administrators and teachers to raise test scores under the pressure of the federal No Child Left Behind Act (NCLB), especially when test scores are published in newspapers school by school, and when pay is tied to score increases, but we must step back and assess the bigger picture. What are the goals of education today?

Richard Rothstein, research associate of the Economic Policy Institute, and Rebecca Jacobsen, a doctoral candidate at Teachers College, Columbia University, shared their thoughts on public attitudes toward historically supported educational goals for American schools in a *Phi Delta Kappan* article (2006). Rothstein and Jacobsen were involved in researching the historical perspectives from the Founding Fathers in the mid-1700s through to the current court battles in numerous states over the definition and financing of an "adequate education."

Historically, education has called for a balanced curriculum that addresses the basic academics of core subjects, as well as the social, emotional, and physical areas of students' growth and development. Different periods of history also called for appreciation and knowledge of the arts and literature, of civic and community responsibility, and of preparation for skilled work. Foundationally, the public school goals required that students learn how to think critically and problem solve.

Rothstein and Jacobsen surveyed representative samples of all American adults, school board members, state legislators, and school superintendents and asked them to rank the relative importance of the historically valued goals. All groups assigned value to each of the diverse goal areas. The average ranking of importance gave "Basic Academic Skills in Core Subjects" the top rank, followed closely by "Critical Thinking and Problem Solving," "Social Skills and Work Ethic," "Citizenship and Community Responsibility," and, finally, "Preparation for Skilled Work."

The authors ask us to consider whether the narrow test focus of the federal NCLB Act on reading, mathematics, and science is preventing schools from addressing the broader goals in American education. That is an interesting consideration. If broader goals are still supported, then it is apparent that test scores for a few subject areas should not be the only focus. Curriculum design and instruction need to take center stage in redesign efforts in schools and school districts to create balanced programs. We can raise academic standards without losing sight of the broader goals in education.

# PRESSURE GROUPS

As schools struggle to define a quality education, they receive conflicting messages from a society carrying multiple agendas and worldviews, which makes the job of educational change very complex. Five pressure groups are especially pronounced: (1) business and the world of work, (2) state governments, (3) social forces, (4) media, and (5) parents. It is important to understand their views and concerns if we are to effectively educate for the diverse needs of society.

## Business and the World of Work

The globalization of economics and trade, stimulated by advances in technology and transportation, has changed the traditional business models forever. Employers decry the quality of education in the United States and lament, "If only workers had the skills we need, our companies could be more economically competitive in the global marketplace."

### The Global Economy

The famed economist Lester Thurow (1993), in his provocative and thoughtful book, *Head to Head: The Coming Economic Battle Among Japan, Europe, and America,* cites the following questions as central to the global economic competition:

> Who can make the best products? Who expands their standard of living most rapidly? Who has the best-educated and best-skilled work force in the world? Who is the world's leader in investment—plant and equipment, research and development (R&D), infrastructure? Who organizes best? Whose institutions—government, education, business—are world leaders in efficiency? (p. 23)

These questions continue to frame global economic competition today. China, India, Mexico, and other countries that can provide less-costly labor draw the production lines of major corporations to their shores—creating complex arterials for product development and dissemination.

In his newer book, *Building Wealth: New Rules for Individuals, Companies and Countries in a Knowledge-Based Economy,* Thurow (1999) acknowledges that as we enter the 21st century the United States is experiencing economic anxieties. The middle class in the United States is shrinking. Although some people are making economic gains, many more are losing ground and experiencing a lowered standard of living. For two-thirds of the workforce, real wages are below where they were in 1973. Since the publication of Thurow's book, workers in the United States are feeling the blunt realities of global competition—from major industries outsourcing jobs to other countries, to cutbacks in employee pension and healthcare plans, to massive layoffs and the need for retraining into new fields of work. Heads are spinning.

Thurow (1999) states that the developing industries at the heart of this global competition are all "brainpower industries":

> Microelectronics, computers, telecommunications, new man-made materials, robotics, and biotechnology are spawning new industries and reinventing old industries. . . . The science behind these new industries is revolutionizing our lives. Internet retailing supplants conventional retailing. Cellular telephones are everywhere. Genetically engineered plants and animals appear. . . . It is an era of man-made brain-power industries. For all of human history, the source of wealth has been the control of natural resources—land, gold, oil. Suddenly the answer is "knowledge." The world's wealthiest man, Bill Gates, owns nothing tangible—no land, no gold or oil, no factories, no industrial processes, no armies. . . . The world's wealthiest man owns only knowledge. (pp. xiv–xv)

Will the traditional U.S. curriculum provide the kind of knowledge and skills that our workforce needs to secure a strong future for all? Regular education is aligning curriculum and instruction to state academic standards to raise achievement levels. Tests, rewards, and sanctions are supposed to motivate excellence, but states vary greatly in the degree to which their standards require conceptual understanding of content knowledge and higher levels of thinking. Some standards are so factually oriented that thinking will never get off the basement floor: "Identify the first governor of _____." Some are so broad and conceptual that it is anyone's guess as to the essential, transferable understandings: "Examine systems." And some are just right—clear and powerful conceptual understandings with enough specificity to bring relevance to the district-defined curricula: "Understand that energy is a property of substances and systems and comes in many forms." Standards need to keep moving toward "just right" in the coming refinements if we are going to develop the kinds of thinking abilities and depth of content knowledge that are required for citizenship as well as for work roles.

The rapid changes occurring in the workplace are also affecting the curriculum of surviving career education programs by emphasizing the infusion of rigorous academic content, problem solving, teamwork, and the use of technology in conjunction with real-world simulations and experiences. The critical need for a quality workforce has been a major impetus for the development of high-level work skills aligned with academic standards in the traditionally differentiated, academic, and career education classrooms. Model programs to blend career and technical education with academic programming are growing around the country through programs such as career pathways and applied academics. These trends need to be supported.

*Salable Skills in the Global Market*

The National Center on Education and the Economy (NCEE) (2007, pp. xvi–xvii) outlines the challenge in creating a competitive workforce for the United States. Students in the United States are in the middle to the bottom of the list when compared with students in other industrial nations. The global economy has rocked our work world—with many well-paying jobs being automated or out-sourced to other countries at an alarming rate. The NCEE report reminds us that

> the best employers the world over will be looking for the most competent, most creative, and most innovative people on the face of the earth and will be willing to pay them top dollar for their services. Strong skills in English, mathematics, technology, and science, as well as literature, history, and the arts will be essential for many; beyond this, candidates will have to be comfortable with ideas and abstractions, good at both analysis and synthesis, creative and innovative, self-disciplined and well organized, able to learn very quickly and work well as a member of a team and have the flexibility to adapt quickly to frequent changes in the labor market as the shifts in the economy become ever faster and more dramatic. (2007, pp. xviii–xix)

Advances in technology have created a time warp in which old methods and ways of thinking leave industries in the dust, and in which expanded communication and interdependence demand big-picture thinking. In business and in our communities, we must now deal with the issues and complexities of global systems: economic, social, and political.

William Greider (1997), in *One World, Ready or Not: The Manic Logic of Global Capitalism,* states, "The national interest must now find expression in the far more complex context of the collective global interest" (p. 470). For example,

> the history of nation-states . . . has been a series of armed contests for territory and domination, but the traditional geopolitical assumptions are now quite confused as global commerce dilutes the meaning of national borders and constructs complex webs of interdependence. . . . It becomes increasingly difficult to select a proper enemy—someone who is not also a major customer or co-producer. (pp. 470–71)

To further complicate this picture of global economics, the 21st century has opened with violent eruptions of conflict in the Middle East, as well as with nuclear threats that create a boiling cauldron of tensions fed by issues of power and control, and by deeply held values and beliefs. Global interaction has spawned global conflict—and economics becomes a nervous bystander waiting for the political dust to settle.

## State Governments

State governments, the second pressure group, have set up commissions and panels to evaluate and plan for a restructured system of education. Goals are defined and standards set. But have state governments required academic standards that would develop the conceptual and critical thinking abilities alluded to by Lester Thurow and the National Council on Economic Education? Have state governments required standards that would develop citizens who are ready to address in a flexible manner the rapidly changing problems and issues of this complex, interdependent world? A review of state standards will show that some states have a conceptual framework for nesting the specific content of the local districts, whereas other states have mandated standards that resemble the district curricular frameworks of old—right down to the last war, date, and general. If only they realized the impact in classrooms: each year, teachers race to cover more material faster, and the goal of intellectual pursuit is forced to compete with trivial pursuit.

State governments in the United States have largely supported the idea of school competition—the panacea offered by business for the problems of education—so they offer vouchers to parents to "buy" the education of choice. A menu of schooling types has sprung up, from religious private schools, to business-run for-profit schools, to public schools.

*The 15th Bracey Report on the Condition of Public Education* (Bracey, 2005) summarizes the ongoing debate over the success of private charter schools. The 2004 NAEP (National Assessment of Educational Progress) test data (NAEP, 2005) did not raise the victory banner for charter schools. According to Gerald Bracey, even though Chester Finn—then head of the National Assessment Governing Board (the 26-member board that sets policy for the NAEP)—had suggested using the NAEP to analyze charter school performance, "he [and other prominent advocates] rejected the NAEP results when they did not show higher achievement when compared to regular public schools." Their argument was that the data was not disaggregated by ethnicity and other socio-economic factors, even though Mr. Finn had vetoed an earlier intent to disaggregate the scores fearing it would "mask poor performance" (Bracey, 2005, p. 144).

In fact, the *Bracey Report* stated that the U.S. Department of Education did not publish the charter school NAEP data along with the regular NAEP results. After an analysis of the NAEP data by the American Federation of Teachers (AFT) and subsequent publication of the charter school results, the U.S. Department of Education presented its own review in December 2004. The results aligned with the AFT analysis: "Of the 22 reading and math comparisons, 20 favored regular public schools, one was a tie, and one favored charters by a single point" (Bracey, 2005, p. 144).

It is really not a puzzle as to why private charter schools generally score similarly or more poorly than public schools when we consider these questions:

- Where are private charter schools finding their teachers?
- Who is designing their curricula? How are they different from the curricula that are currently being taught in public schools? Is it just "more technology" and perhaps "foreign language earlier," or is it truly an insightfully designed masterpiece that meets the needs of developing learners of varying abilities?
- Do the for-profits accept all students, or do they find ways to be selective, thus skewing the results? For many years, there have been accusations of selectivity among private schools.
- Who trains the teachers in for-profit schools, and what is the content of their inservice training? Have they and our regular public school teachers been trained at different preservice institutions?
- Just what are the silver bullets that purport to make for-profit schools succeed over public schools?

I suspect there is little variance between private and public schools after these comparisons have been taken into account.

As a result of the private charter school movement, many public school districts—such as those in Boston, Massachusetts, and Toledo, Ohio—have started their own innovative charter schools rather than pay money and lose students to the for-profit schools.

One thing is certain—to prepare students for today and tomorrow, curriculum and instruction must change from traditional models based on coverage and rote memorization. They must change because these old models do not develop the conceptual, creative, and critical thinking abilities that are now essential for complex problem solving.

So whether schools are public, private, or for profit, they need a deeper understanding of how to redesign curriculum and instruction. Otherwise, the national frustration over schooling will continue.

## Social Forces

Besides the pressure from business and government, social forces affect schools: increasing immigration that brings many cultures and languages into the classroom, ongoing poverty, broken homes, and violence lurking in the shadows. Since the early 1990s, the United States has experienced alarming gun violence in schools from Denver, Colorado, to North Pole, Alaska. The United Nations International Children's Emergency Fund (UNICEF) issued a report in 1999 supporting the Convention on the Rights of the Child, stating that the United States still has one of the highest rates of hunger among children. The United States suffers one of the highest infant mortality rates among industrial countries, with an infant mortality rate of 5 per 1,000 births, which is the same rate as in Poland,

Hungary, Slovakia, and Malta ("U.S. Infant Survival Rates," 2006). Furthermore, nearly three-quarters of all murders of children in the industrial world occur in the United States (UNICEF, 1999).

Another UNICEF report, *Child Poverty in Rich Countries* (UNICEF, 2005), finds that child poverty has risen in 17 of 24 OECD (Organisation for Economic Co-operation and Development) member states since 1990, with Mexico (27.7 percent) and the United States (21.9 percent) having the highest rates, followed by Italy (16.6 percent), Ireland (15.7 percent), Portugal (15.6 percent), and Britain (15.4 percent). The poverty rates decline further in the other member states. It is important to note that the concept of poverty is relative when applied globally; nevertheless, poverty in any nation limits opportunity. For all of our talk of equal opportunity and the American Dream, we are failing a large segment of our young people, and the consequences sting the conscience.

Another factor in the growing poverty rate is the large increase in U.S. immigration. With more than a million legal and illegal immigrants coming across our borders each year (Center for Immigration Studies, 2001), we are feeling the effects on schools and social systems. Illegal immigration has risen more than 185 percent since 1992, and current estimates of illegal immigrants in the Unites States stand between 11 and 12 million according to government census data reported by the *New York Times* ("Plentiful, Productive—and Illegal," 2006).

Increasing migration of peoples worldwide is a reality and schools have been thrust to center stage as they wrap their arms around the children of the world. At times, a teacher may have six or more languages and cultures in the classroom, yet our teachers have had very little training on how to effectively instruct such cultural diversity. Clearly, the schools need to have a focused agenda for meeting the needs of a growing multicultural population. The diversity of the United States is its greatness. No other country in the world has as rich a diversity in customs, perspectives, values, and beliefs, but the United States' inability to assimilate immigrants effectively, while still valuing cultural identities, can threaten the very foundation of our democracy.

Schools must teach the values and principles of democracy and a free society. Separating into ethnic enclaves, without the common bond of shared beliefs outlined in the U.S. Constitution and the Federalist Papers, puts us at risk for the internal ethnic and religious conflict so common in other parts of the world. The reality of global interdependence and interaction requires that schools also prepare students with the knowledge and understanding of diverse cultures and beliefs. Expanded knowledge and perspectives may prevent damaging sociopolitical moves in future delicate international relations, and may help build bridges of understanding to foster cooperation rather than conflict.

## Media

Media are the fourth pressure group. They seem to highlight the negative, whether crime, violence, corruption, or falling standardized test scores. What if publishers insisted that a positive story in education had to be written for every negative story? There are many wonderful things happening in education today, but the push to privatize education and shift funding has had a definite impact on public opinion. The general view is that public education is not teaching enough—yet we teach far more than we ever have in the past. Or the general view is that we are not teaching well enough—yet my experience in working with thousands of teachers and administrators over the past four decades is that the most of them truly care about and strive to educate the students in their classrooms. They work hard to meet all of the instructional demands placed on them by local, state, and national mandates, but they feel whipped this way and that by a parade of so-called critical initiatives that are often ill-conceived, unrealistic in terms of time and resources, or underfunded.

It is true that education needs improvement; it is also true, though, that we have a systems problem. The old system of education is not functional for delivering the highly cognitive, conceptual, and technical skills that are needed for the 21st century. The reality of information overload requires moving to a higher level of abstraction to organize the information base. We need greater attention to the conceptual structure of knowledge, and how to teach the factual knowledge in relation to the organizing **concepts** and principles.

The old system cannot be changed without focused retraining of teachers and administrators, and more effective curricular and instructional models. This retraining needs to include the teacher training institutions that are too often churning out the "same old, same old." Education needs to direct more funding and time to staff development. Tight budgets cut the discretionary funding for curriculum and staff development—the very items that are the heart of educational improvements for students. Our priorities need refinement. State standards are a step in the right direction, but they need to be revised to more clearly reflect the distinction and relationships between the conceptual and factual levels of knowledge for each of the disciplines. Teachers and administrators must be trained on the difference between the factual and conceptual levels of knowledge and how these levels work together to develop deep understanding and intellectual rigor. Improving pedagogy is the key to raising achievement levels, but the pressure to cover so many standards is wearing out the copy machines—and the teachers. Was this the intent?

## Parents

The final pressure group is the parents. What a confusing time for them! Between the mixed messages coming from the media, business, the government, and the schools, parents often do not know what to think. No wonder so many parents are opting for private or home schooling. Never before has the need to include parents in the educational setting been more urgent.

Educational change will only occur in a cooperative, problem-solving partnership among business, the community, and parents. The current aura of blaming impedes progress by generating feelings of hopelessness. Only by addressing the needs at the building level, supporting teachers and administrators, dialoguing as a community, and addressing the desired student outcomes with an analytical systems approach will we be able to align public schooling with societal and individual needs.

# SHARING THE JOB OF QUALITY EDUCATION

## Parents as Partners

Parents need to understand the changing world and how education is working to provide students with the skills for success in the 21st century. Progressive schools cooperatively plan the educational program with parents and see that they are involved in the educational process, whether at the school site or at home.

Traditionally, in education we have opened our doors only slightly to parents. We have engaged them as volunteers for various activities, but have had difficulty communicating our plans for teaching their children. Today, educators must find ways to include parents in defining the aims of education, and to show how the school learning plan is focused toward achieving those aims. Parents want and deserve to be active partners in their children's educational experiences.

Parents are feeling heightened anxiety for the safety as well as the education of their children. In a society that is increasingly violent and threatening, in which guns and drugs appear to be as plentiful as bubble gum and candy, parents naturally hold their children close. They want to see plans to ensure the safety and well-being of children in school. Safety must be an issue for the community as well as for the school.

## Community and Business as Partners

Education is a community venture with schools, churches, health, welfare, and law enforcement agencies working together to provide for the needs of children. In some communities, there are excellent communication networks between the public agencies. Help to families is focused and timely. In other communities, there is a breakdown in relationships. Families wait months for assistance from overburdened case workers, or suffer from duplication of effort between agencies.

One particularly effective model in a small community in Montana calls together an interagency task force that includes representatives from the schools, health and human service agencies, law enforcement, and the clergy. This task force meets on a monthly basis to dialogue and to develop ways to more effectively serve their shared families. Task force members become acquainted as professionals, which opens lines of communication that ultimately serve individual families more efficiently.

Business, as another important segment of the community, also has an important role in education. Certainly, many of the requested changes in schooling are emanating from the needs of business. Businesses have changed their requirements for educated workers: In the industrial age they needed workers who could follow orders and complete assigned tasks in specific time frames. In today's information age they need workers who can process and use knowledge in solving complex problems while working as members of a team.

Today, many businesses around the country provide positive support to schools through business partnerships. These businesses aid schools through activities such as allowing employees to speak to classes during the workday, or providing funding to support the development of curriculum and technology in schools. The business world wants technologically literate workers, but computers and more advanced technologies are still in scarce supply in too many schools. Helping ensure an equitable supply of technology across all schools would be one of the best ways for businesses to help boost relevant curriculum and instruction for the 21st century.

## The Government as a Partner

*The Dilemma of Time and Funding*
*. . . in a Minute . . . With a Nickel*

There are policy makers who have difficulty understanding why education is so slow to change. They believe that if educational standards and tests are developed for students and high stakes are set for students and schools, the change process will occur naturally. But educators know that these changes are a major transformation in outcomes, teaching paradigms, techniques, and materials. They require long-term cooperation and commitment to training and funding.

Two examples come to mind that demonstrate the complexity of curricular and instructional change. The first example deals with the process of curriculum development related to state standards and subsequent classroom implementation; the second revolves around the definition of depth of instruction.

Educators feel the pressure to meet state and local standards. The stakes are high. Some states, such as Florida, are giving letter grades to individual public schools based on their standardized test scores and factored criteria. Grades are published in the newspaper, and merit pay is on the horizon. With stakes this high, teachers deserve quality curricular documents. The reality in many states, though, is that the state standards to which local documents are aligned are very poor. In some states, the standards are so detailed and comprehensive that teachers could never cover the information demanded, let alone help students intellectually process the information. Standards between disciplines also vary in the way they are written and in their expectations.

Because the national science standards are so well conceived and written, the state and local science standards documents usually follow suit. They are concise and clear and can lead to deeper, conceptual understanding. The history standards in too many states, on the other hand, have fallen into the trap of trying to write specific curricula, usually as a set of traditional **objectives**: list, identify, and explain (that is, determine causes and effects).

Teachers need explanations as to how standards are written. They need to know expectations, and what the standards imply for instruction. We cannot assume that by handing these curricular documents to teachers, those teachers will understand them and use them effectively. The formats and expectations vary too much from one discipline to the next.

When state frameworks are poorly conceived, local curriculum committees need to know how to adapt them to address the deficiencies. This is not easy work. After quality curricular and assessment programs have been developed, teachers need intensive inservice training and time to develop new instructional pedagogy and skills for the classroom. It is imperative that school districts have quality leadership in curriculum and instruction at both the central and site levels. The heartbeat of schools is the curricular and instructional program for students.

The second example revolves around the definition of depth of instruction. Under the traditional fact-based paradigm, depth of instruction is too often thought of as teaching more facts about a topic. In a concept-based paradigm, depth of instruction means using the fact base as a tool to teach a deeper understanding of the key concepts and principles of a discipline. This shift in definition highlights the need for changes in instruction as teachers challenge their own thinking to facilitate student thinking. Content serves not as an end product, but as a tool to lead students to deeper thought.

If education is to attract the best and the brightest into teaching and administration, then education as a career must be elevated to a profession on a par with physicians, attorneys, and architects. This means that pay scales must be increased significantly. We get what we are willing to pay for. We could raise standards for the profession and be more selective in our hires if the pay were competitive with other professions. The job of the educator is similar to and no less important than the job of a physician: educators hold the economic and social health of the individual and nation in their hands.

In addition to elevating teachers and administrators to professional status, the issue of staff development on the job needs to be addressed. The increasing emphasis on critical and conceptual thinking in schooling requires a level of staff development that goes far beyond "make it and take it" workshops or five early-release-day presentations by experts. The level of staff development that is necessary to effect the needed changes in curriculum, instruction, and systems planning must be ongoing and weekly. If legislators are serious about wanting an improved educational system, they will concede the time needed for teachers and administrators to interact as professionals in learning new skills.

I have seen the greatest school improvements when teachers and administrators are given time to deal intellectually and in depth with the essential questions related to their profession in a changing world. The school year should be extended so teachers have one morning per week for professional dialogue, curriculum writing, and staff development. It is critical that educators be accountable for this time, however, by showing results to their community.

It is important to hold the staff and curriculum development time in the morning. The high level of staff development and curriculum work to be undertaken requires alert minds. The higher the quality of thinking that is brought to planning, the better the program for students. Results should show for students by the second year if the development time is used effectively.

Some schools are following a model of early release days, but I have found this model to provide insufficient time to complete any meaningful dialogue or work. Early release days often provide only an hour or an hour and a half. Some teachers also feel compelled to attend to other business during that time, which erodes the school-based, professional focus.

If schools would bank time by extending the school day for a few minutes and shortening the passing time between classes, they could effect a three-hour late arrival day for students on alternating weeks. We will not see the kind of school transformation we are seeking without this amount of quality time. Teachers in Germany and Japan have longer school years but less contact time with students during the day. They use the time to dialogue, plan, and learn together.

Big business recognizes the need for quality training of its employees. Education is one of the largest businesses, and the job is human development. This job is far more complex than following a standard blueprint to build a standard product. The job of human development takes the individual child in whatever form and guides and nurtures the mind, body, and self-concept. If we raise the expectations for teachers and administrators, then we owe them the training they need to meet our raised expectations. We get what we pay for. If we expect major change in a minute, with a nickel, we will get what we pay for—minute change.

# A NATIONAL MODEL FOR CONCEPT-BASED CURRICULA

After years of leading local curriculum committees in writing standards-based, concept-based curricula across the United States, I have come to the conclusion that we should develop a model for concept-based curricula at the national level, with teacher teams of our best disciplinary experts representing each grade level. This national model would state clearly what students must know factually, understand conceptually, and be able to do in each subject area. The leaders of the discipline-based writing teams would create a uniform concept-based design across the different disciplines. This means that they would need solid training in the what, why, and how of concept-based curriculum design. The writers would strive for clarity, coherence, and rigor through the grade levels and across subject areas. The current national and state standards are not curriculum documents—they are curricular frameworks. The next step is to provide solid models for classroom curricula.

For science and social studies, the national curriculum model could be in the form of concept-based **interdisciplinary** and **intradisciplinary** instructional units for each grade level and course that are rigorous (intellectually), coherent (internally, horizontally, and vertically), and clear. These grade-level instructional units would be developed using the current national standards as a base, but would focus the content to reflect the most critical knowledge, concepts, and skills of the discipline. Secondary mathematics would also be designed as units of instruction.

Elementary mathematics and language arts would need a developmental skill sequence. The elementary mathematics would also need to develop the statements of conceptual understanding (generalizations) to accompany the necessary skills. Ideally, all other disciplines (fine arts, career and technical education, health and physical education, and so on) would follow suit in designing national concept-based curriculum models for a well-rounded education.

The smaller the school district, the tighter the funding for curriculum development. Because we have not been able to effect quality curricula in all of our local districts across the country, we need to develop one or more concept-based national models so that the local time and money can be better spent on staff development in concept-based pedagogy and disciplinary depth. This would raise standards and be a much wiser use of our limited funding. As it is now, each district is reinventing the same curricular wheel, often with flat results. Whether people know it or not, the national standards have driven a national curriculum that is being reinvented again and again in school districts across the nation. But the shortage of time, funding, and expertise leads to local results that are often lacking in rigor, intellectual depth, and design coherence.

School districts choosing to follow the national model could tweak the curriculum to meet local needs. For example, the national curriculum may include conceptual understanding of a state's economy in relation to its resources; the school district would want to require factual knowledge of its specific resources and economy to support the broader conceptual understanding in the national curriculum. If the idea of a national model for classroom curricula is unworkable because of the commitment to state-level standards, then perhaps each state needs to provide a quality concept-based model for classroom curricula.

In an ideal world, I would want all teachers to be able to guide student-driven inquiries that maintain intellectual rigor, disciplinary and interdisciplinary depth, and conceptual insight. Given today's realities of mandated standards and many teachers who lack disciplinary depth, however, I believe we need to take a more structured half step to our goal. For those school districts and institutions such as the International Baccalaureate diploma schools who are managing to "do it all" with rigor and gusto—bravo!

Certainly, the design of a national curriculum model is contrary to the idea of local control, but there are reasons why I believe it is the solution: writing quality curricula requires a deep knowledge of the disciplines and a commitment of time and funding. It is easier to develop one quality model than thousands of local district curriculums. Because states are invested in frameworks, the development of quality local curricula is a magnified problem when a district lacks expertise and funds to lead the writing. A school district that pays teachers for a full month over two or three summers to write a PreK–12 curriculum for each subject area, and that makes certain they have quality leadership for the writing process, can have excellent results—but how many districts have the funding, leadership, and commitment to make this kind of investment?

It has been my pleasure to work with Channelview Independent School District in Channelview, Texas—a district that has committed the time, funding, and leadership to complete the PreK–12 curricula. More than 100 dedicated and outstanding teachers worked for three years to write quality, concept-based, Web-based curricula for the core areas. Dr. Roxanne Wilson, the assistant superintendent, provided the on-site leadership, tenacity, and expertise to see the project through to the end. The district is working now to train the entire staff on the concept-based pedagogy. Members of the curriculum writing teams are training their colleagues, in many cases. More formal district trainings are also taking place. With continued follow-through, I am confident that Channelview will see student achievement rise significantly over the next few years. I also believe that the engagement of the conceptual level of thinking that is built in to the curricula will increase the motivation for learning and teaching.

In *Concept-Based Curriculum and Instruction for the Thinking Classroom* (Erickson, 2007), I discuss the idea of moving away from traditional verb-driven "content objectives" (we need to retain "skill objectives," however) and instead provide three critical components in classroom curricula for teachers (p. 7):

1. Students will *UNDERSTAND*
   - Transferable generalizations/enduring understandings

   *Examples:*
   o Systems are interdependent. (macro-level)
   o Organisms adapt to changing environments. (micro-level)
   o Rational numbers, including whole numbers, fractions and decimals can be expressed in equivalent forms of standard notation or scientific notation. (micro-level)

2. Students will *KNOW*
   - Factual knowledge, memorized knowledge
   - Critical factual knowledge for understanding the unit generalization(s)
   - Critical factual knowledge for competency with the unit topics
   - Nontransferable—locked in time, place or situation

   *Examples:*
   o Newton's Laws
   o Key vocabulary
   o The causes of the American Revolution
   o The names and contributions of historical figures
   o The formulas for finding the area of quadratics

3. Students will be *able to DO* (processes/skills)
   - The "set" of processes/skills that professionals use in their work (the mathematician, artist, etc.)
   - Transfer across applications within a discipline and at times across disciplines (e.g., language arts or mathematics skills)
   - Not tied to a specific topic (attaching a skill to a specific topic makes it an activity or a performance)

*Examples:*
o Create tables, graphs and charts to display scientific data
o Analyze primary and secondary source documents to evaluate historical information
o Analyze the use of connotative and denotative language in text
o Use context clues in reading to determine meaning

Currently, state academic standards fail to articulate clearly the differences between these three components (factual knowledge, conceptual understanding, and key processes and skills). If teachers had these three sets of expectations articulated clearly for their subject areas they would be able to fuse the skills with content as they design curricula to teach deeper factual and conceptual understanding.

The reason for clearly stating skill sets for teachers by discipline and grade level is to help them internalize the skills of the discipline. They then can apply these skills across a variety of learning experiences in the design process.

With solid instructional units modeled nationally (or at the state level), teachers could gain ownership by developing their classroom lesson plans to develop critical knowledge, understandings, and skills; or they could design their own units following the national or state-provided models. It is the business of the state to provide for the education of its students, but what the state is doing is not working well enough in too many school districts. A quality, concept-based model could be the catalyst we need to create a change in pedagogy. First, though, teachers and administrators must be trained on concept-based instruction, which differs fundamentally from traditional instructional pedagogy.

As soon as I write this proposal, however, I realize that a danger lurks. Suppose the federal government is so enamored with the national model that it makes it a mandate? If that were to occur, I would withdraw my proposal. We need models at this stage, not mandates.

In any case, schools are undergoing change to meet higher standards—and change can be difficult. In the next section, Peter Senge's insights on organizational change can help guide our work.

## MAKING CHANGE THE SYSTEMS WAY

### Senge and Systems Thinking

Two recommended books for all policy makers, leaders, and organizations involved in change are *Dance of Change: The Challenge of Sustaining Momentum in Learning Organizations,* by Peter Senge (1999), and his newly revised and updated edition of *The Fifth Discipline: The Art and Practice of the Learning Organization* (Senge, 2006). Central to Senge's thesis is the view that

learning organizations . . . where people continually expand their capacity to create the results they truly desire, where new and expansive patterns of thinking are nurtured, where collective aspiration is set free, and where people are continually learning how to learn together . . . develop in a culture which embraces systems thinking. (2006, p. 3)

**Systems thinking**, states Senge, is a framework for seeing interrelationships and patterns of change. Too often, events are perceived in isolation, and quick fixes for symptoms are applied. "Systems thinking is a 'discipline' for seeing the structures that underlie complex situations" (Senge, 2006, p. 69). Senge raises our awareness that complexity—caused by information overload, rapid global interdependence, and accelerating change—can overwhelm and undermine the confidence and responsibility of decision makers. "Systems thinking is needed more than ever" (p. 69).

Senge (2006) calls the critical components for a learning organization disciplines. The first four disciplines—Personal Mastery, Mental Models, Building Shared Vision, and Team Learning—are integrated through the fifth discipline, Systems Thinking. Senge gives the following definitions:

- *Systems Thinking.* A conceptual framework, a body of knowledge and tools that has been developed over the past fifty years, to make the full patterns [of interrelated actions] clearer, and to help us see how to change them effectively.
- *Personal Mastery.* The discipline of continually clarifying and deepening our personal vision, of focusing our energies, of developing patience, and of seeing reality objectively.
- *Mental Models.* Deeply ingrained assumptions, generalizations, or even pictures or images that influence how we understand the world and how we take action.
- *Building Shared Vision.* The capacity to build and hold a shared picture of the future we seek to create. People with shared vision have . . . genuine commitment and enrollment rather than compliance.
- *Team Learning.* The ability to dialogue and suspend assumptions while entering into a genuine "thinking together." Team learning also involves learning how to recognize the patterns of interaction in teams that undermine learning. (pp. 7–10)

A major difficulty in the restructuring of schools is a lack of the five disciplines in action. People work in their own comfort zones, and each person tinkers with a piece of the whole. A coordinated, systemic plan for change is too often absent. Policy makers insist on tests; assessment people comply. Principals encourage teachers to focus on raising test scores; teachers comply. A plethora of new buzzwords and innovations sweep into classrooms but are seldom evaluated for their contributions to increased student success. Teachers and principals request time to dialogue, plan, and design effective programs, but there is a breakdown in the system: this essential need remains but a whisper at the budget and policy tables. Educators fear that parents would never support the scheduling change. Parents need to be informed as to the complexity of the changes being asked of us. We must gain their support for these reasonable requests for planning time.

School administrators who have been in the business for a number of years will remember the total quality management (TQM) drive to emulate the principles of Dr. W. Edwards Deming. Peter Senge dialogued with Dr. Deming and found that he had become disillusioned with the ability of organizations to actually implement real TQM. Senge (2006, p. xii) quotes Deming: "We will never transform the prevailing system of management without transforming our prevailing system of education." Deming wrote the following to Senge:

> Our prevailing system of management has destroyed our people. People are born with intrinsic motivation, self-respect, dignity, curiosity to learn, joy in learning. The forces of destruction begin with toddlers—a prize for the best Halloween costume, grades in school, gold stars—and on up through the university. On the job, people, teams, and divisions are ranked, reward for the top, punishment for the bottom. Management by objectives, quotas, incentive pay, business plans, put together separately, division by division, cause further loss, unknown and unknowable. (Senge, 2006, p. xii)

Senge and his colleagues spent many years after Dr. Deming's 1993 death trying to define the characteristics that frame the intractable management system of today. These eight elements are worth sharing here. Could our difficulty in improving our educational system be driven by our allegiance to these old mental models of management?

- Management by measurement
  - Focusing on short-term metrics
  - Devaluing intangibles ("You can only measure 3 percent of what matters."—W. E. Deming)
- Compliance-based cultures
  - Getting ahead by pleasing the boss
  - Management by fear
- Managing outcomes
  - Management sets targets
  - People are held accountable for meeting management targets (regardless of whether they are possible within existing systems and processes)
- "Right answers" versus "wrong answers"
  - Technical problem solving is emphasized
  - Diverging (systemic) problems are discounted
- Uniformity
  - Diversity is a problem to be solved
  - Conflict is suppressed in favor of superficial agreement
- Predictability and controllability
  - To manage is to control
  - The "holy trinity on management" is planning, organizing, controlling

- Excessive competitiveness and distrust
  - Competition between people is essential to achieve desired performance
  - Without competition among people there is no innovation ("We've been sold down the river by competition."—W. E. Deming)
- Loss of the whole
  - Fragmentation
  - Local innovations do not spread (Senge, 2006, pp. xiv, xv)

Education is still bound by these system structures with the carrot and stick approach to standards attainment, competition between schools, and perceived lack of time to collaboratively solve problems. This is not to say that systems should disavow leaders and structures; nevertheless, we have to consider how people operate within the system structures and how they are designed.

The five disciplines as defined by Senge (2006, p. xii) center on the development of three core learning capabilities: fostering aspiration, developing reflective conversation, and understanding complexity. The focus in education on the development of professional learning communities (PLCs) provides hope that we can address Senge's core learning capabilities.

## Professional Learning Communities

*On Common Ground: The Power of Professional Learning Communities* (DuFour, Eaker, & DuFour, 2005) is a collection of chapters by noted, contemporary educational authors who support the tenets of PLCs. Richard DuFour et al. cite three driving questions to frame the work of a school's PLC:

- What do we want each student to learn?
- How will we know when each student has learned it?
- How will we respond when a student experiences difficulty in learning? (p. 33)

PLCs respond to these questions as a collaborative team rather than as individuals. Principals in PLCs regard themselves as "leaders of leaders" rather than "leaders of followers" (DuFour et al., 2005, p. 23). Followers wait to be told; leaders engage intellectually. It is clear why the PLC premise has more promise in improving schooling.

There is another reason why I think the PLC model is important to the change process. After decades of work on concept-based curriculum and instruction, I have come to realize that unless the personal intellect is engaged in learning, student motivation for that learning is poor. When the conceptual mind (the personal intellect) is processing and problem solving, motivation is high. The reason for this is that humans are intellectual beings. When we are invited to use our minds, contributing and working collaboratively, we feel valued. When we are told what to do or what to say, we feel little personal fulfillment.

## OVERCOMING OBSTACLES:
## OVER, UNDER, THROUGH, AND AROUND

Educators have an indomitable spirit. Despite a lack of coordinated problem solving and systems thinking in school districts, teachers and administrators strive to improve education for the students in their schools. A powerful point made by Senge (2006) is that learning organizations move forward on the collective vision and actions of people. They overcome obstacles and achieve their goals because they are all headed in the same direction, toward a shared vision. Individual schools appear to be more successful in creating a shared vision, but school districts find it more difficult to create that collective synergy so necessary for focused change.

Systems design considers all players when building a shared vision. When business works with government to require certain standards from schools, business becomes part of the system. Parents, too, are part of the system. So are the community agencies that support children and families. It is admittedly difficult to effect a coordinated and coherent vision because of diverse perspectives and a natural resistance to change, but let's start the discussion of change where it has the greatest benefit for children—with curriculum and instruction.

The next chapter presents an introduction to the idea of concept-based curriculum design. This book provides guidance for school districts who are designing their own concept-based curriculum. Concept-based curriculum provides a more efficient model for handling the massive amounts of information available today, focuses teaching and learning to more sophisticated levels, and provides hope for raising standards in education. Without addressing the inherent problems in the basic structure of traditional curriculum designs, educational change will fall short of the goal of raising standards.

## SUMMARY

Teachers and administrators are caught in the crosshairs of conflicting messages and actions from pressure groups. Everyone wants higher academic standards for schools, but legislators create cattle-prod policies of punishment and reward, vouchers, choice, and competition. They want educational excellence but encourage state standards that at times are antithetical to excellence because they promote low-level coverage over intellectual and emotional engagement. The focus is on assessment before teachers have been trained to teach to higher standards. Media have a field day reporting test scores and school letter grades, and parents question, worry, and shuffle their children around, shopping for the best deal.

A committed partnership among schools, parents, business, and the community is essential to a quality plan for education. A systems approach to the education of each child brings the parts into a coherent whole—with the children the winners.

Curriculum and instruction are critical focal points for educational change. This job cannot be done effectively without providing quality time each week for professional dialogue, staff training, and curriculum development. Teachers deserve quality curriculum documents that will help them raise intellectual and academic standards. Perhaps it is time to admit that many local school districts lack the time, funding, and expertise to develop quality concept-based curricula for the classroom. It is time to consider the development of one or more national, concept-based curriculum models (grade level and course units of instruction) that local districts could tweak to fit their needs. The national models would be offered for voluntary use by school districts. For school districts using the national model, district funds could be spent on improving disciplinary knowledge and pedagogy among teachers, and on improving the leadership skills of administrators. Those school districts that do have the resources to design a concept-based model locally would be able to more easily gain ownership among teachers by developing their own curriculum, but for others the national model can be a viable option.

There is so much work to do in schools that collaborative team planning is a must. The idea of PLCs can provide the structure for getting the job done. Besides, it just makes sense to problem solve and plan collaboratively.

The purpose of educational change is to better meet the needs of our students today and to prepare them for the future. Change for the sake of change is wheel spinning. Change for the sake of children is our job, and we are ready and willing. All we need to start is quality systems planning.

## EXTENDING THOUGHT

1. Why must education become a community partnership in the systems view?

2. What questions should parents ask of educators today?

3. How would you respond to those questions as an educator?

4. What impediments to quality education do you perceive today?

5. Describe your vision of an insightful and appropriate curricular and instructional program for students in the new millennium.

6. The dilemmas of little time and short funding are school realities. How can you creatively and practically "make time" and "find funding"?

7. What kind of training do teachers need to raise standards for all students?

8. What should be included in a well-rounded education for students today?

*(Continued)*

(Continued)

9. What issues would you raise in your PLC for each of these topics in your school?
   - Raising academic achievement
   - Academic success for *all* students
   - Our goals and aims for education

10. What do you think of the idea of developing a voluntary concept-based, national curriculum that would be tweaked at the local level? Discuss the pros and cons of such a curriculum.

11. What are the main impediments to change in your school or district? How would you address those impediments as a leader?

12. How would you characterize quality leadership?

# Concept-Based Curriculum

We are caught in a curious blend of old and new content. Pressures to meet academic standards have left a pot of mulligan stew at the schoolhouse door. Schools purchase this program and that, trying to address the breadth of content and skills delineated in state standards and district curricular frameworks. Teachers cringe to hear that they must toss in "just one more thing." This continual addition of ingredients into the simmering curriculum stew has created a pot of mush. We are in a crisis. Just what should we be teaching? Significant knowledge and ideas are becoming lost in the mix.

Process outcomes address the personal abilities that students will need for responding to the trends, but they do nothing to address the problems of subject area content. How do we make decisions on what content is most valuable to include in our limited school hours? And how do we ensure that meaningless content will be replaced with worthwhile content?

- Elementary teachers collect myriad instructional material through the years. But how can they ever use all that material? The current wisdom is that less is more, making much of that "stuff" obsolete.
- American history classes live in the past and race toward the future but often crash at the end of World War II. (Some determinedly speed through to U.S. involvement in Vietnam.) The dogged pursuit of a chronological compendium of events contributes to the loss of significant understandings—which are the lasting lessons of history.

## TRADITIONAL CURRICULUM

Many teachers still rely heavily on textbooks to tell them what to teach. Yet textbooks, because of their topic focus, cover too much content and fail to address the lasting ideas that can be applied to current and future trends.

Historically, curriculum has been governed by discrete subject areas and topical organizers for content. Figure 2.1 shows the traditional model of a burgeoning array of topics sprouting from science and history. The unwavering focus in schooling has been on memorization of an increasing body of facts and the practice of skills.

The problem with this model is that the information base in our world is challenging the best of microchips. School districts try to keep up with this information explosion by looking to state standards as the parameters for what to teach. Local **curriculum frameworks**, however, usually resemble the traditional booklets and lists of isolated student learning objectives that were prevalent in the early 1980s, because that is what we know. Although we do need skill-based objectives, the format for writing content objectives usually tickles only the lowest cognitive levels, serving as fodder for a trivia pursuit intellect.

There is more than one effect of this lower-level love affair with trivia. Perhaps most significantly, studying topics and facts as information to be memorized fails to engage the deeper intellect of students. When students are encouraged to think beyond the facts and to connect factual knowledge to ideas of conceptual significance, they find relevance and personal meaning. And when students become personally and intellectually engaged, they are more motivated to learn because their emotions are involved: they are mind-active rather than mind-passive. Could the curricular lack of personal, intellectual engagement be a major reason why so many students are apathetic toward their studies?

A second effect of content coverage is that we miss the deeper, transferable understandings. Kings, queens, dates, and the presidents and all their men: what significance do they hold for understanding our world and the human condition? Certainly, as isolated bits of stored memory they hold little significance, but as key historical players in life's drama their social situations, actions, and reactions hold lasting lessons for understanding the human condition today and for predicting the world of tomorrow.

There is ongoing debate between historians and social studies educators as to the best approach for teaching content. Both groups have developed a set of national standards for their disciplines, and both integrate economics, politics, sociology, anthropology, and geography. The primary differences between them appear to be in pedagogy and approaches to content:

- Historians use specific events and people to promote historical thinking, and avoid conceptual generalizations.
- Social studies educators use specific events and people to teach historical thinking, but encourage students to identify the lessons of history and the human experience by relating specific content to conceptual generalizations.

Sam Wineburg, who at the time was a professor of educational psychology and history at the University of Washington, wrote a powerful article for the *Phi Delta Kappan* titled "Historical Thinking and Other Unnatural Acts" (Wineburg, 1999). Wineburg includes in the article a cogent explanation as to why historians

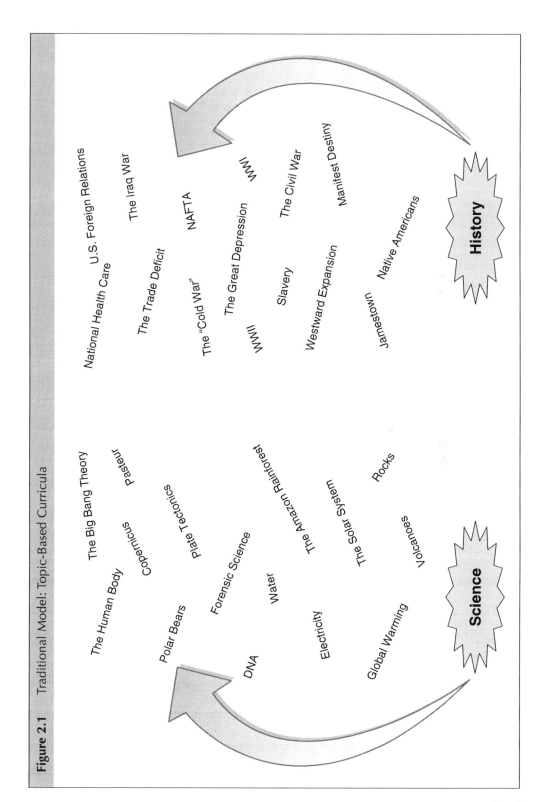

**Figure 2.1** Traditional Model: Topic-Based Curricula

National Health Care
U.S. Foreign Relations
The Iraq War
The Trade Deficit
NAFTA
The "Cold War"
The Great Depression
WWI
WWII
Slavery
The Civil War
Westward Expansion
Manifest Destiny
Jamestown
Native Americans

**History**

The Big Bang Theory
Pasteur
Copernicus
Plate Tectonics
The Human Body
Forensic Science
Polar Bears
Water
The Amazon Rainforest
DNA
Electricity
The Solar System
Rocks
Global Warming
Volcanoes

**Science**

basically eschew the practice of generalizing in history, and he balances this view with the realization that one cannot understand the past without relating to the thread of human experience:

> The study of history pivots on a tension between the familiar and the strange, between feelings of proximity to and feelings of distance from the people we seek to understand. . . . [But] we discard or just ignore vast regions of the past that either contradict our current needs or fail to align easily with them . . . [and] we contort the past to fit the predetermined meaning we have already assigned to it. . . . Yet, taken to extremes, regarding the past "on its own terms"—detached from the circumstances, concerns, and needs of the present—too often results in esoteric exoticism . . . which fails to engage the interest of anyone except a small coterie of professionals. (p. 490)

Wineburg (1999) goes on to quote the philosopher Hans-Georg Gadamer:

> How can we overcome established modes of thought when it is these modes that permit understanding in the first place? . . . Trying to shed what we know to glimpse the "real" past is like trying to examine microbes with the naked eye—the very instruments we abandon are the ones that enable us to see. (p. 492)

Historians have a valid concern in one respect: generalizations may make it too easy for students of history to wrap the complexities of events, issues, and people from different times and places into neat little summary statements. I have seriously considered this argument—then I look at the current history standards and am struck with the realization that historians want it both ways. They want students to develop historical thinking (a laudable aim), and they want students to know every war, date, and general, figuratively speaking (a not-so-laudable aim). We cannot have it both ways because each goal takes a great deal of time. If the breadth of content forces teachers to choose, they are going to emphasize the study of facts because they perceive that is what will be tested—and in most cases they are correct. It is harder to assess historical thinking because it includes factual knowledge, conceptual understanding, and reasoning ability. Nevertheless, it is historical thinking that will develop depth of understanding and the ability to reason critically.

As I have watched and worked with history teachers, I have seen the generalizations and guiding questions actually stimulate historical thinking abilities. When students (and teachers) consider specific events, issues, and historical figures through a **conceptual lens**, they are forced to analyze, evaluate, and investigate at deeper levels as they consider the transferable legitimacy of an idea.

Wineburg (1999) concludes in his article that our best chance at having students understand the past is to develop their sensibility to the time, culture, perspectives, and people. They must engage with primary source documents and literature that convey the emotions and perspectives of the time. They will naturally want to use their experience as a frame of reference, but we can broaden that frame by heightening their sensibilities. Wineburg points out that most history textbooks are written in a dispassionate, dry discourse and do little to develop historical sensibility. (And we wonder why history is one of the least favored subjects among students!) All history teachers would enjoy reading *Historical Thinking and Other Unnatural Acts,* Wineburg's 2001 book that extends his earlier writings.

The model presented in this book will show how the events of history can become lessons of history with the focused exploration of concepts and representative examples viewed through time. Culture, change and continuity, trade, justice, law and order, and diversity and commonality can serve as conceptual lenses. A conceptual lens forces students to think through and beyond the facts to consider the transferable lessons of history—the generalizations that highlight patterns and connections of human experience.

SOURCE: Cartoon by David Ford, davidford4@comcast.net.

In *The Disciplined Mind,* Howard Gardner (1999) states that

it should be clear by now why a "fact-based" approach will make even less sense in the future. One can never attain a disciplined mind simply by mastering facts—one must immerse oneself deeply in the specifics of cases and develop one's disciplinary muscles from such immersion. (p. 126)

Gardner is a leader in the popular view that understanding is a performance—a public exhibition of what one knows and is able to do. Gardner (2006) provides many examples of quality performances in his revised and updated book, *Multiple Intelligences*—performances that reflect conceptual or disciplinary depth and breadth. Nevertheless, the reality in many classrooms is that the rich performances that Gardner advocates materialize as shallower activities that fall short of a demonstration of understanding. This happens because our curriculum designs do not explicitly state the deeper ideas to guide instruction. Consequently, classroom performances demonstrate a skill tied to a topic rather than to a deeper, conceptual understanding.

Some state standards unknowingly reinforce this confusion of activity for performance of deeper understanding. For example, the following **performance indicator** might be suggested for teachers as evidence that a student understands that governments influence the lives of citizens: "Identify the rules that people are asked to follow." This performance indicator shows us that students can identify rules, but stops short of showing whether students understand the idea of governmental influence.

A concept-based curriculum raises the bar for curriculum design, instruction, and assessment in history because it forces students to use meta-analysis to evaluate historical issues. The big ideas, guiding questions, and understanding performances cause students to examine and understand the particular perspectives, emotions, causes, and effects of events and issues in different times and places.

## CONCEPT-BASED CURRICULUM

Concepts are the foundational organizers for both interdisciplinary curriculum and single-subject curriculum design. They serve as a bridge between topics and generalizations.

Hilda Taba (1904–1967), a visionary educator in the 1950s and 1960s, saw the value of conceptual organizers for content. Her research on developing higher levels of thinking was funded through a Federal Department of Education research project, which she completed in February 1966 at San Francisco State College. Today, more than ever, we need to reexamine Taba's views and extend her work: she provides positive direction for increasing the intellectual functioning of students. Development of critical and creative thinking is essential for the challenges of the 21st century.

## HISTORICAL PERSPECTIVE: HILDA TABA

Taba (1966) refers to concepts as "high level abstractions expressed in verbal cues and labels, e.g., interdependence, cultural change and causality" (p. 48). She states that a person's understanding of a concept grows as he experiences increasingly complex, conceptual examples. In science, for example, a student might learn about the concept of "Force" at Grades 4, 8, and 12, but the specific examples used at each grade level would represent increasingly complex principles as the child progressed (see Table 2.1).

**Table 2.1** Gradated Examples of Force

| Grade 4: General Science | Grade 8: Physical Science | Grade 12: Physics |
| --- | --- | --- |
| Force as action/reaction | Newton's second law of momentum | Friction<br>Hydraulics |
| Pulleys and force | Machines and gravity | Pneumatics |
| Gravity as a force | Pressure | Torque |
| Reduction of force | Energy transfer | Electromagnetism |

Taba (1966) refers to generalizations and principles as the main ideas of the content under study. She differentiates generalizations from principles by stating that generalizations usually include qualifiers in their statements, such as conflict is often caused by differences in values and beliefs (p. 49). Taba proposes that content coverage could be focused and delimited by letting the main ideas—the generalizations—determine the direction and depth for instruction. She holds that specific content should be sampled rather than covered (p. 49).

Another insightful Taba truism is the observation that learning has multiple objectives—the learning of content and the learning of increasingly sophisticated behaviors in thinking, attitudes, and skills—and that these objectives call for different forms of instruction at different levels of complexity.

Taba's (1966) study consisted of an experimental research design using a trained group of 12 teachers and a control group of 12 untrained teachers. All of the elementary grade teachers instructed students with a social studies curriculum that used topics and facts as a vehicle for teaching major concepts and main ideas.

The trained teachers received 10 days of intensive instruction on using the social studies curriculum to develop students' cognitive processing abilities. Trained teachers learned to sequence and pace instruction to allow for maximum student response. The concept "Formation Strategy" required students to identify what they were seeing, formulate groupings of items by common characteristics, and label and subsume like items under organizing concepts.

Taba (1966) found that the cognitive maps of the teacher are critical to facilitating the cognitive development of the student. By "cognitive map," Taba refers to the levels of understanding related to the content under study, as well as the nature of the thinking processes. The teacher's task of "protecting the student's creative and autonomous thinking" (p. 60) while reinforcing the logic of content calls for high sensitivity in the instructional setting.

Taba's (1966) research found that students in the trained groups showed a greater number of thought units, which were also longer and more complex than the control groups. The trained students exhibited the convergence of low- and high-level thought units into logical generalizations (the main ideas) that were related to the content.

Although the greatest problem for the teachers was a feeling of pressure to cover the curriculum (sound familiar?), test results demonstrated that the time spent on process teaching and learning did not impede strong achievement in learning the fact-based information (Taba, 1966).

# CONCEPTUAL ORGANIZERS

A conceptually organized curriculum helps solve the problem of the overloaded curriculum. Concepts bring focus and depth to study and lead students to the transferable, conceptual understandings. (These conceptual ideas are commonly referred to as "enduring understandings" [Wiggins & McTighe, 1999], "essential understandings" [Erickson, 1995], or "big ideas" in today's educational jargon. In this book, I will use the term "enduring understanding" or "generalization" to create less confusion over terminology.) It is important to clarify the issue of concepts in general before we return to their value in curriculum organization.

## What Is a Concept?

A universal concept is a mental construct that is timeless, universal, and abstract (to different degrees). Although the specific examples of a concept may vary, the general attributes of the concept will always be the same. "Symmetry," as a concept, has many different examples, but the attributes of symmetry (balance and equivalence) are the same across all examples. "Symmetry," as a concept, can be found across disciplines, such as in art, science, mathematics, or music.

Concepts are a higher level of abstraction than facts in the structure of knowledge. They serve as cells for categorizing factual examples. Conceptual understanding continues to grow more sophisticated as new examples fill each concept cell. Because concepts are timeless, they provide lessons through the ages. Because they are universal, their examples may be derived from any culture.

It is common in educational circles today to hear the word "theme" being used for the ideas I am defining as concepts. The problem with this practice is that the definition of theme is so loose that topics sometimes become confused with concepts. This is a significant problem in interdisciplinary curriculum if the goal is higher-level, integrated thinking. Units centered on a **topical theme** (e.g., "Dinosaurs") will only result in a coordinated, **multidisciplinary** curriculum. This means that multiple subjects coordinate facts and activities related to a common topic. Interdisciplinary curriculum, described in detail in Chapter 4, requires a conceptual as well as a topical focus if thinking is to be integrated. (For instance, "The Extinction of Dinosaurs" is a conceptual theme.) Themes, therefore, can be either topical or conceptual. In this book, I avoid the term "theme" and use the term "unit title" for the sake of clarity when discussing the design of instructional units.

## Where Do Concepts Fall in the Structure of Knowledge?

Figure 2.2 illustrates the relationship of concepts to topics and facts, generalizations, principles, and theories in the structure of knowledge. Traditionally in education, we have spent the majority of our content study on the lowest cognitive level: the memorization of isolated facts.

The oft-quoted Third International Mathematics and Science Study (TIMMS) study that compared U.S. curriculum to higher achieving industrial countries really characterizes the problem best: "American curriculum is an inch deep and a mile wide" (Schmidt, McKnight, & Raizen, 1997). Although there is controversy over whether the TIMMS research is an unbiased and accurate international comparison, no one can argue that schools in the United States cover far more content than do schools in other industrial nations. Common sense tells us that massive content coverage will be intellectually shallow when time is limited.

I was surprised to realize, through my work in curriculum, the generally shallow cognitive level most of us have experienced as students in our educational paths. I now think this is largely the result of fact-based rather than idea-based emphases in textbook and curriculum design. Later in our lives, we often teach as we were taught. Educators today, however, know that students must be actively and mentally engaged in their learning. As a result, educators are adjusting the

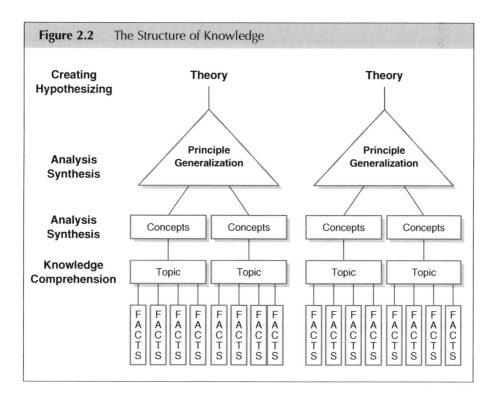

**Figure 2.2    The Structure of Knowledge**

learning experience. Unfortunately, many textbook materials and some standards continue to be structured with low cognitive expectations and a continued emphasis on coverage over intellectual engagement.

Some people would argue that students cannot apply higher-level thinking processes until they have a wealth of factual knowledge, but I disagree. As a first-grade teacher, I enlisted creative and critical thinking from my students to solve problems. For example, using the concept of "Need Versus Want," my students built new homes for our two imaginary pets, Chalk Mouse and Pencil Mouse. Chalk Mouse ate the teacher's chalk, and Pencil Mouse ate the pencils. They lost their homes in a natural disaster, when the custodian accidentally disposed of them. The challenge for students was to decide what Chalk Mouse and Pencil Mouse would need and what they would want in a home.

Students gathered their materials for the project and went to work. The students had chalk and pencils for the mice to eat, water for them to drink, ladders for them to climb up and down from desks, and soft straw for them to lie on. Needless to say, this exercise was the expression of critical and creative thinking at its finest. The room was buzzing with discussion of need versus want. The critical point is that the students were responsible for solving the problem. (I'm sorry to say that Chalk Mouse turned to dust with the invention of the white board in classrooms.)

Perhaps in the days of relatively unsophisticated technology and global isolationism, it was not as critical to think at high levels. Nevertheless, the game has changed. Global interdependence and sophisticated technologies require that we raise the intellectual as well as the content standards in classrooms.

SOURCE: Cartoon by David Ford, davidford4@comcast.net.

## What Are Some Examples of the Subject Area Organizing Concepts?

Teachers frequently want to know if there is a master list of concepts for each subject area. Except for the field of science, there are no formal lists at this time. It would be helpful to have national subject area organizations develop their lists of the most significant organizing concepts as frames for the critical content. Certainly, the dialogue among the professionals has started, but the task of delineating grade level and subject area concepts is not yet complete.

We need not wait, however. I have seen some of the most intense professional dialogues occur among subject area staff as they relate the content they teach to the organizing concepts. This process forces teachers to consider the most important ideas for instruction. Table 2.2, Resource A, and Resource B show examples of concepts for different subject areas. Note the macroconcepts that cut across disciplines. Because these concepts rise above the fact base and can be exemplified through multiple disciplines, they are often used as organizers for integrated, interdisciplinary curriculum, which will be the focus of Chapter 4.

The sample science concepts in Table 2.2 are taken from the national science standards (National Research Council, 1996). The macroconcepts are referred to as integrating concepts in the national science standards because they can be applied across all three science disciplines—earth, life, and physical. They lead to the encompassing, enduring ideas that explain our world and universe. The

**Table 2.2**    Examples of Subject Area Concepts

| Macroconcepts | | |
| --- | --- | --- |
| *Science* | *Social Studies* | *Literature (Thematic)* |
| Change | Change/continuity | Change |
| System | System | System |
| Order | Patterns | Relationships |
| Interactions | Interactions | Interactions |
| Interdependence | Interdependence | Interdependence |
| Microconcepts | | |
| *Science* | *Social Studies* | *Literature (Thematic)* |
| Organism | Culture | Perception |
| Energy conservation | Landforms | Character |
| Waves | Scarcity | Passion |
| Heat/light/sound | Immigration/migration | Love/hate |
| Bond energy | Inventions | Family |
| Phase changes | Trade | Conflict |

microconcepts are the more discipline-specific concepts, although some of them also transfer across disciplines.

Another source for identifying discipline-based concepts is in the national standards for each discipline (see Resource B). In some standards, such as the national science standards, the concepts are easily identified and labeled. In other standards, such as standards for history, one must know the difference between a topic and a concept and be able to draw out those differences. I would suggest the use of a highlighter pen to note the concepts in standards before beginning curriculum development work at the local level.

Please note in Table 2.3 that literature has three types of concepts: One type arises out of the literature itself—out of the themes of literature. "Family," "Love," and "Conflict" are examples of the first type of concept. The second type is drawn from the author's craft. How does the author use concepts such as "Character," "Symbolism," "Allegory," "Foreshadowing," and so on to convey meaning or create effects? Recently, I have come to appreciate that there is a third type of concept for literature—the reader's craft. What do we want students to understand conceptually from the reader's frame of reference? We want students to understand that readers use context clues and connotative language to interpret the meaning of text, for example. The concepts in Table 2.3 for reader's and writer's craft were suggested by my friend and colleague, Dr. Lois Lanning, Assistant Superintendent for the Pomperaug Regional School District 15, Middlebury, Connecticut. Sample macroconcepts for the reader's craft are "Comprehension" (of text), "Reader Response" (to text), "Critical Stance" (to text), and "Purpose" (for reading). Each of these macroconcepts is supported by microconcepts such as text structure, imagery, or personal reflection. An English teacher I hold in high regard—Del Whitmire, from Green Bay, Wisconsin—suggests two additional microconcepts for the author's or writer's craft:

*Illumination.* The identification of particularly descriptive or significant passages

*Connecting Epiphanies.* Identifying emotional connections based on similar situations. (Whitmire, personal communication, February 17, 2007)

Identifying the major concepts for a topic of study is not as difficult as it seems. If you were asked to name the major concepts for a unit on "U.S. Trade," "The Economic Concepts of Scarcity," "Supply and Demand," and, of course, "Trade" would spring to mind. Once you have a list of terms related to the unit title, you can run them through the concept definition test.

## Concept Definition Test

Does the term you are considering as a higher-level concept serve as a mental frame or construct for a class of examples? Does it meet the following criteria?

- Broad and abstract (macrolevel to microlevel, but must transfer)
- Represented by one or two words

**Table 2.3** Literary Concepts

| Concepts in Themes | Reader's/Listener's/Viewer's Craft (Macroconcepts/Microconcepts)* | Writer's/Speaker's Craft (Macroconcepts/Microconcepts)* |
|---|---|---|
| Power | Comprehension (of text) | Voice |
| Identity | • *Strategies/Skills* | • *Tone* |
| Survival | • *Directionality* | • *Mood* |
| Fear | • *Matching* | • *Dialect* |
| Inner Conflict | • *Self-regulation* | Organization |
| Courage | o Problem solving | • *Transitions* |
| Love | o Metacognition | • *Text structure* |
| Relationships | o Self-correction | • *Leads* |
| Loss | o Reading rate | • *Details* |
| Friendships | • *Text language* | Fluency |
| Caring/Sharing | • *Inference* | • *Rhythm* |
| Jealousy | • *Summary* | • *Cadence* |
| Tolerance | • *Connections* | • *Flow* |
| Idealism | • *Imagery* | Word Usage |
| Isolationism | • *Genre* | • *Conventions* |
| Greed | • *Text Structures* | o Grammar |
| Sacrifice | • *Background knowledge* | o Mechanics |
| Compromise | Response (to text) | o Format |
| Control | • *Interaction (of text and reader)* | o Epithets |
| Justice | o Connection | o Epigrams |
| Humanity/ Inhumanity | o Discourse | • *Onomatopeia* |
| | • *Perspective* | o Language |
| | • *Personal reflection* | • *Alliteration* |
| | • *Literary criticism* | • *Symbolism* |
| | • *Motivation* | |
| | Critical Stance | |
| | • *Evaluation* | |
| | • *Judgment* | |
| | • *Text evidence* | |
| | • *Synthesis of ideas/information* | |
| | Purpose (for reading) | |
| | • *Audience* | |
| | • *Information* | |
| | • *Entertainment* | |
| | • *Explanation* | |
| | • *Research* | |
| | • *Reading rate* | |
| | • *Goals* | |

SOURCE: Reprinted with permission from Dr. Lois Lanning, Avon, Connecticut.

*Macroconcepts are formatted as regular text; microconcepts are italicized and listed with bullets.

- Universal in application
- Timeless (carries through the ages)
- Represented by different examples that share common attributes

*Example:* "Conflict," as a concept, has many different examples, but the examples share the characteristics of opposing forces and friction.

Let's try it. Which of the following are concepts? Apply each of the following terms to the test:

- Conflict
- Family
- Culture
- Change
- Fitness
- Human rights
- China

- Persuasion
- Power
- Revolution
- Model
- Dinosaurs
- Polar bears
- Cooperation

SOURCE: Cartoon by David Ford, davidford4@comcast.net.

How did you do? If you recognized that China, dinosaurs, and polar bears are topics that hold learning to the fact and activity base, then you are correct. But remember that you can apply a concept to the study of a topic, and to shift learning to a higher cognitive plane. In the following examples, consider the effects on instruction and learning when the conceptual lens is focused on the topics under study:

| Topic Example | Possible Conceptual Lens |
|---|---|
| Polar bears | Habitat/survival |
| Global warming | Sustainability |

## Why Should Curriculum Documents Provide a Conceptual Structure for the Content of Different Subject Areas?

● A conceptual structure for curriculum is important because conceptual understanding requires content knowledge, but the reverse is not necessarily true. National and state standards include the statement, "Students will understand the concepts and principles of mathematics, science, social studies, and so on." It is recognized that an understanding of concepts and principles signifies a deeper understanding of content knowledge.

● A conceptual structure is efficient for handling the growing body of information. Concepts focus and streamline the breadth of content.

● A conceptual structure forces students to think about topics and facts in terms of their transferable significance.

● A conceptual structure allows kindergarten teachers through postsecondary professors to become a team as they systematically build conceptual understanding and develop student intellect.

● A conceptual structure provides an instructional model that is idea centered, rigorous, and engaging for both students and teachers.

● A conceptual structure ensures that teachers are clear on the concepts and generalizations that students must understand at each level of schooling. It is not assumed that students and teachers will reach deeper understanding of ideas by covering the course objectives.

## Why Are Concepts Better Than Topics Alone as Curricular Organizers?

Curriculum design in the United States today is flawed in most subject areas because it relies on topics alone to organize content. If we are to truly raise standards, then a conceptual overlay for the topics and facts is critical.

Table 2.4 compares the value of concepts and topics as curricular organizers.

**Table 2.4**   Solely Topical Organizers and Conceptual Overlays

| Solely Topical Organizers | Conceptual Overlays |
| --- | --- |
| Frame a set of isolated facts | Provide a mental schema for categorizing common examples |
| Maintain lower-level thinking | Lead to higher levels of thinking |
| Hold learning to the fact or activity level | Aid in the development of higher-order generalizations |
| Have short term use—to cover an event, issue, or set of facts | Serve as a tool for processing life events |
| Increase the overloaded curriculum | Reduce the overloaded curriculum by framing the most salient, or critical examples of the concepts |

# GENERALIZATIONS

### What Are Generalizations? Why Are They So Important for 21st-Century Education?

Generalizations are the enduring understandings, the answer to the "so what" questions of study. They synthesize the factual examples and summarize learning. An excellent discussion of generalizations can be found in *Teaching Strategies for Ethnic Studies* by James Banks (1991). Banks differentiates between lower-level, intermediate-level, and universal-level generalizations that are related to a factual example:

*Fact:* The Chinese immigrants who came to San Francisco in the 1800s established the *hui kuan.*

*Lower-Level Generalization:* Chinese immigrants in the United States established various forms of social organizations.

*Intermediate-Level Generalization:* All groups that have immigrated or migrated to the Unites States have established social organizations.

*Universal-Level Generalization:* In all human societies, forms of social organizations emerge to satisfy the needs of individuals and groups. (pp. 43–45)

It is interesting to note that Banks (1991) differentiates the levels by the statement's degree of generalizability. I would consider Banks's lower and intermediate levels to be facts rather than generalizations, however, because these two levels give specific noun subjects and use past tense verbs. The parts of the sentences that generalize are the conceptual phrases; when these phrases are linked to specific nouns, they fall into the category of facts. The past tense verbs do not permit transfer through time, which is a critical attribute of universal generalizability.

In this book, the focus is on the **universal generalizations**—the enduring understandings that have applicability through time and across cultures. These are the lessons of history that can be used as references in considering and comparing new situational examples. Some possible generalizations for a unit on Native American culture and change might include the following:

- Cultures change over time.
- Cross-cultural interaction fosters the exchange of ideas, goods, and services.
- Social, political, or economic change can cause conflict within a society.
- Dominant cultures can disrupt minority cultures.
- Merging cultures create social, political, and economic change.

When people do not understand the significance of teaching to conceptual understandings they may be alienated by the abstract statements. They may think, "These ideas are too difficult for children to understand. Why not just write straightforward facts?" But the truth is, when students can discuss conceptual ideas and use the facts to support those ideas they gain a deeper grasp of knowledge. They also gain the ability to transfer knowledge. We want students to be able to use and understand conceptual language. This is certainly possible if we build conceptual brain schemata from grade level to grade level in a **developmentally appropriate** manner.

Teachers do not usually tell students the generalizations at the beginning of a lesson. They teach inductively to develop students' abstract thinking abilities as they relate specific facts to transferable understandings. Students will develop their own insights as they learn to synthesize facts to the level of abstract relevance. It is important to ensure that student generalizations are supported with facts. At times, students may make inaccurate generalizations, leaps of abstraction in their zeal to know the answer. Teachers must think on their feet as they foster the development of students' higher-level abstraction through reasoning and critical thinking. They teach students to use primary and secondary sources to support their generalizations. They question students to help them clarify their thinking. (Chapter 7 discusses additional strategies and provides examples for concept-based instruction.)

Because the path from specific topics to the concepts and generalizations is a new and somewhat difficult skill, teachers' first attempts at teaching to ideas may be very broad surface learnings, such as "Governments influence culture." But as they question the broad ideas with "How?" or "Why?" and delineate the ideas more specifically, these surface learnings become powerfully stated, clear statements. An example of a more specific idea might be "Governments structure a society to maintain order." The learning curve for thinking from facts to conceptual understandings is very steep. Teachers around the country are becoming very skilled at writing clear and powerful generalizations for instruction.

Some educators feel that young children are not capable of abstracting to the level of generalizations, but children are capable of abstract thought and generalization when they are called for in the context of developmentally appropriate content.

As one example, a group of kindergarten and first-grade teachers in Richmond, Indiana, developed a unit around the concept of "Color" for their young students. The unit title they chose was "The Value of Color in Our Rainbow World." They engaged students in many activities such as the following to demonstrate the concept:

- Using scarf draping to decide as a group whether each child looks best in winter, spring, summer, or fall colors
- Taking environmental walks to note and appreciate how the different colors create interest for the viewer
- Identifying how color is used to keep people safe

When asked how color helps us in our world, the children were able to generalize (with a little help on the lead-in) that color "can make us pretty," "makes our environment more interesting," and "keeps us safe."

Generalizations are summaries of thought and answer the relevancy question, "What do I understand as a result of my study?" Generalizations are deeper understandings that transfer through time and across cultures. They hold truth as long as they are supported by the situational examples. Banks (1991) explains that even though a generalization is capable of being tested or verified, it can never be proven absolutely to be correct. Because of the complexity of human behavior, generalizations in the social and behavioral sciences are necessarily tentative and often contain qualifiers. Generalizations are important, however, as conceptual summaries of thought.

## A Universal Generalization Defined

A *generalization* is defined formally as two or more concepts stated in a relationship. Universal generalizations have characteristics similar to concepts:

- Broad and abstract (macrolevel to microlevel)
- Universal in application
- Generally timeless—may need to be qualified as "often, can, or may" if the ideas do not hold through time in all cases
- Represented by different examples which support the generalization

Apply the characteristics to the following idea: "Cultures regulate social behavior through norms and mores." Does this idea meet the criteria to qualify as a generalization?

Universal generalizations, as they are written, use no past, past-perfect, or present-perfect verb tenses. To do so would identify them in time as facts. For example, the sentence "Poverty was a catalyst for migration" is past tense and may be a factual generalization referencing a particular time and place, but it is not a timeless, universal generalization as stated. How could we change this fact into a timeless generalization?

Although generalizations are usually timeless, they are more susceptible to demise than are concepts. Concepts are timeless; because generalizations are interdependent variables, they may not hold over time. For example, a current generalization could be, "Trade stimulates an economy." If a nation's trade deficit makes it overly dependent on other countries, however, the generalization eventually breaks down. Generalizations are helpful constructs for summarizing conceptual relationships, but their timeless validity must be tested continually through analysis of contemporary, factual examples. If a generalization is an important idea, but does not hold across all cases, then the qualifiers "often," "can," or "may" can be used in the sentence.

Universal generalizations avoid proper and personal nouns. "Japanese trade affects the American economy" is a fact because it states specific examples. The universal generalization is written, "Trade affects an economy." This statement can be supported through time by numerous examples. As students progress through the grades, the generalizations should become more sophisticated by drawing on more complex concepts. Concepts and generalizations provide a framework for the articulation and coordination of curriculum in both single-grade and multiage schooling structures.

Chapter 3 looks at state standards and considers their impact on local curriculum design. Do standards support or impede concept-based curriculum and instruction at the local level? Chapter 3 shares examples of district curricula that adhere to a concept-based design as they align to state standards.

# SUMMARY

The use of universal and lasting concepts to structure the massive amount of content that educators present to students provides a rational plan to teach for the transfer of knowledge. Concept-based curriculum and instruction solve problems:

- How to reduce an overloaded curriculum
- How to systematically articulate K–12 curriculum to engage higher-level, complex thinking and develop deepened understanding
- How to raise academic standards by bringing relevance and rigor to learning through idea-centered curricula

Concept-based curriculum designs allow the teacher to control rather than be controlled by the subject matter, and provides the flexibility to allow students to search for and construct knowledge.

## EXTENDING THOUGHT

1. How does concept-based curriculum design reach beyond the memorization of isolated facts?

2. When students dialogue about issues at a conceptual level, they may be debating a variety of perspectives. What are the ramifications for instruction? What are teachers' responsibilities?

3. What role do topics and facts play in a concept-based curriculum design?

4. Why is a conceptual schema important as a framework for learning in today's world?

5. What is the value of a universal generalization to the learning process?

6. What are the dangers of generalizing related to
   - Shallow thinking and low-level generalizations?
   - Leaps of abstraction without supporting data?
   - Bias in generalizing?

# State Academic Standards and Local Curriculum Frameworks

3

## STATE STANDARDS

State standards are driving curriculum and instruction in the United States today. On the positive side, standards have dramatically increased the attention and time that schools and school districts spend on curriculum development and assessment. On the negative side, standards vary greatly in the quality of their design from state to state, and curriculum design does affect classroom instruction. Let's look at a few examples from state standards and consider how they will affect local curricular documents.

Although the implied or implicit content of state standards is virtually identical from state to state, the language of standards varies greatly. Some content standards are specific and factual; others are broad and abstract. It is important to understand how these standards are written because their impact on classroom instruction is significant. State curriculum committees and legislative oversight committees make a conscious decision to write the content standards either in the form of a conceptual framework or as a delineated curriculum of specific topics and skills. Most states emphasize the conceptual approach with science and the topic approach with history, following the lead of the national science and history standards. (Note: Skill-based standards, such as the language arts area, have not changed much over the years except in degree of emphasis for various skills. Skill-based standards are driven by verbs of necessity. This discussion of concept-based versus topic-based does not relate to these skill areas.)

Can you determine from the following examples of state standards whether the emphasis and expectations are for conceptual understanding or for factual knowledge?

*Typical History State Standards: Grade 5*

I. The student will know how early cultures developed in North America.
   a. Locate the settlements of early Native American tribes, including Arctic (Inuit, or Eskimo), Northwest (Kwakiutl), Plains (Sioux), Southwest (Pueblo), and Eastern Woodland (Iroquois).
   b. Explain how geography and climate influenced the daily lives of Native American peoples.

II. The student will know the reasons for and effects of European exploration and settlements in North America.
   a. Describe the motivations, hardships, and accomplishments of the Spanish, French, Portuguese, and English explorers.
   b. Describe the cultural interactions leading to conflicts and cooperation between the Europeans and the early Native Americans.

Factual or conceptual? How will teachers address these standards in their instruction?

---

*Typical Science State Standards*

*Early Elementary*

12.B.lb. Describe how living things depend on one another for survival.

*Middle School or Junior High School*

12.B.3a. Identify and classify biotic and abiotic factors in an environment that affect population density, habitat, and placement of organisms in an energy pyramid.

*High School*

12.B.4b. Simulate and analyze factors that influence the size and stability of populations within ecosystems (e.g., birth rate, death rate, predation, and migration patterns).

Factual or conceptual? How will teachers address these standards in their instruction?

How will local committees design their curricula when aligning to these two approaches to standards? Will both approaches use specific topics to ground the standard? Certainly! You cannot teach conceptual understanding without covering specific content topics. But should we write traditional content objectives at the state level, complete with the verbs from Bloom's taxonomy (Bloom, Engelhart,

Furst, Hill, & Krathwohl, 1956)? Or should we write important conceptual understandings at the state level, listing critical content topics (without verbs) that must be included in the local curriculum documents? Which format—conceptual or topic driven—will facilitate deeper levels of thinking, transfer of knowledge, and active student engagement when translated into curriculum at the local level? Which will allow the teacher greater intellectual engagement as she designs for learning?

## Objectives, Outcomes, and Standards

Educational terms shift in the wind with each wave of reform. In the 1970s and early 1980s, the essential component for quality education was a set of clear, specific, and measurable objectives for each subject. Educators practiced writing objectives using just the right verb. Then, in the mid-1980s, the outcomes movement came roaring along. Objectives were out—outcomes were in. Outcomes were used to show through performance what students could do with what they know. The philosophy held on, but the term "outcome" became a target for political harpoons, and we moved on to the term "standards." This term survives, and the intent is to have students demonstrate what they know. When we get right down to it, though, we are back to the old objectives in most states. Adding the current focus on high-stakes testing to the "what goes around, comes around" objectives phenomenon leads to predicted results in classrooms: "Cover more faster" and "More discrete skill drill, less talk."

The trouble with traditional objectives is that they choose a verb, link it to a topic, and assume that teaching and learning will move beyond memorization. For example, consider the following typical objective (often called a **benchmark** or performance indicator in today's jargon): "Describe life in early America before and after European contact." Now consider the question, "Why should we describe life in early America?" We should ask this question every time we align to a content standard.

It is easy to "do the verb" with the topic—but is that really the point? Do we instead want students to understand that "Interacting cultures create social, political, and economic changes"? Too many standards assume that teaching and learning will go beyond the objective to arrive at a deeper understanding. I can assure you, though, based on 13 years of intensive work with teachers, that thinking beyond the facts to the level of conceptual relevance is a difficult and new skill for most educators. Traditional curriculum designs and lower-level assessments do not require going beyond the facts. The structure of traditional content objectives is a large part of the problem in helping teachers raise the bar for students.

## THE TRIPARTITE MODEL OF CURRICULUM DESIGN

To truly raise standards, we must move from a solely fact-based model to a **tripartite model of curriculum design**. Figure 3.1 shows the usefulness of the tripartite model for single-subject area curriculum design, as well as for the interdisciplinary curriculum model, which will be described in Chapter 4.

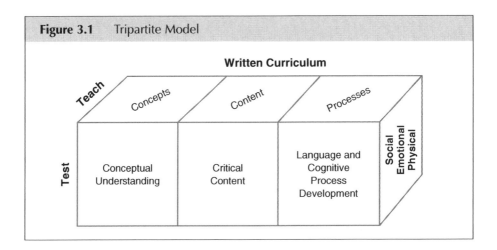

**Figure 3.1** Tripartite Model

Written Curriculum

Teach

Concepts

Content

Processes

Test

Conceptual
Understanding

Critical
Content

Language and
Cognitive
Process
Development

Social
Emotional
Physical

In the traditional model of curriculum, the focus for teaching and learning is on the fact base. The facts are organized by topics. As the world information base expands, more topics are added to the bulging curriculum. We lack a rational plan for reducing content, and teaching becomes a skim of surface information.

In the tripartite model, content topics are set within a conceptual framework. When an educator teaches conceptually, the focus shifts from memorizing isolated facts as the end game to using facts as a tool for understanding the deeper, transferable concepts and principles. The aim is to develop conceptual understanding and to build brain schemata to intellectually manage the expanding information base.

Figure 3.1 shows the balance between conceptual understanding, critical content knowledge, and process development. If we are to increase the development of critical content knowledge, conceptual understanding, and process and skill abilities, then we must find more instructional time in the school day. This can only be accomplished by systematically reducing and focusing the factual content load. The standards movement can conceivably make this task more difficult. If teachers view standards as a set of objectives that they have to check off and race through, then learning will be shallow.

The move toward a more balanced curriculum of concept, content, and process development is really a move toward greater depth in teaching and learning as well as a focus on higher-level thinking. If we want all children to be successful in developing the conceptual understanding implied in many standards documents across the country, then we will need to design curriculum that moves from topic-based to concept-based curricula, from lower-order to higher-order **process skills,** and from meaningless activities to meaningful learning experiences.

### How Can Curriculum Developers and Committees Organize Content Related to the Major Concepts?

In Chapter 2, I advocated the creation of national (or state-level) concept-based models for classroom units. But the precedent of local control of curriculum may forestall this idea, so this chapter and the next provide guidelines for district-level curriculum development.

## Curriculum Mapping

Before a district, school, or classroom can design a concept-based curriculum, it must identify the required critical content topics. These topics, along with processes and skills, and assessments, are noted through the process of curriculum mapping, so aptly described by contributors to *Getting Results With Curriculum Mapping* (Hayes-Jacobs, 2004).

Curriculum mapping is a procedure for collecting data about the actual curriculum in a school district, using the school calendar as an organizer. Data need to be collected on the content being taught at each grade level, and on the processes and skills being emphasized. Curriculum maps help teachers to see what is actually going on in curriculum through the grades; to adjust for gaps, overlaps, and redundancies in content topics and skills; and to see where connected topics can work together in an integrated, interdisciplinary unit. Hayes-Jacobs (2004) expands the use of curriculum mapping as a tool in planning for instruction. See Table 3.1 for a basic curriculum-mapping format.

## Content–Concept Matrices

Once the critical content has been identified by topics on curriculum maps, it is helpful to identify related concepts. A simple format is the matrix. Tables 3.2 and 3.3 show examples from high school chemistry and economics. These examples were developed by teachers in the Federal Way, Washington (State), School District. Although these matrices have been replaced over the years with other curriculum documents, they illustrate an effective method for relating critical content subtopics and subconcepts to organizing concepts in different disciplines.

**Table 3.1**    Curriculum-Mapping Format

| Grade Level 4 | September | October | November | December | January |
|---|---|---|---|---|---|
| Science topics | | | | | |
| Science skills | | | | | |
| Social studies topics | | | | | |
| Social studies skills | | | | | |

**Table 3.2** Chemistry, Concepts, and Critical Content

| Organizing Concepts | Content Strands | | | | | | |
|---|---|---|---|---|---|---|---|
| | Processes and Methods | Energy/Thermo Dynamics | Atomic Theory | Bonding | Matter | Kinetic Theory | Reactions |
| Cause and Effect | Controlled experimentation<br>Safety | Entropy: activation and potential energy | Significance of electron configuration<br>Periodicity | Attachment between atoms | | Heat and temperature<br>Factors affecting reaction rate | Ionic reactions<br>Molecular reactions |
| Change | Dimensional analysis | Conversion of energy<br>Phase changes<br>Entropy | | | Physical change<br>Chemical change | Phase changes | Stoichiometry<br>Oxidation reduction reactions |
| Energy Matter | Naming compounds | Forms of energy | Light emission<br>Absorption<br>Ionization | Bond energy | Varieties of matter physical or chemical properties | Heat and temperature<br>Phase changes<br>Enthalpy<br>Entropy | Energy and chemical reactions |
| Equilibrium | Chemical formulas solutions | Phase changes | | | Conservation of matter<br>Conservation of atoms | Phase changes | Le Chatelier Principle |
| Fundamental Entities | Mole | | Atoms<br>Molecules<br>Electron<br>Proton<br>Neutron | Electrical interaction | Mole | | Balancing equations<br>Mole, pH scale |
| Interaction | | | | Ionic bonds<br>Covalent bonds<br>Hydrogen bonds<br>Polar bonds | Solubility<br>Colligative properties | Factors affecting reaction rate | Limiting reaction<br>Acid/base reaction |
| Model | Problem solving | Ionization | Dalton model<br>Thomson model<br>Bohr model<br>Quantum model<br>Charge cloud<br>Electron configuration<br>Electron distribution<br>Energy levels | VSEPR model<br>Lewis structure | Conservation of mass | Gas laws<br>Collision theory<br>Hess's law | Collision theory<br>Acid/base reaction |
| Probability | Percent error | | Atomic weight<br>Mass | | | | |
| Quantification | Percent composition<br>Graphing SI units<br>Significant figure precision<br>Concentrations of solutions | Scientific notation<br>Measurement<br>Heat | | | Mole<br>Percent composition | | Stoichiometry |

SOURCE: Federal Way Public Schools, Federal Way, Washington. Used with permission.

**Table 3.3**   Economics Concept/Content Matrix

| Concept | Content | Generalizations and Principles |
|---|---|---|
| Scarcity | Opportunity Costs<br>Choices<br>• Personal<br>• Country | The basic economic problem is scarcity. At any given time each society has a given amount of labor, capital, and natural resources. People's wants for goods and services are greater than what can be produced. Because we cannot do, or have, everything all at once, we must make choices. Much of economics deals with analyzing how and why individuals, institutions, and societies make the choices they do. |
| Comparative Systems | Command Economy<br>• Communism<br>• Socialism<br><br>Market Economy<br>• Business Cycles<br>• Capitalism | Every economic system institutionalizes the manner in which people decide what to produce, how to produce, and for whom to produce. Each economic system uses different means to answer these questions, based on its prevailing philosophic assumptions. Several economies rely more heavily on government and less on markets. |
| Investments | Stocks<br>Bonds<br>Mutual Funds<br>Others | Investment capital comes from the people buying stocks and bonds from companies who use the needed capital to expand their production capacities and increase their productivity. |
| Supply and Demand | Competition<br>Utility<br>Equilibrium | Markets are institutional arrangements that enable buyers and sellers to exchange goods and services. Changes in supply, or demand, or both, will cause changes in prices, and in the amounts of goods or services produced and demanded. Competition thus forces the use of resources in an efficient manner. |
| Government Regulation | Budget, Debt<br>Taxation<br>Controls | Government guides the market in decision making by forcing it to respond to rules and regulations which are designed to achieve the objectives society has set, and to answer its basic economic questions of what to produce, how to produce, and for whom to produce. |
| Monetary/Fiscal | Federal Reserve<br>Government | Monetary policy attempts to regulate the general level of economic activity. It regulates the money supply by its activities. Governments use taxing and spending policies to shape fiscal policy. |
| Labor | History<br>Unions<br>Bargaining | Labor movements reflect the working supply and demand in the job market. Unions are formed to maintain some control over working conditions and seek fairness in the workplace through collective bargaining. |
| International Trade | Comparative Advantage<br>Balance of Trade<br>Restrictions Versus<br>Free Trade | The concept of "Comparative Advantage" explains why nations benefit from specialization and trade with each other. Comparative advantage can allow goods and services for the least cost to be exchanged. However, this specialization might force a nation to become dependent upon others for basic needs. As a consequence, government often takes steps in with regulations designed to balance the flow of trade to insure jobs and resources for itself. |

SOURCE: Federal Way Public Schools, Federal Way, Washington. Used with permission.

A concept–content matrix allows the teacher to evaluate the content load of the course. If there are too many topics to cover, there will be less time for the student to develop the essential processes and skills for accessing, interpreting, and displaying knowledge.

Three criteria are especially helpful in deciding which topics (subtopics or subconcepts) qualify as critical content to be included on the matrix:

1. What do students need to know to be successful at the next level of learning? Multiplication, for example, is necessary prior knowledge for success with division.

2. What do you, as a professional, feel that students need to know to understand the subject? For example, the American Revolution and the Civil War are two topics critical to an understanding of the subject of U.S. history.

3. What critical content topics and concepts are reasonably expected and identified in state academic standards?

# SCOPE AND SEQUENCE CHARTS FOR PROCESSES AND SKILLS

Processes and skills noted on the curriculum maps need to be articulated in a scope and sequence format. Processes and skills also need to be aligned to state standards to prevent gaps. Some disciplines, such as mathematics and art, are both skill based and concept based. Yet, too often, the curriculum documents address directly only the skill component and make an assumption that students will infer the key concepts and principles of the discipline. That assumption is a fallacy. Why is it that so many people feel that they are weak in mathematics or art knowledge? Is it because they never really developed understanding of the deeper knowledge base—the key concepts and principles? Could they do the skills of mathematics, yet never really understand why mathematics worked? And how could they really show sophisticated performance in art without being able to use the language of art to articulate their understandings?

Meridian School District in Meridian, Idaho, has developed concept–process curricula for all subject areas from kindergarten through Grade 12. Tables 3.4 and 3.5 share excerpts from the curricular frameworks of two subject areas that traditionally tend to focus more on the skills and activities in curriculum documents—elementary and secondary mathematics. Key concepts are italicized in the generalizations.

Districts such as Meridian, which take on the intellectual challenge of identifying the deeper, conceptual understandings, are to be commended. It is hard work to think beyond the facts and activities to answer the relevancy questions "Why?" "How?" and "So what?" These excerpts from Meridian continue to be refined by curriculum committees to meet the expectations of new state academic standards.

**Table 3.4**   Elementary Mathematics

**Generalizations (Enduring Understandings)**

- *Numbers* are *quantities*.

- *Numerals* represent *quantities*.

- *Numbers* name *things* and place things in *order*.

- *Mathematical operations* (+, −, ×) help solve *problems*.

- *Quantities* can be *added together* or *taken apart*.

| Introduce | Develop | Master |
|---|---|---|
| Numeral recognition to 200 | Numeral recognition to 200 | Numeral recognition to 100 |
| | Counting 1–100+ | Counting 1–100+ |
| | Counting backward from 10 | Counting backward from 10 |
| | Matching numeral to number<br>2 ☐☐<br>5 ☐☐☐☐☐ | Matching numeral to number<br>2 ☐☐<br>5 ☐☐☐☐☐ |
| Place value to 100—counting days in school, grouping 1s to 10s and 10s to 100s | Place value to 100—counting days in school, grouping 1s to 10s and 10s to 100s | |
| | | Numeral writing 1–100 |
| Ordinal numbers 6th to 10th and vocabulary | Ordinal numbers 6th to 10th and vocabulary | |
| | Count by 2, 5, 10, to 100 | Count by 5 and 10 to 100 |
| Addition—connecting concrete form to symbolic form (5 + 2 = 7) | Addition—connecting concrete form to symbolic form (5 + 2 = 7) | Addition—connecting concrete form to symbolic form (5 + 2 = 7) |
| Addition—2 digits without carrying | Addition—2 digits without carrying | |
| Addition—single-digit sums to 18 | Addition—single-digit sums to 18 | Addition—single-digit sums to 10 |
| Subtraction—symbolic form (5 − 2 = 3) | Subtraction—symbolic form (5 − 2 = 3) | Subtraction—symbolic form (5 − 2 = 3) |
| Subtraction—2 digits without regrouping | Subtraction—2 digits without regrouping | |

*(Continued)*

(Continued)

| Introduce | Develop | Master |
|---|---|---|
| Subtraction—single-digit differences from 18 | Subtraction—single-digit differences from 18 | Subtraction—single-digit differences from 10 |
| Concept of "Zero" in addition and subtraction facts as a quantity | Concept of "Zero" in addition and subtraction facts as a quantity | Concept of "Zero" in addition and subtraction facts as a quantity |
| Doubles (2 + 2 to 9 + 9) | Doubles to 9 + 9 | Doubles to 5 + 5 |
| Doubles +1 (2 + 2 = 4, so 2 + 3 = 5) | Doubles +1 (2 + 2 = 4, so 2 + 3 = 5) | |
| Greater than, less than, equal to—terms, not symbols | Greater than, less than, equal to—terms, not symbols | |

**Sample Generalizations**

| Fourth Grade | Fifth Grade | Sixth Grade | Seventh Grade |
|---|---|---|---|
| The placement of a *number* determines its *value*. | *Long division* is a *repeated-step* process. | Estimation approximates exact values. | *Rational numbers* can be written as *fractions* or *decimals*. |
| The *decimal placement* determines *place value* in *addition* and *subtraction*. | The placement of the *decimal* in a *product* is determined by the *parts of the whole* that are multiplied. | *Division* splits a *whole* into *equal parts*. | *Relationships* exist between *factors, multiples,* and *rules of divisibility*. |
| The *borrowing process* depends on a *comparative value* of the *numbers*. | | *Divisibility rules* control *factoring* and *dividing*. | *Fraction* and *decimal numbers* can be *expressions* of the same *quantity*. |

SOURCE: Meridian Mathematics Committee, Meridian Joint School District No. 2, Meridian, Idaho. Used with permission.

The mathematics curriculum in Meridian provides the necessary scope and sequence based on skills to be introduced, developed, and mastered. The mathematics committee also looked for the key concepts implied in the skills to be mastered and asked themselves, "What are the key, conceptual ideas (generalizations) that students need to internalize?" The scope and sequence charts and the generalizations were written for the following mathematics strands:

- Number
- Patterns, functions, algebra
- Measurement, geometry, spatial sense
- Data analysis, statistics, and probability

Table 3.4 shows an excerpt from the Meridian first-grade scope and sequence for the number strand only. The generalizations at the top of the page are the *enduring understandings*—the key conceptual ideas framing the skills to be mastered. Meridian chose to make the generalizations for kindergarten through Grade 3 the same, but the skills become more sophisticated to bring depth to the understandings. At Grade 4 and each subsequent grade, the generalizations become more sophisticated as additional concepts enter the curriculum.

Table 3.5 excerpts the increasingly sophisticated generalizations from Grades 4 through pre-calculus as students work with the concept of "Number" in Meridian.

**Table 3.5** Secondary Mathematics

| Pre-Algebra | Algebra 1/2 | Pre-Calculus |
|---|---|---|
| *Proportion* expresses an *equivalent relationship* between two *parts*. | The *distributive property* allows *options* in *problem solving*. | *Logarithms* represent *exponents* and follow *exponential rules* of *operation*. |
| *Scientific notation* is an efficient way to represent *extended numbers*. | *Absolute value* measures the *distance* from *zero*.  *Variables* represent *unknown quantities*. | All *real* and *imaginary numbers* can be written as *complex numbers*. |
| The *properties* of *numbers* and the *order of operations* establish a *universal language*. | *Rational numbers* are a *subset* of the *real number system*. | *Conjugates* are used to simplify *complex rational expressions*. |

SOURCE: Meridian Mathematics Committee, Meridian Joint School District No. 2, Meridian, Idaho. Used with permission.

Table 3.6 shows a Grade 5 geometry framework excerpt from Pomperaug Regional School District 15 in Middlebury, Connecticut. The Enduring Understandings and the Essential Question provide the extended focus for the Performance Standards.

Table 3.7, from Meridian, Idaho, shows an excerpt of the generalizations for music. The basic elements of music are the organizing concepts that structure the knowledge and provide the language to discuss music. When students can perform the skills and deepen their conceptual understanding of the content and language of music, they move toward artistry. Notice how this curriculum benchmarks the enduring understandings by grade bands for each organizing concept. Their

**Table 3.6** Grade 5 Mathematics Framework Excerpt

**Strand**

Geometry and Measurement

**Concepts**

Shapes; Geometric Comparisons; Measurement

**Enduring Understandings**

1. Changing the position of an object does not affect its attributes.
2. Lines and angles can be described using geometric attributes.
3. The perimeters, areas, and volumes of objects depend on their dimensions.
4. The perimeter, area, and volume of a geometric figure may change as angles, sides, and lengths change.

**Essential Question**

How do geometric relationships and measurements help us to solve problems and make sense of our world?

**Students Should**

3.1. Use properties and characteristics of two- and three-dimensional shapes and geometric theorems to describe relationships, communicate ideas, and solve problems.
3.2. Use spatial reasoning, location, and geometric relationships to solve problems.
3.3. Develop and apply units, systems, formulas, and appropriate tools to estimate and measure.

| Performance Standards | Expected Performances | Focus Questions | Assessments | Resources |
|---|---|---|---|---|
| Use geometric relationships to describe polygons and solids. | 1. Use geometric relationships such as parallel, perpendicular, and congruent to describe the attributes of sets and subsets of shapes and solids.<br><br>2. Make and test conjectures about geometric relationships. | 1. How do you describe the attributes of geometric shapes and solids?<br><br>2. What does change in position mean? | Use various suggested Trailblazer assessments to monitor progress. | *Math Trailblazers (MTB)*<br><br>Unit 6: Geometry<br><br>Unit 4: Division and Data<br><br>Unit 14: Using Circles |
| Recognize that changes in the perimeter of a polygon may affect its area, and changes in area may affect the perimeter. | 1. Explore the relationship between area and perimeter when the dimensions of a polygon change.<br><br>2. Develop formulas to find the perimeter and area of squares, rectangles, and triangles. | 1. How do you find area and perimeter of any given shape or solid?<br><br>2. How are the area and perimeter of a polygon interdependent? | Use various suggested Trailblazer assessments to monitor progress. | *MTB*<br><br>Unit 4: Division and Data<br><br>Unit 9: Connections to Division<br><br>Unit 15: Developing Formulas With Geometry |
| Identify, describe, and build nets for solid figures and objects. | 1. Represent the surface of 3D objects through the use of 2D nets.<br><br>2. Investigate and develop strategies to determine the volume of rectangular solids. | 1. How do you find volume of a solid figure?<br><br>2. How do you build a model of a 3D solid using a net? | Use various suggested Trailblazer assessments to monitor progress. | |

SOURCE: Mathematics Curriculum Committee, Pomperaug Regional School District No. 15, Middlebury/Southbury, Connecticut. Used with permission.

**Table 3.7** Meridian Music Generalizations

| Grade | Melody | Rhythm | Harmony | Form |
|---|---|---|---|---|
| K–2 | Melody has direction. | Rhythmic patterns exist in the natural and constructed worlds. | Combining two or more pitches creates harmony. | Music has structure. |
| 3–6 | Melodies are organized into tonalities. | Manipulation of rhythm creates musical patterns. | Combining two or more sounds in different ways creates variety in harmony. | Musical structure is caused by repetition and contrast of same and different parts. |
| 7–12 | Distinct melodic patterns indicate culture and style. | Distinct rhythmic patterns differentiate musical styles. | Harmonic movement through chord construction and progression follows a deliberate order. | Structure creates order and clarity in music. |

| Grade | Timbre | Texture | Expressive Elements |
|---|---|---|---|
| K–2 | Sounds have recognizable/distinguishing characteristics. | Music has layers of sound. | Music has a variety of expressive elements. |
| 3–6 | Timbre conveys mood and culture. | Layers of sound (texture) are associated with historical musical periods. | Dynamics, tempo, articulation, and text express and enhance the message of music. |
| 7–12 | Timbre can be modified to reflect style, mood, and culture. The authentic recreation of style requires appropriate timbre. | Manipulation of textures creates complexity and interest—aural, visual, and kinesthetic. | The message of music elicits an emotional response. Expressive elements drive the artistry in music. |

SOURCE: Meridian Joint School District No. 2, Meridian, Idaho. Used with permission.

curriculum also includes a scope and sequence for the music skills to be taught in the different grade bands.

Visual art is another discipline that traditionally has been reflected in curriculum documents as a set of skills to be learned and applied, although the content of art is structured with a language that students need to understand at a conceptual and skill level.

Public schools in Tacoma, Washington, designed a K–12 visual arts curriculum that addresses conceptual understanding as well as skills. Figures 3.2a through 3.4b share excerpts from classroom lessons related to the concept of "Line" at different grade levels. The generalization and essential question set the focus for the lesson. As students learn and practice skills, they build conceptual understanding. The art generalizations become more sophisticated as students progress through the grades. Teachers need to have the generalizations clearly stated in the grade-level curricula. We cannot assume that practicing the skills will produce conceptual understanding. Instruction needs to follow through to the conceptual level. Susy Watt, art instructor for elementary and secondary education at Pacific Lutheran University in the state of Washington, and consultant for the Tacoma visual art curriculum, shares her thoughts on concept-based art:

> Whether looking at, talking about, or making visual art, a concept-based approach to teaching gives teachers a clear, intentional focus, and gives students the resulting opportunity to apply new knowledge and skills in their everyday living. Generalizations and essential questions advance art in the classroom from a singular activity to vital study for school, work, and home. Long after the excitement of art making, students recognize the practice of art in their lives. Students learn a concept, practice the concept again in a new context, change the subject of their art, change the art materials, and are still left with enduring understandings. (Watt, personal communication, February 2000)

Figure 3.4 shows an excerpt from the Tacoma high school course, Drawing 2. Notice that the students are still working with the concept of "Line," but that their prior knowledge of the concept and related skills allow them to perform with greater sophistication and deeper understanding. The generalizations that describe conceptual relationships are more complex. This curriculum design is strong because it brings relevance to skills by highlighting the related concepts and transferable understandings.

There are many different formats for designing district-level curricula to meet state and national standards. This chapter shares examples of district frameworks that express all three components of the tripartite curriculum model: conceptual, factual, and processes and skills. It is important for subjects such as mathematics, language arts, and fine arts that have a heavy skill emphasis to delineate the curriculum for their own discipline before they create interdisciplinary connections in social studies or science units.

Once members of a discipline have identified their subject area concepts, generalizations, critical content, and processes and skills, they can work with social

*(Text continues on page 66)*

**Figure 3.2a** Curriculum Content for Solving Problems Using the Visual Arts: Kindergarten

Curriculum Content for Solving Problems Using the Visual Arts

# Kindergarten

Essential Learning 1: The student acquires the **Knowledge and Skills** necessary to create, to perform, and to respond effectively to the arts.
Component 1.1. Applies arts concepts and vocabulary; 1.2. Organizes compositions; 1.3. Uses arts skills and techniques; 1.4. Produces quality work
Benchmark 2. Understands concepts that structure thinking in the arts; changes the impact of a composition; selects tools and materials; demonstrates craftsmanship
The student **Identifies and Explores Arts Elements** (in nature, constructed world, own art).

**Line**
- Straight
- Curved
- Wavy
- Zigzag
- Interrupted

**Color**
- Primary

**Texture**
- Rought
- Smooth

**Shape/Form**
- Edges
- Faces
- Angles
- Naming shapes

**Take Knowledge**

**Add**

**Materials and Tools**
(3+ surfaces)
- 12" × 18" + paper (sulfite, kraft, butcher, construction, tissue)
- Tools (pencils, brushes, crayons, payons)
- Paints (liquid tempera, finger paint, watercolor)
- Fasteners (white glue, glue sticks, tape)
- Found materials (cardboard, coated wire)
- Blunt scissors
- Clay premixed ceramic and oil-based
- Yarn

**Skills and Techniques**—*Uses safe procedures/maintains studio organization*

**Markmaking**
*Uses full arm movement*
*Uses sides and paints of tools*
*Invents drawing techniques (spinning, twisting, multiples)*

**Cutting**
*Cuts straight lines*

**Constructing**
*Rolls and flattens clay*

**Fastening**
*Pastes paper to paper*

**Printmaking**
*Stamps with objects on paper or clay*

**Talk About and Create a**

**Composition**

*Identities components within a composition by looking and naming*

Calm ↔ Harmony ↔ Variety ↔ Chaos

SOURCE: Tacoma School District No. 10, Visual Arts Curriculum, Tacoma, Washington. Used with permission.

**Figure 3.2b** Curriculum Content for Solving Problems Using the Visual Arts: Kindergarten (Continued)

# Kindergarten

| Essential Learning 1 | + | Essential Learnings 2–4 | = | Assessments | Teaching/Learning |

## Essential Learning 1

### Questions/Problems to Solve
### Generalizations

1. *How can I make a variety of lines?*
   G1: Straight and curved LINES combine to form all other types of lines (interrupted, wavy, spiral, zigzag).

2. *How will I make many different colors?*
   G2: ALL COLORS/hues are created from the primary colors.

3. *How can I make a variety of shapes?*
   G3: SHAPES have names, edges, faces, and sometimes angles.

4. *How does this texture feel?*
   G4: TEXTURE is surface quality perceived through touch (rough, smooth).

### Interdisciplinary Connections

*Conceptual Connections*
Math: Geometric shapes/puzzles classification of lines
Science: Identification of pars of animals and insects
H&F: Moving in space on a line

*Contextual Connections*
Social Studies: Directions traffic shapes and colors
Language Arts: Prepositions to describe location in space
Music, Drama, Dance: Marks to movement, marks to music

## Essential Learnings 2–4

### Life Applications

- Student uses lien, shapes, and color in visual images.
- Student associates actual textures with visual textures.
- Student recognizes lines, colors, textures in nature, constructed world and own art.

### Essential Learnings 2–4

2.1. Identifies and explores sensory information from a variety of sources
2.2. Finds one artistic solution to a problem (gathers and investigates information).
2.3. Describes, analyzes, interprets, and evaluates in guided talk about art selections
3.1. Communicates about personal experiences
3.2. Describes art; recognizes images/symbols used in home
3.3. Explores more than one art medium
4.1. Finds use for lines, shapes, colors, and textures in other disciplines
4.2. Uses art to create images for self
4.3. Makes personal decisions using arts knowledge with teacher guidance
4.4. Identifies art from at least two different cultures
4.5. Shares materials and studio space

**Narrative Focus**
Telling stories with images
**Cultural/Historical Focus**
Storybooks
**Self-Expression Focus**
Painting to music

## Assessments

### Assessment Strategies

Selected Response
Constructed Response
- ☑ Checklist
- ☐ Student journal entry
- ☐ Portfolio entry
- ☑ Teacher anecdote
- ☑ Performance-based art production
- ☐ Photo/video

### Target Learnings and Criteria

The student
TL1 Identifies and makes a variety of LINES.
C1 uses straight, curved, wavy, spiral, zigzag, and interrupted LINES.
TL2 identifies and uses primary COLORS.
C2 makes COLORS in addition to primary colors.
TL3 identifies and makes basic SHAPES.
C3 makes and names at least 4 basic SHAPES.
TL4 identifies and describes different TEXTURES.
C4 can describe associations with different TEXTURES.

## Teaching/Learning

### Instructional Strategies
- ☐ Direct instruction
- ☑ Activity-based instruction
- ☑ Modeling/Demonstration
- ☐ Guided Instruction
- ☐ Group collaboration
- ☐ Group critique

### Creative Process
- ☑ Gathers Information
- ☐ Generates solutions
- ☑ Uses arts criteria
- ☑ Manipulative exercises
- ☑ Process drawing
- ☐ Preliminary composition
- ☑ Direct use of materials
- ☐ Redraft and elimination
- ☐ Resolution

### Art Products For Learning
- ☑ Manipulatives (clay)
- ☑ Drawings
- ☑ Paintings
- ☑ Collages

### Resources and Examples
Line: P. Klee
Color: W. Kandinsky, J. Lawrence, P. Manarion
Shape: G. Braque, S. David, H. Frankenthaler, J. Lawrence
Texture: Actual objects, mask portfolio
Narrative: Faith Ringgold

SOURCE: Tacoma School District No. 10, Visual Arts Curriculum, Tacoma, Washington. Used with permission.

**Figure 3.2c** Sample Art Lessons: Kindergarten

## TACOMA PUBLIC SCHOOLS
### *SAMPLE ART LESSONS: KINDERGARTEN*
## LESSON ONE: MAKING LINES

*Essential Question:* How can I make a variety of lines?
*Generalization:* All lines are made of straight and curved lines.

Student Art Images

**Brief Description of Lesson**
The students investigate a variety of basic lines and make lines to music.

**Resources**
*Art Objects:* Paul Klee, Twittering Machine
*Art Materials:* black crayons, 18 × 24 in. white sulfite paper
*Music:* instrumental music: jazz, classical, etc. (various tempos and rhythms)

**Target Learning**
*The student:*
Makes straight and curved lines.

Invents drawing techniques and makes lines to music.

**Assessment Criteria**
*The student:*
Uses straight, curved, zigzag and interrupted lines.
Uses more than on approach to using tools while making lines to music.

**Instructional Strategies**
**What the Teacher Does** (Activity-Based Insturction and Modeling Demonstration)

1. Leads students in discussion using Paul Klee's *Twittering Machine* and asks students to name different kinds of lines (straight, curved).
2. Demonstrates making straight lines and using straight lines to make zigzags.

3. Demonstrates making curved lines.
4. Demonstrates interrupting lines by lifting the tool and starting again and encourages students to find other ways to make lines with the crayon.
5. Plays music and demonstrates making lines to music.

**Creative Process**
**What the Student Does** (Manipulative and Direct Use of Materials)

1. Runs fingers over the lines on *Twittering Machine* and names the lines.

2. Makes straight lines and zigzag lines. (Placement of lines is not important. Lines can overlap, intersect or not touch.)
3. Makes curved lines.
4. Practices lifting drawing tool (crayon) to make interrupted lines, and explores other ways to use crayon.
5. Makes a variety of lines while listening to music

**Assessment Strategies**
Performance Assessment (Constructed Response)
Checklist: multiple tool approaches and use

**Evidence of Student Learning**
Student drawings include a variety of straight, curved, zigzag and interrupted lines. Student drawing techniques include a variety of approached (examples: twisting, spinning, and multiple tool use).

**Vocabulary**
- Curved
- Interrupted
- Straight
- Zigzag

**Life Applications**
Student recognizes lines in nature and constructed world, and consciously makes a variety of lines in own art. (*ARTS Els 1.1 concepts and vocabulary: line*)

SOURCE: Tacoma School District No. 10, Visual Arts Curriculum, Tacoma, Washington. Used with permission.

| Figure 3.2d | Sample Art Lessons: Kindergarten (Continued) |
|---|---|

## TACOMA PUBLIC SCHOOLS
### *SAMPLE ART LESSONS: KINDERGARTEN*
## LESSON ONE: MAKING LINES

*Essential Question:* How does line describe different objects and effects?
*Generalization:* Variations in line can generate alternate effects: interrupted, spiral, and textural.

Student Art Images

**Brief Description of Lesson**

The student makes an observational landscape drawing that includes a horizon, overlap, and a variety of descriptive lines.

**Resources**

*Art Object:* Vincent Van Gogh, *Harvest, the Plain of LaCrau; Cypress Trees*
*Art Materials:* conte, 12 × 18 in. white sulfite paper, 12 × 18 in. preliminary drawing paper (newsprint)

**Targed Learning**
*The student:*
Observes and makes a high horizon line in drawing.

Uses overlap to create space.

Observes and interprets a place using a variety of lines.

**Assessment Criteria**
*The student:*
Consciously includes a high horizon line in a drawing of a landscape.

Uses overlap to show one object in front of another.

Uses interrupted, spiral, and textural lines to interpret a place.

**Instructional Strategies**
**What the Teacher Does** (Guided Instruction—Modeling/Demonstration)

1. Introduces Vincent Van Gogh's drawing. *P: Find the horizon line in van Gogh's drawings (where the sky meets the ground). Find all the different types of line the artist uses to describe the space.*
2. Demonstrates drawing a horizon line at least half way up the page.
3. Creates one large dominant object.

4. Demonstrate making interrupted lines and spiral lines for both sky and ground.
5. Demonstrate using any lines with a textural quality to fill in space.

**Creative Process**
**What the Student Does** (Direct Use of Materials)

1. Observes and points to the horizon line.

2. Draws a high horizon line.

3. Creates one large object to overlap the horizon to create attention with scale (size).
4. Practices making interrupted, spiral and textural lines on preliminary drawing paper. Then makes interrupted, spiral, and textural lines to fill in space in scape.

**Assessment Strategies**
Performance Assessment (Constructed Response)

**Evidence of Student Learning**
Student scape includes a high horizon line and multiple types of lines to fill space.

**Vocabulary**
- Horizon
- Interrupted
- Overlap
- Spiral
- Textural

**Life Applications**
Student recognizes horizon lines in natural world and use of varied lines in natural and constructed world.
*(ARTS ELs 1.1 concepts and vocabulary: interrupted, spiral, invented textural lines: 1.2 composition: horizon)*

SOURCE: Tacoma School District No. 10, Visual Arts Curriculum, Tacoma, Washington. Used with permission.

**Figure 3.3a** Curriculum Content for Solving Problems Using the Visual Arts: Third Grade

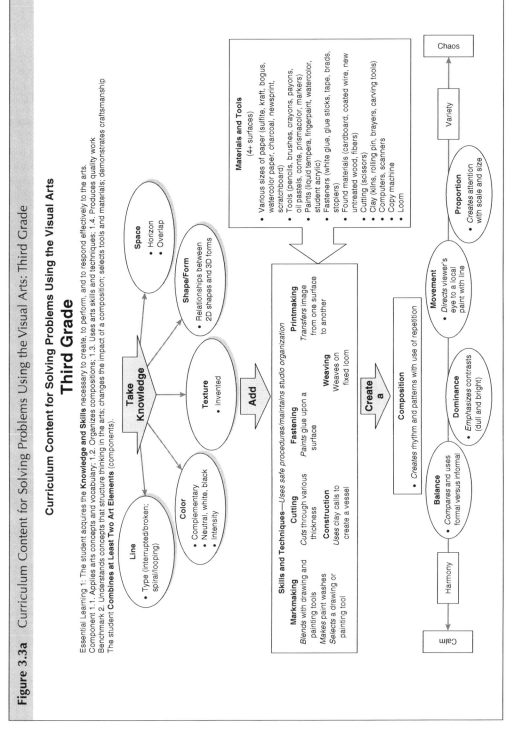

Curriculum Content for Solving Problems Using the Visual Arts

**Third Grade**

Essential Learning 1: The student acquires the **Knowledge and Skills** necessary to create, to perform, and to respond effectively to the arts. Component 1.1. Applies arts concepts and vocabulary; 1.2. Organizes compositions; 1.3. Uses arts skills and techniques; 1.4. Produces quality work Benchmark 2. Understands concepts that structure thinking in the arts; changes the impact of a composition; selects tools and materials; demonstrates craftsmanship The student **Combines at Least Two Art Elements** (components).

SOURCE: Tacoma School District No. 10, Visual Arts Curriculum, Tacoma, Washington. Used with permission.

62

**Figure 3.3b** Curriculum Content for Solving Problems Using the Visual Arts: Third Grade (Continued)

# Third Grade

| Essential Learning 1 | + | Essential Learnings 2–4 | Assessments | = | Teaching/Learning |
|---|---|---|---|---|---|

## Essential Learning 1

### Questions/Problems to Solve Generalizations

1. *How does line describe different objects and effects?*
   G1: Variations in LINE can generate alternate effects–interrupted, spiral, and textural.
2. *How can color separate two objects?*
   G2: Complementary COLORS create contrast.
3. *How is a 3D form represented on a 2D surface?*
   G3: 3D FORMS can be represented by 2D SHAPES.
4. *How does adding texture tell more about an object? How does texture add a personal viewpoint?*
   G4: TEXTURE provides information to define an object. Invented texture generates a personal interpretation of a surface.
5. *How does placing one object in front of another add another dimension to space?*
   G5: The overlap of one object in front of another object creates visual DEPTH.
6. *How does the viewer's eye travel through a work of art?*
   G6: Repetition creates rhythm and patterns in a COMPOSITION.

### Interdisciplinary Connections

*Conceptual Connections*
Math: 2D–volume objects denote whole versus fractions
Science: Visual observation of organization in the environment

*Contextual Connections*
Social Studies: Topography and texture in geography
Language Arts: Different perspectives, artist's intention

## Essential Learnings 2–4

### Life Applications

- Student uses color to create contrast in nature, constructed world, and own art.
- Student represents 3D world in 2D.
- Student recognizes the functional rate of art in life.

### Essential Learnings 2–4

2.1. Discriminates between similarities and differences.
2.2. Elaborates on ideas.
2.3. Describes, analyzes, interprets, and evaluates art with project criteria.
3.1. Communicates ideas to the community.
3.2. Responds critically to illustrations and art in the city.
3.3. Combines 2 art forms.
4.1. Estimates, uses spatial sense, critiques, problem solves.
4.2. Uses art to create images for the community.
4.3. Uses art knowledge to support a collaborative decision.
4.4. Considers function for art in culture. compares similarities and differences between art of different cultures.
4.5. Completes a project with a team.

### Narrative Focus
Rhymes
**Cultural/Historical Focus**
Function of art in culture
**Self-Expression Focus**
Functional objects
Artist's Intent

## Assessments

### Assessment Strategies
Selected Response
Constructed Response
☑ Checklist
☐ Student journal entry
☑ Portfolio entry
☑ Teacher anecdote
☑ Performance-based art production
☐ Photo/video

### Target Learnings and Criteria

The student
TL1 uses a variety of LINES for effect.
C1 LINES vary for different effects.
TL2 uses complementary COLORS to create contrast.
C2 COLORS separate one object from another.
TL3 makes 2D SHAPES appear to be 3D forms.
C3 2D SHAPE appears to be 3D form.
TL4 uses representational and invented TEXTURES.
C4
TL5 uses overlap to represent SPATIAL depth.
C5 overlaps one object in front of another to develop SPACE.
TL6 repeats an image to create rhythm and pattern in a COMPOSITION.
C6 repetition in art creates both rhythm and pattern in a COMPOSITION.

## Teaching/Learning

### Instructional Strategies
☑ Direct instruction
☑ Activity-based instruction
☑ Modeling/demonstration
☐ Guided instruction
☑ Group collaboration
☑ Group critique

### Creative Process
☑ Gathers Information
☑ Generates solutions
☑ Uses arts criteria

☑ Preliminary composition
☑ Direct use of materials
☑ Redraft and elimination
☑ Resolution

### Art Products for Learning
☑ Drawings   ☑ Prints
☑ Paintings  ☑ Textiles
☑ Collages   ☑ Ceramics
☑ Sculptures

### Resources and Examples
Line: P. Klee, H. Matisse, Van Gogh
Color: G. Braque, Hartley, W. Thiebound, G. Seurat
Shape: C. Dermuth, E. Hopper
Texture: R. Rouschenberg, mask portfolio, kachina dolls
Narrative: Faith Ringold
Space/Composition: Constable, F. Kahlo

SOURCE: Tacoma School District No. 10, Visual Arts Curriculum, Tacoma, Washington. Used with permission.

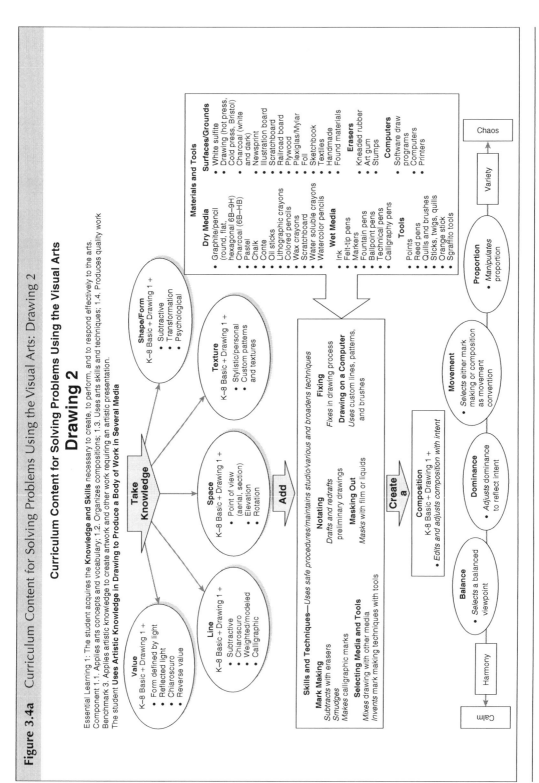

**Figure 3.4a**   Curriculum Content for Solving Problems Using the Visual Arts: Drawing 2

Curriculum Content for Solving Problems Using the Visual Arts

# Drawing 2

Essential Learning 1: The student acquires the **Knowledge and Skills** necessary to create, to perform, and to respond effectively to the arts. Component 1.1. Applies arts concepts and vocabulary; 1.2. Organizes compositions; 1.3. Uses arts skills and techniques; 1.4. Produces quality work Benchmark 3. Applies artistic knowledge to create artwork and other work requiring an artistic presentation. The student **Uses Artistic Knowledge in Drawing to Produce a Body of Work in Several Media**

**Take Knowledge**

**Value**
K–8 Basic + Drawing 1 +
• Form defined by light
• Reflected light
• Chiaroscuro
• Reverse value

**Line**
K–8 Basic + Drawing 1 +
• Subtractive
• Chiaroscuro
• Weighted/modeled
• Calligraphic

**Space**
K–8 Basic + Drawing 1 +
• Point of view (aerial, section)
• Elevation
• Rotation

**Texture**
K–8 Basic + Drawing 1 +
• Stylistic/personal
• Custom patterns and textures

**Shape/Form**
K–8 Basic + Drawing 1 +
• Subtractive
• Transformation
• Psychological

**Materials and Tools**

**Dry Media**
• Graphite/pencil (round, flat, hexagonal 6B–9H)
• Charcoal (6B–HB)
• Pastel
• Chalk
• Conte
• Oil sticks
• Lithographic crayons
• Colored pencils
• Wax crayons
• Scratchboard
• Water soluble crayons
• Watercolor pencils

**Wet Media**
Ink
• Felt-tip pens
• Markers
• Fountain pens
• Ballpoint pens
• Technical pens
• Calligraphy pens

**Tools**
• Points
• Reed pens
• Quills and brushes
• Sticks, twigs, quills
• Orange stick
• Sgraffito tools

**Surfaces/Grounds**
• White sulfite
• Drawing (hot press, Cold press, Bristol)
• Charcoal (white and dark)
• Newsprint
• Illustration board
• Scratchboard
• Railroad board
• Plywood
• Plexiglas/Mylar
• Foil
• Sketchbook
• Textiles
• Handmade
• Found materials

**Erasers**
• Kneaded rubber
• Art gum
• Stumps

**Computers**
• Software draw programs
• Computers
• Printers

**Add**

**Skills and Techniques**—*Uses safe procedures/maintains studio/various and broadens techniques*

**Mark Making**
*Subtracts* with erasers
*Smudges*
*Makes* calligraphic marks

**Selecting Media and Tools**
*Mixes* drawing with other media
*Invents* mark making techniques with tools

**Notating**
*Drafts and redrafts* preliminary drawings

**Masking Out**
*Masks* with film or liquids

**Fixing**
*Fixes* in drawing process

**Drawing on a Computer**
*Uses* custom lines, patterns, and brushes

**Create a**

**Composition**
K–8 Basic + Drawing 1 +
• *Edits and adjusts composition with intent*

**Balance**
• *Selects* a balanced viewpoint

**Dominance**
• *Adjusts* dominance to reflect intent

**Movement**
• *Selects* either mark making or composition as movement convention

**Proportion**
• *Manipulates* proportion

Harmony

Calm

Chaos

Variety

SOURCE: Tacoma School District No. 10, Visual Arts Curriculum, Tacoma, Washington. Used with permission.

**Figure 3.4b** Curriculum Content for Solving Problems Using the Visual Arts: Drawing 2 (Continued)

# Drawing 2

## Essential Learning 1

### Sample Questions/Problems to Solve—Generalizations

1. *How can lines be created on a dark value?*
   G1: Using a subtractive process can create LINES.
2. *How can lines make an object or figure seem to recede into space?*
   G2: Thick and thin LINES appear to advance or recede.
3. *How can texture become an expression of personal style?*
   G3: TEXTURAL qualities can be represented by a variety of stylistic approaches.
4. *What is the relationship between manipulative drawing and drawing on the computer?*
   G4: Custom LINES, pattern, and brushes parallel qualities of manipulative art work.
5. *How can a shape be transformed?*
   G5: Simplification and exaggeration transforms SHAPES.
6. *How can a sectional view be represented?*
   G6: A sectional view relates to fictional layers of SPACE.
7. *How can different points of view be represented?*
   G7: Changing the point of observation changes the representation of the viewpoint.
8. *How does light affect perception of forms?*
   G8: The representation of VALUE gives forms the illusion of 3D.

### Interdisciplinary Connections

**Conceptual Connections**
Biology: Botanical illustration
Geology/Architecture: Cross sections/elevations

**Contextual Connections**
Psychology: Dreams

## Essential Learnings 2–4

### Life Applications

Student uses drawing knowledge, skills, and techniques draw representationally and abstractly.

Student uses drawing knowledge and skills in design.

### Essential Learnings 2–4

2.1. Evaluates the sensory environment in relation to rendered imagery.
2.2. Uses preliminary sketches to analyze and produce solutions before drawing a resolved image.
2.3. Critiques formal considerations of work.
3.1. Selects mark making and tools for a specific purpose: subtractive, architectural, mechanical
3.2. Reflects and responds critically to the use of drawing technical areas.
3.3. Combines drawing knowledge and skills in use of computer graphic imagery.
4.1. Uses knowledge and skills in drawing to support mechanical subjects.
4.2. Selects personal content for drawings.
4.3. Uses drawing to plan and support school or community decision-making.
4.4. Recognizes the influence of drawings in culture and history.
4.5. Uses drawings to broaden the representation of work in a portfolio.

**Realistic Focus**
Architecture
**Abstract Focus**
Fantasy

## Assessments

### Assessment Strategies

Selected Response
Constructed Response
☑ Checklist
☑ Student journal entry
☑ Portfolio entry
☐ Teacher anecdote
☑ Performance-based art production
☐ Photo/slide/video

### Sample Target Learnings and Assessment Criteria

The student
TL1 makes LINES using a subtractive process.
C1 makes LINES on a dark ground.
TL2 makes an object or figure recede into space.
C2 uses thicker LINES in the foreground and thinner lines as the object or figure recedes.
TL3 uses personal mark making and patterning to create TEXTURE.
C3 adopts a distinct approach to making TEXTURES.
TL4 uses computer to draw.
C4 replicates qualities of the object or figure.
TL5 transforms a SHAPE.
C5 alters form through simplification or exaggeration.
TL6 represents a sectional view.
C6 represents portions of an object.
TL7 represents different elevations between drawings.
C7 shows a variety of elevations
TL8 represents a 3D form.
C8 varies value in relationship to the amount of light and the source of the light.

## Teaching/Learning

### Instructional Strategies

☑ Direct instruction
☐ Activity-based instruction
☑ Modeling/demonstration
☐ Guided instruction
☐ Group collaboration
☑ Group critique
☑ Artist-in-residence

### Creative Process

☑ Gathers information
☑ Generates solutions
☑ Uses arts criteria
☐ Manipulative exercises
☑ Process drawing
☑ Preliminary composition
☑ Direct use of materials
☑ Redraft and elimination
☑ Resolution

### Art Products For Learning

☑ Drawings    ☐ Prints
☐ Paintings   ☐ Textiles
☐ Collages    ☑ Computer imagery
☐ Sculptures  ☐ Photographs

### Resources and Examples

Personal textures: Dubuffet, Van Gogh, Guiseppe Archimboldo, Paul Taylor
Transformational shape: Dali, Roger Kutz
Sectional views: Haas
Points of view: Rubens
Value and light: Benion, Ruscha

SOURCE: Tacoma School District No. 10, Visual Arts Curriculum, Tacoma, Washington. Used with permission.

*(Text continued from page 57)*

studies or science teachers to create interdisciplinary units. Some local districts have chosen to develop curriculum frameworks for each subject area at the district level through teacher committees. They encourage teachers at each school site to design classroom units (interdisciplinary or intradisciplinary). It is expected that the classroom units will be aligned to the district curricular frameworks. Other school districts are using teacher committees to develop interdisciplinary units for the system in social studies and science. Mathematics, art, and the language arts committees articulate curriculum frameworks for their individual disciplines, but then fuse their concepts and skills into the science and social studies units whenever possible. Chapter 4 will deal with interdisciplinary, integrated curricula in greater detail.

## SUMMARY

As school districts design local curricular frameworks, they rely on state standards to clarify what students must know and be able to do at each grade level. The state standards vary in the way they are written, however—from broad, conceptual language to specific, topic-driven objectives. Teachers need to understand the language of standards because they drive different expectations and types of instruction in the classroom.

Some educators think that the more specific and factually oriented the standards, the better they are. In my opinion, though, well-written concept-based standards have a better chance of raising the bar for teaching and learning. Conceptually driven standards cause curriculum committees at the local level to determine how the grade-level content can be used to teach to the deeper understanding of the concepts and principles specified in the state standards. Conceptually framed state standards value the intellectual pursuit and deeper understanding of knowledge. It is important, however, to list the critical content topics for each grade level and subject—with the exceptions of skills and processes—without verbs. If teachers see the skill sets for grade levels and subjects, they can internalize the skills and apply them appropriately in lesson plans and assessments. This is their job: it is the art and the science of teaching.

Curriculum mapping is a necessary strategy for determining what teachers are currently teaching. These maps will provide the information for identifying gaps and redundancies in content and skills when aligned to expectations from standards.

Curriculum maps also provide a base for identifying content that can be brought together for interdisciplinary units, for linking content to discipline-based concepts, and for assisting in the articulation of processes and skills for areas such as mathematics, art, or language arts.

# EXTENDING THOUGHT

1. How can you identify whether a standard is factual, conceptual, or skill based?

2. How are the standards in your state written in the area of science? In the area of history? In each case, are the standards more conceptually or factually driven?

3. How do local curriculum committees use their grade-level topics and content to align to conceptually driven standards? Relate a specific example from history to the following standard: "Understand that as the economy of a nation expands, the demand for goods and services increases."

4. What value do curriculum maps have in the articulation of critical content and skills?

5. Why is it important to articulate discipline-based curriculums for subjects such as mathematics, art, physical education, and other skill-based subjects prior to making interdisciplinary connections?

6. Why do skill-driven subjects such as mathematics and art also need to identify grade-level generalizations?

# Designing Interdisciplinary, Integrated Curricula

Teachers in elementary schools jump in and tenaciously pursue interdisciplinary unit teaching. The thought of reducing the burden of content by connecting subject matter across disciplines is an appealing motivator for teachers to design interdisciplinary units, but the task has not been easy. A lack of well-articulated models has caused teachers to piece together design components from trial and error and from tidbits of training.

Student benefits from interdisciplinary unit design have become more apparent as teachers continue to explore the idea. An interdisciplinary curriculum is a more difficult undertaking at the secondary level because of the standards-driven expectations for each discipline, class schedules, and issues of collaboration and teaming. For these reasons, and because of the need to preserve disciplinary integrity, there is less interdisciplinary unit work in secondary schools. It can and should be implemented when feasible because it helps students understand complex issues from different disciplinary perspectives, but interdisciplinary work should enhance but not supplant a quality discipline-based curriculum. Schools that are allowed greater flexibility in their approach to curriculum, such as theme-based academies, will find it easier to design interdisciplinary units.

This chapter will address the definition and value of interdisciplinary, integrated curricula and present a step-by-step model for getting started. The chapter will end with answers to questions that have been raised by elementary and secondary school teachers.

# DEFINING INTERDISCIPLINARY, INTEGRATED CURRICULA

A common precursor to interdisciplinary, integrated curricula is coordinated, multidisciplinary curriculum (see Figure 4.1). This model relates facts and activities across subject areas to a common topic, such as dinosaurs, polar bears, Africa, or the American Revolution. Students learn facts about the topic and develop their process skills through the varied activities. Nevertheless, a conceptual focus to force the **integration of thinking** is usually missing from the curriculum. Integration, then, is not the same thing as interdisciplinary curriculum. *Interdisciplinary curriculum* refers to what we do with different subjects that focus on a common topic; *integration* is the cognitive process of seeing patterns and connections between factual knowledge, and conceptual ideas that transfer through time, across cultures, and across situations. Teachers often begin learning about interdisciplinary curriculum by using the coordinated model, and then progress to the higher intellectual form.

It is important for primary grade teachers to be assured that teaching units on bears or dinosaurs is fine as a supplementary unit if those teachers recognize that the major benefit will be the development of language skills and some content knowledge around a motivational topic: certainly, all students love bears and dinosaurs! But teachers will also want to provide units that challenge the higher-level thinking abilities of their students. They could achieve both language development and higher-level thinking in the same unit by linking a relevant concept to the topic study, such as hibernation, as a conceptual lens for the study of "Bears in Winter" or of "Extinction" as a lens for the study of "Dinosaurs" (see Figure 4.1b).

**Figure 4.1**    Coordinated, Multidisciplinary Versus Integrated, Interdisciplinary Unit Web

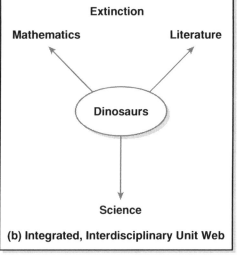

(a) Coordinated, Multidisciplinary Unit Web

(b) Integrated, Interdisciplinary Unit Web

The higher form of concept-based integration presented in this chapter rests on the following definition: concept-based integration examines a topic of study through a "conceptual lens" such as "Interdependence" or "Conflict." The goal of concept-based integration (in both interdisciplinary and intradisciplinary contexts) is to cause students to "integrate their thinking" at a conceptual level. Students see patterns and connections between factual knowledge and transferable, conceptual ideas. This integration of thinking provides deeper understanding and greater insight into the study.

*Interdisciplinary,* as used in this chapter, refers to a variety of disciplines sharing a common, conceptual focus for the topic under study. The *conceptual lens* creates a synergy, or interactive energy, between the factual and conceptual levels of thinking. This synergistic thinking leads to integration of thinking and differentiates interdisciplinary from multidisciplinary unit work.

*Multidisciplinary* refers to a variety of disciplines coordinating to a specific topic of study. A unit on contemporary Iraq is multidisciplinary unless a conceptual lens such as "Stability and Instability" is used to force the mind to process information on both the factual and conceptual levels.

The common focus on the conceptual lens does not mean, however, that all disciplines must work through the lens in an interdisciplinary unit. A discipline may or may not relate directly to the lens. For example, if I am an art teacher participating in a unit titled "Contemporary Iraq: Stability and Instability," I might use artwork that illustrates social instability in some way, but I will have students explore how the artist used the conceptual elements of line, shadow, or form to express the mood of the times. If I am a mathematics teacher, however, I may not be illustrating the lens of "Stability and Instability" directly, but I rather will choose an economics topic from social studies to illustrate a mathematics principle. I may have students do a mathematical analysis of Iraq's economy based on statistics. I would be teaching mathematics concepts through the unit topic, and I would indirectly be supporting the conceptual lens. Each discipline teaches to its own subject-specific concepts—but it develops these discipline-based concepts through the interdisciplinary unit study. Each discipline directly or indirectly relates to the conceptual lens. The purpose of the lens is to provide an overall conceptual direction for the topic under study.

Integration (of thinking) can also occur within a single discipline (which means it is intradisciplinary work). Figure 4.2 illustrates an intradisciplinary, integrated history web that would compare 20th-century conflicts illustrating the lens of "Freedom and Independence" when fleshed out. Resource D has an intradisciplinary unit for ninth-grade world geography for a more complete unit.

## THE INTEGRATED, INTERDISCIPLINARY CURRICULUM MODEL

When content from separate disciplines is focused on a common problem, topic, or issue viewed through a conceptual lens, the study leads to the integration of

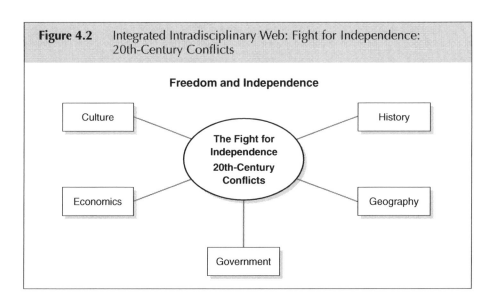

**Figure 4.2** Integrated Intradisciplinary Web: Fight for Independence: 20th-Century Conflicts

thinking. It is the lens that draws thinking to higher cognitive levels and sets up a *synergy* (interactive energy) between the lower- and higher-order processing centers of the brain. Process skills interact with content in learning experiences and performances to enhance conceptual and content understanding, as well as to develop the process skills. The use of Gardner's (2006) multiple intelligences is another example of how processes and skills enhance "know, understand, and able to do" expectations. Processes and skills provide invaluable support for concept-based curriculum and instruction.

## Purpose and Value

Some educators feel that interdisciplinary curriculum work should obliterate the separate disciplines to avoid fragmentation of knowledge. I agree with Gardner (1999), however, that the separate disciplines have value and should not be sacrificed in this design process.

One of the problems with a seamless curriculum is that even though disciplines have many foundational concepts in common, they also have discipline-specific concepts that would leave gaps in critical content knowledge if not addressed. Mathematics, for example, has the concepts of "Number," "Order," "Ratio," and "Proportion," which hold heavy content meaning. If subjects such as mathematics, literature, and art lose their unique conceptual structure, they will perform poorly inside or outside interdisciplinary units.

The purpose of interdisciplinary instruction goes back to the definition stated previously—to cause students to integrate their thinking at a conceptual level by seeing the patterns and connections between transferable, conceptual ideas and the topic under study.

Interdisciplinary integration should proceed at a pace that allows for developing understanding and consideration of the following questions:

- Which concepts, critical content, and skills, by subject area, do state standards consider essential for the 21st century?
- What criteria will we use to decide on the significant topics, problems, or issues around which thinking will become integrated?
- How many interdisciplinary, integrated units should be taught in a year at the elementary level? At the secondary level? When should content and skills not be taught in the context of interdisciplinary units?
- How do we address discipline-based standards and benchmarks in instructional units?
- How will we ensure that we are maintaining the integrity of concepts, critical content, and skills from the separate disciplines as we design interdisciplinary units?
- If we use an issues orientation in the design of an interdisciplinary curriculum, what curriculum framework will ensure developing sophistication of conceptual understanding, critical content, and process skills?

As we continue to explore the idea of interdisciplinary curriculum, the answers to the above questions become clearer. Clearly, interdisciplinary curriculum offers great value for teaching and learning. Table 4.1 lists oft-cited benefits of interdisciplinary curricula.

**Table 4.1**    Benefits of Concept-Based, Interdisciplinary Curriculum

| Student Benefits | Rationale |
| --- | --- |
| Reduces curricular fragmentation. | Interdisciplinary curriculm facilitates connections. |
| Provides depth to teaching and learning. | Students gain depth of thought and ideas, not depth of facts stacked higher. |
| Provides teaching and learning focus. | Teaching and learning are guided by the high-level generalizations arising from the concepts and critical content. |
| Engages students in active learning. | Students search for and construct knowledge using a variety of learning styles and modalities. |
| Challenges higher levels of thinking. | The conceptual lens and generalizations force thinking to the analysis and synthesis levels. |
| Helps students connect knowledge. | The best minds rise above the facts and see patterns and connections as they transfer knowledge. |
| Addresses significant problems, issues, and concepts. | Teacher-designed units typically address critical real-life issues. |
| Forces an answer to the relevancy question, "Why study these facts?" | Facts are not the end but the means to deeper understandings. |
| Draws on multiple styles of learning. | Auditory, visual, and kinesthetic activities are designed to engage many different modalities. |

Because the interdisciplinary curriculum format draws from a wider information base than the single-subject area textbook, the teacher cannot hope to know all of the information prior to instruction. This provides an environment of greater freedom and flexibility to learn. It also ensures that students take responsibility for thinking and answering questions, and that they do not depend on the teacher to dispense all knowledge.

In addition to the benefits for students, teachers find that the process of designing units facilitates the teachers' own development as learners. As they work collaboratively to plan units, teachers challenge their thinking in defining the critical outcomes for content and process development and in anticipating enduring understandings—the transferable generalizations. Interdisciplinary units provide pathways for creating new knowledge for teachers and for students.

### Integrated, Intradisciplinary Units

Thinking can be integrated conceptually in *intradisciplinary units* (units designed within a subject area) as well as in *interdisciplinary units* (units designed among subject areas). Integration is a cognitive process that requires a conceptual level of work within the study. Resource D provides an example of an intradisciplinary ninth-grade unit in world geography written by Kelly Coats, social studies department head from Channelview Independent School District, Channelview, Texas.

## DESIGNING CONCEPT-BASED TEACHING UNITS

Teachers who seek information on how to design concept-based instructional units, which can be either interdisciplinary or intradisciplinary, ask for a step-by-step process that provides a model yet allows them to use their own critical and creative thinking in the design process. Although I cringe to think that the model presented in this section will be looked on as another Hunter-like set of steps, I also trust that teachers will also see its value as a flexible springboard for engaging students in the design of concept-based units as well as for engaging them in relevant learning experiences.

Figure 4.3 lists 12 steps for designing concept-based teaching units. I have worked with elementary and secondary grade teachers around the country for the past 13 years to develop and refine these steps. Clarifying notes follow each step.

Figures 4.4a–4.4g provide a set of unit-planning pages as a possible format to use with the steps for designing a concept-based unit. It is not necessary to use this particular format for laying out a unit, however. The various unit components can be arranged in a variety of formats. Teachers want a format that is coherent and usable for them. Resource A provides two alternative formats for unit plans. Secondary teachers may prefer these alternative formats.

To move from the overall unit plan to classroom lessons, the teacher may want to use the lesson-planning pages similar to the example in Figure 4.5. Lesson plan pages can be written to cover one day up to a week. There may be 5 to 10 lesson plans, for example, to carry out unit work.

| Figure 4.3 | Steps for Designing Concept-Based Teaching Units |
|---|---|

1. Decide on a unit title, which is the focus of the unit work. (See Figure 4.5.)

2. Identify a major concept to serve as a suitable integrating or conceptual lens for the study. Which conceptual lens would shed a deeper light on this unit topic? The conceptual lens draws thinking above the topic and facts; thinking becomes integrated as students see the conceptual patterns and connections between facts and transferable ideas. Different conceptual lenses change the unit focus (e.g., a unit on "Our Community" through the conceptual lens of "Interdependence" would be a different study with the lens of "Change and Continuity"). (See page 85.)

3. Web the subtopics and subconcepts for study, by subject or strand, around the unit title and conceptual lens. Subtopics listed around this content/concept web may be specific (names of community leaders, historical dates and events, etc.), or they may be subconcepts (needs and wants, roles, leadership, etc.). After brainstorming, underline all of the subconcepts. These become the fuel for writing developmentally appropriate and powerful enduring understandings. (The more complete the web with subconcepts, the more powerful the enduring understandings. Be sure to contextualize the subconcepts and subtopics from your academic standards onto the unit webs so you are aligned to required content.) (See page 86.)

4. Write a unit overview to engage student interest and to introduce the unit. (This step can actually be completed after you have drafted out the entire unit.) (See page 87.)

5. Brainstorm some of the enduring understandings (generalizations) that you would expect students to derive from the study. Enduring understandings answer the question, "So what? Why should I learn these facts?" Enduring understandings go beyond the facts to the conceptual and transferable level of understanding. (This facilitates conceptual thinking and deeper understanding.) (See page 87.)

6. Brainstorm guiding or essential questions to facilitate the student's thinking toward the enduring understandings. Guiding questions combine specific "what, why, or how" questions related to specific topics and facts within the unit, with open-ended "why and how" questions to develop the transferable level of understanding. A unit will have a few provocative debate questions, which have no right or wrong answer but develop interest, engagement, and defense of a position. These provocative questions are sometimes referred to as essential questions. It is helpful to code these different kinds of questions in the design process to make certain you are addressing different levels of questions (F = factual questions; C = conceptual questions; and P = provocative, debate questions). (See page 93.)

7. Identify the specific knowledge (key topics) and skills that a student must internalize. For instance, students will "know critical facts" and exhibit "critical skills." (See page 95.)

8. Code the knowledge and skills with assessment codes to show the other evidence that is planned beyond the culminating performance task. Include these other assessments in your unit packet. (See page 96.)

9. Write the culminating performance task to show the depth of learning. The performance task answers the questions, "What do I want students to know, understand, and be able to do as a result of this unit of study?" Use the formula "what, why, and how" in writing to ensure that the performance assesses to the level of deep understanding (the statement that follows the "why" question). You may decide to use more than one performance task in your unit. (See page 96.)

10. Design the scoring guide (criteria and standard) to assess the performance task. For each criterion assessed in a given mode, ask yourself, "What does it look like?" at each level of the performance. (See page 97.)

11. Once the culminating performance task is written, design backward (Wiggins and McTighe 2005) and design the instructional plan or learning experiences to address the critical knowledge, understandings, and skills of the unit. This step comes after the performance task(s) is written, so that the learning experiences can be designed to prepare the students and set them up for success on their performance assessments. (Note: this step is taught prior to the culminating performance task, however.) (See page 101.)

12. Identify unit resources and include teacher notes to assist with instruction. (See page 101.)

**Figure 4.4a**  Critical Content and Concept Web

## Critical Content–Concept Web

### Unit Planner

Unit Title: _____

Conceptual Lens: _____

Unit Time Frame: _____

**Unit Overview**

Grade Level: _____

Course: _____

**Unit Title**

Designer(s): _____

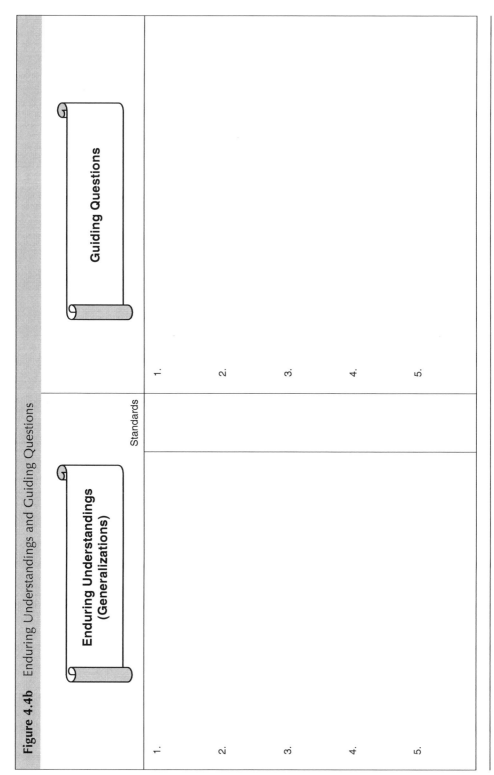

**Figure 4.4b** Enduring Understandings and Guiding Questions

**Enduring Understandings (Generalizations)**

Standards

1.

2.

3.

4.

5.

**Guiding Questions**

1.

2.

3.

4.

5.

77

**Figure 4.4c**  Critical Content and Skills

AC = Assessment Code:

Q-Quizzes
T-Tests
WS-Work Samples
SA-Student Self-Assessment

P-Prompts
O-Observations
D-Dialogues

## Critical Content and Skills

**Students Will Know . . .**
(Key Topics/Facts)

| | Standards | AC | | Standards | AC |
|---|---|---|---|---|---|
| 1. | | | 4. | | |
| 2. | | | 5. | | |
| 3. | | | 6. | | |

**Key Skills . . .**
(Able to Do)

| | Standards | AC | | Standards | AC |
|---|---|---|---|---|---|
| 1. | | | 4. | | |
| 2. | | | 5. | | |
| 3. | | | 6. | | |

NOTE: No correlation needed between the Know and Key Skills boxes here.

**Figure 4.4d**  Step 1: Performance Task Planner

# WHAT: Investigate . . .
(Unit title or major topic here)

# WHY: In order to understand that . . .
(1–2 unit generalizations from Figure 4.4b here)

# HOW: (Engaging Scenario-Performance)
(Performance to meet the WHY generalization(s) above as well as unit critical content and skills)

**Figure 4.4e** Scoring Guide Planner

## Scoring Guide Planner

Performance:

| Mode(s) | Criteria | Descriptors |
|---------|----------|-------------|
|  |  |  |

## Scoring Guide

Mode: _____

| Criteria | Excellent | Highly Competent | Competent | Novice |
|----------|-----------|------------------|-----------|--------|
|  |  |  |  |  |

**Figure 4.4f** Suggested Learning Experiences

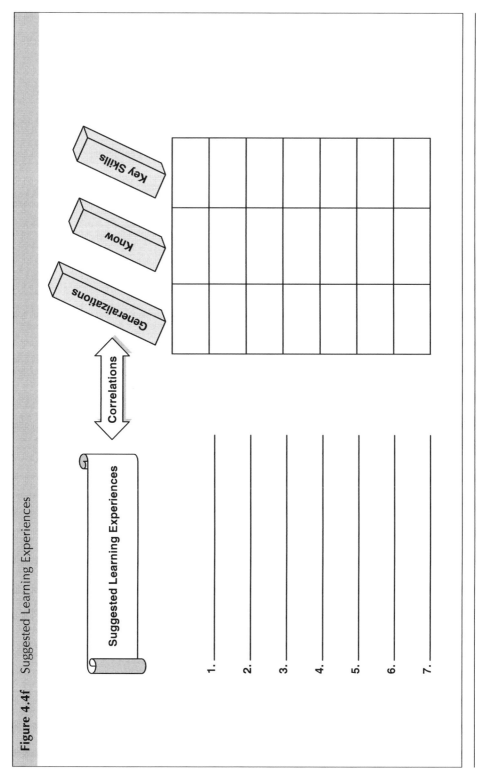

**Figure 4.4g** Unit Resources and Teacher Notes

Unit Resources

Teacher Notes

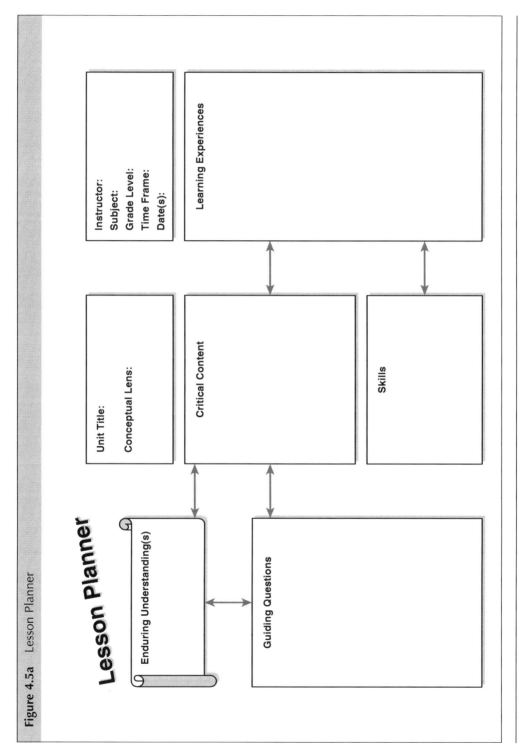

# Lesson Planner

Instructor:
Subject:
Grade Level:
Time Frame:
Date(s):

Learning Experiences

Unit Title:

Conceptual Lens:

Critical Content

Skills

Enduring Understanding(s)

Guiding Questions

**Figure 4.5b** Lesson Planner (Continued)

# Lesson Planner

Instructor: _____

### Instructional Strategies

- Direct instruction
- Interactive lecture
- Inquiry
- KWL (Know, Want to Know, Learned)
- Question—All Write
- Think-Pair-Share
- Whip around ( . . . the circle with responses)
- Note taking
- Graphic organizers
- Summary reflection statements
- Reflective discussion: Socratic questioning, open-ended questions
- Cooperative learning
- Independent study/research
- Writing as Thinking (The I-Search Essay, framed paragraphs . . .)

### Differentiation Strategies

- Multiple intelligences (perform in different modalities)
- Peer tutoring
- Leveled "gig ideas" (generalizations)
- Leveled guiding questions
- Differentiated instructional materials
- Differentiated assessments (alternative and leveled)
- Extension activities

### Assessment Strategies

- Performance task
- Forced choice (multiple choice, T/F . . .)
- Open-ended response
- Interview
- Observation
- Peer assessment
- Metacognitive response (reflecting upon own thinking)
- Self-assessment

### Materials and Resources

### Teacher Notes

# UNIT DESIGN STEPS: QUESTIONS AND ANSWERS

Questions arise as teachers work together to design concept-based units. To answer some of these questions, let's take each of the unit design steps and discuss major issues.

## 1. The Unit Title (Theme)

*A. What is a theme?*

A theme can be a topical theme such as "The U.S. Presidency" or a conceptual theme such as "Leadership and the U.S. Presidency." Including the conceptual lens of "Leadership" as part of the unit title converts a topical theme into a conceptual theme. Which type of theme requires a greater degree of complex thinking? Why? Did you discover that conceptual themes take thinking to the transferable level, which requires a greater degree of complex thinking? Congratulations! You understand a basic premise of concept-based instruction.

You can state your unit focus as a topical theme, but for higher-level integrated thinking, you will also want to identify a conceptual lens for the unit. Because of the confusion over the term "theme," I will simply use the term "unit title" in this book when referring to the focus topic for an instructional unit.

*B. How does the number of disciplines participating in a unit affect the unit title?*

Generally, the more subjects involved in the unit, the broader and more abstract the unit title. To allow each discipline to enter the integration process, the title has to be broad enough to encompass the different curricula. For example, I could do a unit titled "Wildlife Populations in the Northwestern United States" with a conceptual lens of "Habitat," but if I want to include social studies in the same unit, then I would have to make the title more abstract and broad, such as "Populations in the Northwestern United States." As you can see, this makes the title so obtuse that it provides little focus and the unit will lack coherence. Beware the pit of "title obtusity" or you will end up with unfocused coverage over depth. There would also be the problem for the "Habitat" lens: it would have to be broadened to something like "Interdependence" to cross disciplines.

## 2. Concept (Conceptual Lens)

*A. Why use a conceptual lens for my topic of study?*

- A conceptual lens forces the integration of thinking. Students see patterns and connections at a conceptual level as they relate the topic to the broader study framed by the lens.
- Without a conceptual lens, a topic of study remains at a lower cognitive level, and students seek to memorize the "facts" related to the topic.
- The conceptual lens facilitates and requires deeper understanding and allows for the transfer of knowledge.

*B. How do I select a suitable conceptual lens?*

Examine the title and focus of your unit and select a conceptual lens that will provide a direction for the thinking process. For example, do you want thinking to center on the title of "Interdependence Between Nations" or "Competition Between Nations"? For beginners in concept-based unit design, it sometimes helps to refer to the concepts suggested in Figure 2.5 (or Resource B), realizing that there are other choices available that are not shown on the sample lists. You may use either macro- or microconcepts for the lens, depending on the unit focus. Sometimes, a more specific microconcept, such as "Identity," produces deeper conceptual thinking.

There are some concepts that are just too narrow (e.g., "Organism") to serve as a suitable lens. In *Concept-Based Curriculum and Instruction for the Thinking Classroom* (Erickson, 2007, p. 12) I provide a listing of popular conceptual lenses.

*C. Shouldn't I decide on my conceptual lens before I decide on the title of my unit?*

Not usually. How would you know which lens would provide the greatest thinking power unless you relate it to the specific unit focus? Occasionally, you can decide as a teaching team that a particular concept is so important that you want to focus the study on that concept and the lessons related to it. In these special cases, the unit title might be selected after the lens is identified. A literature unit, for instance, may want to explore the lens of "Survival" in historical fiction. In this case, the lens would focus the selection of relevant novels.

## 3. Webbing the Topics for Study

*A. Should the strands around the web always be different subject areas?*

No. There are two key considerations when deciding on strands to display the specific subtopics and subconcepts of study related to the unit title:

1. Is the unit interdisciplinary? If it is, then web the different subject areas that are participating in the unit as your strands.

2. Is the unit intradisciplinary? If so, then web the major subconcepts of study as your strands. For example, if I am doing a unit within the field of social studies, my strands would be history, geography, economics, government, and culture.

Another intradisciplinary method for webbing is to determine the strands that best break down the unit title into its significant components. For example, foreign language teachers may choose to do a unit related to the concept of "Culture" (e.g., "Hispanic Influence on U.S. Culture") and would define the categories around the web by the elements of culture: language, customs, music, art, and so on. A unit on "Chemical Bonding" would use strands such as "Bond Energy," "Atomic Structure," "Electronegativity."

## 4. The Unit Overview

*A. Is there a specific pattern for writing the unit overview?*

No. The key is to convey the content focus of the unit in an engaging way. The overview would include the unit focus and a description of the unit work, but this overview can be accomplished with a combination of narrative and engaging questions.

## 5. Generalizations (Enduring Understandings)

*A. What are generalizations?*

- Generalizations fall on the synthesis level of thinking in the structure of knowledge (see Figure 2.2). Generalizations may be referred to as enduring understandings, because they are the deeper, transferable ideas that arise from fact-based studies.
- Generalizations are statements of conceptual relationship.
- Generalizations transfer through time and across cultures and situations. They are exemplified through the fact base but transcend single examples.

*B. How do we identify generalizations for our topics of study?*

In units of study, use the content web to look for concepts that can be paired to make statements of enduring understanding. Why are you studying this unit topic? What do you want students to understand at a conceptual, transferable level—beyond the specific topic?

*C. How do we write generalizations?*

- When first learning, it is helpful to use the sentence starter, "Students understand that . . ." Complete the sentence by pairing two or more concepts from your unit of study into a sentence that conveys an important idea that will transfer through time and across cultures or situations.

- When writing generalizations, do not mention your topic of study. In other words, do not use proper or personal nouns. Move beyond the example provided by your topic and look for the transcendent understandings.

- When writing generalizations, use active, present-tense verbs to convey the timeless characteristic. Avoid passive voice and past-tense verbs. Try to avoid the verbs "to be" or "to have." A pitfall in writing generalizations, which are statements of conceptual relationship, is to write them as simple definitions of concepts. An example might be the statement, "A *ratio* is a *relation* in *degree* or *number* between two *things*." This statement has many concepts (italicized) but is mainly a definition of the concept of "Ratio." The use of "is," a form of the verb "to be," can be a clue that a definition has been offered. The danger would be in overusing definitions and missing the deeper conceptual relationships of the discipline. A few definitions are fine for baseline understanding but are better left for vocabulary study.

- Use qualifiers (may, can, often) if your generalization will not hold across all examples but is still a significant understanding.

Let's put two or more of the following concepts together and state a generalization. (You can generate at least five generalizations out of these concepts.) You may use other concepts if you need to add to the list for your idea.

---

| | |
|---|---|
| Organisms | Disease |
| Migration | Environment |
| Survival | Populations |
| Resistance | Adaptation |
| Change | |

The student understands that _____

_____

_____

_____

---

Is your idea important for students to understand in a broader context? Did you remember to use an active, present-tense verb? Do you have a full sentence? Did you avoid using proper and personal nouns? Did you use a qualifier (often, may, can) if the generalization is important but may not hold across all examples? (For instance, "Natural disasters may create an imbalance in the ecosystem.")

## D. What is the difference between a generalization and a principle?

*Generalizations* are statements of conceptual relationship that transfer across examples. They must be continually tested for truth because they may not hold over time. When generalizations are important ideas for a discipline but do not hold across all related examples, they include a qualifier. For example, "Nations with different ethnic or religious factions may experience severe conflicts that lead to civil war."

Principles are also statements of conceptual relationship, but they are always true (based on our best evidence) and use no qualifiers. They are the cornerstone or foundational truths of a discipline such as Newton's Three Laws of Motion or the axioms of mathematics. For example, "An object that is not being subjected to a force will continue to move at a constant speed and in a straight line."

### E. How do we tell the difference between less sophisticated and more sophisticated generalizations?

If we think of generalizations according to levels of sophistication, then we can look at what characteristics differentiate Level 1 (less sophisticated) from Level 3 (sophisticated) generalizations. The following generalizations, which might be appropriate for the elementary grades, show three different levels of sophistication.

---

Level 1: People use *machines* to do *work*.

Level 2: *Machines* supply *energy* and/or *special functions* to complete *tasks* efficiently.

Level 3: *Work efficiency* increases *productivity* and generates more *business* income.

---

As we move forward from Level 1, the generalizations become more specific, and the concept load becomes heavier. The concepts (in italics) require more background knowledge to understand as the levels increase. As the levels increase, we won't necessarily find more concepts in the sentence, but the idea presented will be more cognitively challenging. Note: Sometimes Level 3 will be more general than the specificity found in Level 2, but the Level 3 idea will extend the Level 2 thinking to a new idea.

Let's look at a set of generalizations that would be developmentally appropriate at the high school level:

---

Level 1: *Governments* regulate the exchange of *goods*.

Level 2: A national imbalance in the *supply* and *demand* of *goods* can lead to an *economic dependence* on *foreign products*.

Level 3: *Economic dependence* on foreign products to meet *basic needs* may jeopardize the *political* and *economic stability* of a *nation*.

---

*F. How do we scaffold thinking to
write generalizations at more sophisticated levels?*

To take thinking to more sophisticated levels in writing generalizations, you should use open-ended guiding questions, just as you would in the teaching situation. Notice the guiding questions following each generalization in the examples below. The questions are formed by asking a "how," "why," or "so what" (not just a "what") question related to the generalization. In the unit planning process, teachers discuss the possible answers to the guiding question and listen for any concepts that could be used to form a more sophisticated and conceptually specific understanding (generalization). Make certain that the generalizations answer the question, and avoid the error of restating the previous generalization in different words.

---

*Elementary Grades*

Level 1: Changing environments affect organisms. (How do changing environments affect organisms?)

Level 2: Changing environments require that organisms adapt. (So what? What would the effect be if organisms did not adapt?)

Level 3: Organisms that do not adapt to changing environments will not survive (survival).

*Secondary Schools: Visual Art*

Level 1: Texture can be real or implied. (How is texture implied?)

Level 2: Artists imply texture through repeated patterns of lines, shapes, and spaces. (So what? What is the value of texture in visual art forms?)

Level 3: Texture adds variety and balance to visual art forms and can offer visual complexity and interest.

---

Take the Level 1 generalization provided below and scaffold by asking a "how" question (flip the generalization into a question) that will take the thinking to the next level. (There are times when a "why" question works better than a "how" question when scaffolding thinking from Level 1 to Level 2.)

---

Level 1 Generalization: "Art is a method of communication."

Scaffolding Question: "Why . . . ?" _____

_____

---

Level 2 Generalization: _____

_____

Scaffolding Question: "So what . . . _____?"

Level 3 Generalization: _____

_____

Did you experience difficulty moving from Level 2 to Level 3? This is common when first learning the strategy. I think it is because our traditional curriculum design does not require much thinking beyond Levels 1 or 2, and teachers feel so pressured to cover the content that there is little time in classrooms to probe students' thinking. So here is a tip to help you reach Level 3: After you have written the Level 2 generalization, ask the significance question, "So what? What effect or significance does this understanding (Level 2 generalization) have for society, the individual, and so on?" After thinking about and discussing the effect or significance, write the response in the form of a Level 3 generalization.

*G. Aren't generalizations too abstract to mean very much?*
*Isn't it more important to have clarity and topic specificity?*

The most specific and clear piece of information is a fact (see following example), but is it the desired end for teaching and learning? What do you think? Why? What role do facts play in concept and process curriculum and instruction?

SOURCE: Cartoon by David Ford, davidford4@comcast.net.

- *Fact:* According to census data, the United States population is growing.
- *Generalization:* Increasing populations can lead to environmental stress and depletion of natural resources.

Do not underestimate the power of a seemingly bland generalization. The questions that are generated from the generalization challenge thinking and lead to discussions at deeper levels. The generalizations are the summary of higher-level thought. They bring closure to previous learning and invite further questions.

### H. Why should we scaffold generalizations?

When teachers are asked why they are teaching a topic, the first answer is usually a summary of the facts they want students to know. After learning how to identify and write generalizations, teachers begin to state the important transferable ideas they want students to understand. But this new skill takes practice. The first generalizations are more often Level 1, no matter what the grade level. The learning curve is very steep, however, and after a few practice sessions, the generalizations become more sophisticated. Learning how to scaffold thinking also helps the thinking and writing processes. Learning to use precise language to state generalizations (enduring understandings) brings focus to teaching and learning. The verbs "to influence," "to affect," "to impact," "to be," or "to have" usually develop into Level 1 generalizations, making the statements so general that they say very little. I encourage teachers to drop the Level 1 generalizations (because they are weak and unclear) and focus instruction at Level 2, and challenge students to reach Level 3.

It is important to scaffold those generalizations that are so simplistic that they beg to be carried forward. You have students in your classrooms that fall at all levels of conceptual sophistication. If you identify and teach to Level 2 and 3 generalizations, you will be able to differentiate curriculum and instruction for the different ability levels while still centering on the same topics. This helps in this age of inclusionary programming. Scaffolding helps tap the depth and breadth of enduring understandings.

### I. Why should I determine so many of the generalizations for a unit? Why not let the students come up with their own generalizations?

If a student comes up with a generalization in the group discussion, then celebrate! You have a thinking student! But if you are just beginning to work with concept-based instruction, the more likely scenario will be students who think to the level of facts (we have trained them well) and who resist thinking beyond the facts. (Do some of your brightest students come to mind?)

The reason teachers identify unit generalizations is that we are learning how to think conceptually ourselves and need the practice of extrapolating transferable understandings from our content. Even more important, we identify unit generalizations because we are "systematically" teaching students how to think.

This is generally an inductive teaching model using guiding questions and learning experiences to direct thinking toward enduring understandings. To teach students how to think conceptually, we have to know where the thinking is going (at least a direction), so that we can plan a questioning path. We do not want to be so rigid that we miss teachable moments when a student discovers a big idea that we can build on, or when student questions take the discussion in a certain direction. We cannot always wait and see where students want to go, though, if we want to teach conceptual thinking and illuminate enduring understandings for a unit of study.

## 6. Guiding Questions

*A. What are guiding questions?*

Guiding questions are a critical driver for teaching and learning. They engage students in the study and create a bridge between learning experiences and deeper, conceptual understandings.

*B. Why are guiding questions*
*important in the teaching-learning process?*

There are a number of reasons why guiding questions are important:

- They can help students to discover patterns in knowledge and to solve problems.
- They support inductive teaching, guiding students to discover meaning, which increases motivation to learn.
- They are one of the most powerful tools for helping students think at more complex levels.
- They engage the personal intellect—something that traditional objectives usually fail to do.

Read the following objectives directing the learning of a unit on "Famous People in American History." Do these objectives have a familiar ring?

---

*Famous People in American History: Objectives*

- Identify famous historical figures in American history.
- Identify significant events related to these historical figures.
- Recall how the following historical figures shaped the course of American history: John Adams, Martin Luther King, Jr., Adam Smith, Harriet Tubman, Rosa Parks, and George Washington.

Now read the guiding questions related to the same topic.

---

*Famous People in American History: Guiding Questions*

- What does it mean to be a leader?
- Who were some of the famous leaders in American history?
- Why are these leaders famous?
- How did John Adams shape the future of America?
- How did Martin Luther King, Jr., and Rosa Parks influence the views of a nation?
- Why do we remember leaders long after their lives have ended?
- Are all leaders good?
- Can you think of a leader in the world today that America does not support? Why do we not support this leader?
- What are the characteristics of a good leader?
- Can someone who is not in politics or in the military be a leader?

---

What did you notice as you read the questions that differed from what you noticed as you read the objectives? Did you find that your mind was on autopilot as you read the objectives but that you were thinking as you read the questions? Did the questions engage your interest because you wanted to know how you would answer the questions based on your own knowledge and perspectives? Looking at factual content through a conceptual lens, such as "Leadership," engages the personal intellect. Why do so many curriculum documents attempt to drive content teaching through the use of objectives when they create so little passion for thinking and learning? Could it be that objectives are easier to test and score? We definitely need skill objectives, but do we really need content objectives if we have clearly identified the following?

1. The critical content topics (without verbs) that students are to study
2. The enduring conceptual understandings to be drawn from content
3. The key processes (complex performances) and skills that students are to learn

Let's allow our professional teachers the latitude in lesson planning to fuse the processes and skills with content to guide student learning.

## C. Why are guiding questions so difficult to write?

We can only pull so many questions out of the air related to a topic. Consequently, most of the questions end up being "what" questions directly related to the topic of study. However, overemphasizing "what" questions won't guide thinking to deeper waters.

One reason that some teachers have trouble writing guiding, or essential, questions is that they have not consciously identified the conceptual understandings toward which the questions should drive. Consequently, the questions keep flowing toward the specific topic. In a concept-based curriculum, it is not enough to teach only the facts related to a specific topic: we also want to use questions to take thinking to the level of conceptual understanding and help students build brain schemata for knowledge transfer. We need "why" and "how" questions as well as "what" questions to extend thinking.

Although fact-based questions are important to ensure the foundations of knowledge, the open-ended, conceptually based questions challenge the thinking of students beyond the facts. Open-ended questions that transfer across time and situations usually specify the enduring understanding as an embedded statement. It is the use of these questions as a follow-up to specific, topic-related questions that will help students build a bridge to deeper understanding.

## 7. Specific Knowledge and Skills

*A. How should we identify the specific knowledge for the unit?*

The specific knowledge is a list of the critical content topics to be studied in the unit. These topics can be pulled off the unit web and delineated further with bullets, or they can be listed as key facts that you feel students must know.

*B. Where do the skills come from?*

The skills can be drawn from the standards documents for the different subject areas such as language arts, mathematics, or science. The skills listed need to have been taught directly either as a part of the unit or at another time during the day. Notice that we are not yet writing the learning experiences: we are just identifying

SOURCE: Cartoon by David Ford, davidford4@comcast.net.

the key skills that will be taught directly by the teacher. The learning experiences, which link the skill with a topic, are developed in Step 9.

## 8. Assessment Codes

*A. What are the assessment codes?*

The assessment codes allow you to plan and identify the different ways you wish to assess knowledge, skills, and understandings within your unit. You will need to develop and include the different assessments in your unit packet. Different assessment types are suggested by the codes, but you may choose to add some other types. These assessments are in addition to the performance task, which is designed in Step 10.

## 9. Instructional Plan and Suggested Learning Experiences

*A. When do we design this step? When do we teach this step?*

This step is actually designed following the development of the culminating performance and other unit assessments. As Wiggins and McTighe (2005, pp. 17–19) explain we need to design backward to make certain we prepare students with the knowledge and skills to be successful on the unit assessments, although we teach forward. The instructional step of learning experiences precedes the administration of the various assessments when instruction is carried out.

*B. What is the purpose of the*
*instructional plan and learning experiences?*

Teachers have a choice in this step. They can either suggest learning experiences to explore and develop the critical content and enduring understandings, or they can list the instructional steps for carrying out the unit plan. What would you do first in implementing this unit? What would you do second? The instructional plan uses a teacher's frame of reference and describes how the teacher will engage students in the learning. The learning experiences use the students' frame of reference.

There should be a coherent link between the understandings, the questions, and the learning experiences. The purpose of the instructional plan and guiding questions is to develop the enduring understandings based on the specific content examples. Students will learn specific content knowledge and also develop deeper, conceptual understanding when there is evident coherence. (When you write suggested learning experiences, infuse the skills identified on the specific knowledge and skills page of the unit plan.)

*C. How do the secondary school unit-planning pages*
*differ from the elementary pages?*

The secondary school remains quite departmentalized across the country, though some have moved to interdisciplinary teams and block schedules. With the reality of departmentalization, the unit-planning pages are used somewhat differently at the secondary level. Although the interdisciplinary team works together to develop the unit title, conceptual lens, and web, the other unit components, up to the culminating performance, can be completed independently by teachers in each discipline. This difference between elementary and secondary levels is because secondary teachers in a departmentalized situation will be teaching their own subjects within their classrooms. They will still be providing interdisciplinary instruction with their team because they share a common unit focus and conceptual lens. There will be a few major generalizations that all disciplines support, but it is critical that each discipline maintain instructional integrity by also teaching to its own concept-specific generalizations, reached through guiding questions and learning experiences. The experiences will draw on the processes and skills important to each discipline. Once the unit-planning pages have been completed by each discipline, it is important that the interdisciplinary team come back together once again to share their work and discuss what the overall student learning experience will be throughout the unit. Teachers will want to maintain a holistic sense of the interdisciplinary learning experience for students.

## 10. Culminating Performance Task

*A. What is the culminating performance task?*

The culminating performance allows you to make a final assessment on how well students relate content to transferable, conceptual ideas and on how well they are able to perform with their knowledge. It answers the question, "What do I want students to know, understand, and be able to do as a result of this unit of study?" We are assessing understanding of one or more major ideas (generalizations) for the unit, supported by critical content knowledge and demonstrated by one or more authentic performances.

*B. How do we evaluate the culminating performance?*

A scoring guide is developed as part of the unit planning process to assess the level of performance. It is important to realize that students could easily get overloaded with major projects due in all classes at the same time in interdisciplinary units. This problem can be eased if teachers plan a common performance (e.g., a play) that would draw from the different disciplines or if they work together to stagger the due dates. Another option would be a unit portfolio, developed throughout the length of a unit, which would include the work of the different disciplines. The assessment criteria might differ by discipline.

*C. Is the culminating performance the only assessment in the unit?*

Definitely not. Throughout a unit, you will use an array of assessments that match the kinds of learning students are to demonstrate. Interviews, true-false assessments, multiple choice, writing tasks, oral presentations, and projects are just a few examples of assessments that provide information about different kinds of learning. These other assessments are noted in Step 8 (Assessment Codes).

### D. How do we write the culminating performance?

A major problem with many performance tasks is that there is too often little or no display of deep understanding. I think this is once again because our traditional curriculum design only takes us to the superficial level of topics and facts. How, then, can we write assessments for deep understanding? Figure 4.6 shows a simple model for writing a culminating performance task. This format ensures an assessment of deep understanding.

Complete the formula in Figure 4.6 as follows: What do you want students to do?

---

**WHAT:** Begin this statement with a cognitive verb such as "Investigate" and tie it directly to the title of your unit. The title of the unit in the example following is "The Holocaust: Man's Inhumanity to Man."

*Example:* Investigate the Holocaust . . .

**WHY:** In order to understand that. . . . Complete this statement by thinking beyond the topic to the importance or significance of the study. What is the transferable lesson (generalization) to be taken from this particular study?

*Example:* . . . to understand that leaders may abuse political or social power.

**HOW:** Begin a new sentence that frames how you want students to demonstrate their understanding of the "why" statement. This is a critical step. If you want to measure deep understanding, then this "how" statement needs to demonstrate the "why," and not just demonstrate knowledge of the facts learned in the "what" statement.

*Example:* You are a prosecutor with the War Crimes Tribunal. Prepare a case trying Adolph Hitler for his alleged war crimes against the Jewish people in Germany during the Holocaust. Research primary and secondary documents and build your case around the themes of "Crimes Against Humanity" and "Abuse of Power." Using multimedia and clear and specific arguments, present your case to the court.

In a follow-up discussion, ask the students what arguments the defense may have presented to support Hitler's actions. Then pose the question, "Under what criteria would humanity consider a person's actions indefensible?

---

Notice that the performance, the "how" statement, demonstrates understanding of the "why" statement. This takes the performance beyond a simple recitation of facts related to the Holocaust.

**Figure 4.6**  Culminating Performance Task

**WHAT:** Investigate . . . (unit title or major topic)

_____

_____

_____

_____

_____

_____

_____

**WHY:** In order to understand that . . . (enduring understandings)

_____

_____

_____

_____

_____

_____

_____

**HOW:** (Performance)

_____

_____

_____

_____

_____

_____

_____

What are the complex performances required in this task? Can you underline them? What kinds of criteria will be used in the scoring guide related to the multimedia presentation? (clarity of presentation, organization, depth and breadth of knowledge, etc.).

Carla Hassell, a dedicated eighth-grade science teacher at Alice Johnson Junior High in Channelview Independent School District, Channelview, Texas, allowed me to share a draft, and a revised Performance Task for one of her units. See if you can tell why Carla's revised task is stronger than her draft:

---

*Draft*

**WHAT:** Compare the climate of various cities around the world.

**WHY:** In order to understand that uneven heating produces convection currents that transfer energy from one place to another, creating diverse weather patterns.

**HOW:** Locate Prince Rupert, British Columbia; Mexico City, Mexico; and Ushuaia, Argentina, on your world map and highlight them. Research the climate for each city using the following Web sites: www.wunderground.com and www.weather.com. Design a data table that will describe the temperature, precipitation, and humidity for each city during the months of December through May. From your data, create a travel brochure for each city that will describe how the sun, oceans (if applicable), and elevation create weather for the perfect vacation.

**Revised**

**WHAT**: Compare the climate of various cities around the world

**WHY**: In order to understand that uneven heating produces convection currents that transfer energy from one place to another, creating diverse weather patterns.

**HOW**: Locate Prince Rupert, British Columbia; Mexico City, Mexico; and Ushuaia, Argentina, on your world map and highlight them. Research the climate for each city using the following Web sites: www.wunderground.com and www.weather.com. Design a data table that will describe the temperature, precipitation, and humidity for each city for the months of December through May. Analyze the data and write an article for *Science Today* that describes how the sun's heat energy is transferred at each city and how the elevation and oceans affect the convection currents that move the weather.

---

Did you discern that building the language of the generalization into the revised task in the last sentence provides greater focus on the deeper understanding, which is the goal of the assessment? Also notice that the travel brochure idea suggests identifying the ideal climate for a vacation, but does not provide criteria for an "ideal" climate. A climate that is ideal for a skiing vacation would differ from a climate that is ideal for underwater diving. The science journal article is a stronger performance task for determining a student's conceptual understanding.

## 11. Scoring Guide for Culminating Performance

*A. What is a scoring guide?*

A scoring guide assesses performance on a task according to defined criteria and a scaled set of performance indicators. A scoring guide assesses student progress toward the standard. The standard is the expected quality of performance.

Perhaps the most difficult part of writing scoring guides is finding effective and precise language to describe performance at the various levels. Too often, the defining language sounds vague and wishy-washy, using words such as "always," "often," "sometimes," or "seldom." We need to keep working on this language problem. We can find descriptive terms that are more precise and helpful to students, but it means that teachers will need to help students develop a mental construct for what these terms "look like" in the performance or product.

Students need to see specific *exemplars* (standards-level examples) of work. They need practice in applying the various descriptors that will be used in the assessment of their own work. This process of internalizing the "look" of various levels of performance through the descriptors must be engaged prior to the student's own work on a culminating performance. It is helpful if

- Teachers use the descriptors throughout the year on a variety of different performance assessments
- Teachers on a grade level agree to a common language of descriptors and applications to the various levels of performance
- Students can participate in choosing and defining the various descriptors of performance

Chapter 6 provides examples of scoring guides developed by teachers for classroom performances.

## 12. Unit Resources and Teacher Notes

*A. Do I have to list all unit resources?*

Unit planners need to think through the generalizations, questions, learning experiences, and skills and try to identify relevant and obtainable resources. Certainly, all teachers who implement the unit will add their own resources or continue to select the best resources over time. The Internet is a valuable tool for locating unit resources.

*B. What is the purpose of the teacher notes?*

These notes help the teacher implement and facilitate instruction. Again, any teacher who uses the unit will add to these notes.

## LESSON-PLANNING PAGES

The lesson-planning pages can take the unit plan into classroom instruction. These pages are a tool for teachers. Lesson plans may be a day long, or a few days long, or even a week long. Which enduring understandings, topics, questions, skills, and so on will be put together to form the actual lessons? Once a unit plan has been entered into the computer's word processing software, a "copy-and-paste" method can speed up the lesson planning and may just require a little embellishment on the questions and learning experiences. The second page allows teachers to differentiate instruction and assessment for special-needs students.

Chapter 5 shares some unit excerpts from the elementary and secondary grade levels.

## SUMMARY

Perspectives on the design of integrated, interdisciplinary curricula continue to evolve. My own views have developed over the past 13 years of intensive work with teachers around the country. This chapter shares a concept-based model for curriculum that integrates thinking in both interdisciplinary and intradisciplinary unit design. Unit design formats can vary from district to district. The design steps and unit- and lesson-planning pages in this book are provided to show a set of critical components for a quality concept-based design.

---

### EXTENDING THOUGHT

1. What is the value of integrated curriculum and instruction for students? For teachers?

2. What is the difference between a coordinated-multidisciplinary and an integrated-interdisciplinary curriculum?

3. Why is a conceptual lens essential for content integration?

4. What is the difference between macroconcepts and microconcepts? Why do instructional units need to identify enduring understandings at both the macrolevel and microlevel?

5. How does intradisciplinary differ from interdisciplinary in unit design? Can both be integrated? What is the key to integration?

6. Why is "scaffolding" a helpful skill in writing powerful, crisp, and clear generalizations?

7. How can you ensure that performance tasks go beyond simple activities to the level of deep, enduring understandings?

# Concept-Based Units

*Samples and Questions*

## FROM COORDINATED TO INTEGRATED UNITS

It is a simple matter to rework a topically based unit into a concept-based unit by deciding on a conceptual lens to draw thinking from the factual to the conceptual level. For example, an integrating conceptual lens for a supplementary unit on "Butterflies" might be "Life Cycles." In a supplementary unit on "African Art," in the upper grades, the teacher might choose the lens of "Form and Function."

At this point, it might be helpful to review some definitions that are critical to understanding this section:

- *Concept.* A mental construct that frames a set of examples sharing common attributes; concepts are timeless, universal, and abstract (to varying degrees). Specific examples (e.g., cycles, diversity, and interdependence) of the concept may vary, but the attributes are the same. For example, a cycle is a timeless concept. Although specific examples of a cycle differ—water cycle, rock cycle, historical cycle—they all have the attribute of a being a repeating, circular pattern.
- *Universal Generalizations.* Two or more concepts stated in a relationship (enduring understandings). Ideas that transfer through time, across cultures, or across situations. Example: Living organisms adapt to changing environments.
- *Conceptual Lens.* The integrating, focus concept for a topic-based study. The conceptual lens pulls thinking to the conceptual and transferable levels, and integrates thinking between the factual and conceptual levels.
- *Subtopics.* The content to be experienced through the unit learning experiences. The subtopics are brainstormed on the overview web under each strand surrounding the unit title.
- *Subconcepts.* Concepts to be explored through the unit learning experiences. The subconcepts are brainstormed along with subtopics for the unit overview web.

Figure 5.1 shows a concept–content web for a concept-based, integrated unit. This web-planning tool shows a unit title, "Ancient Egypt," which is viewed through the conceptual lens of "People, Places, and Environments." This design forces thinking to the conceptual level as students are led through unit questions and learning experiences to enduring understandings of social change and cultural identity. A major goal in concept-based instruction is to teach students how to think beyond the facts—to conceptualize and understand the lasting significance of content study.

The design in Figure 5.1 meets the criteria of a strong interdisciplinary, integrated unit using the definition of interdisciplinary curriculum presented in Chapter 4. This unit also meets the additional criterion of a strong, integrated unit because each of the subject areas has depth of study—it is not composed of a few activities. The conceptual lens brings cohesion and focus to the unit study. The students know the focus for learning, but the search for understanding is their responsibility.

Figures 5.2 through 5.13 are additional examples of the brainstormed concept–content webs that elementary and secondary teachers have developed in planning interdisciplinary, integrated units. Each figure has been chosen to illustrate one or more of the steps for design. Accompanying each figure is a discussion of the illustrative points.

The webs show the initial brainstorming efforts in planning the content focus for the unit study. It is important to realize that these figures do not intend to convey the personal process skills that students will develop and apply to the content study. Those will appear in unit and lesson plan experiences through formats such as drama; debates; panel presentations; technology displays; plays; or musical, oral, or written presentations.

Figure 5.2 is a kindergarten unit on "Transportation." Although transportation is actually a concept, the teacher has chosen to use the more sophisticated lens of "Motion and Energy" to begin developing student understanding of those concepts.

Figure 5.3 demonstrates a template model. Though most states do not teach about all of the regions of the United States in this much detail any longer, this model of the conceptual template works well for any subject matter that studies the same concepts applied in different contexts (e.g., world geography, cultures, or ancient civilizations).

Figure 5.4 shows that teachers are drawn to issues of social significance when asked to design units of study. These issues need to be addressed in classrooms. Violence in America is certainly a topic of great concern to students, parents, and teachers today. Addressing issues of social significance is one of the best uses of interdisciplinary curriculum. Students view complex social issues from multiple perspectives and develop problem-solving skills, which are essential to effective citizenship.

Culture-based units, such as the one shown in Figure 5.5, teach students how interacting cultures influence each other. Cultures are compared and studied through various cultural aspects, from language to trade to technology.

Elementary grade units, such as Figure 5.6 on "My Family," are common. Notice how this teacher develops important enduring understandings with young students.

*(Text continues on page 124)*

**Figure 5.1** Ancient Egypt: Grade 6 Social Studies Unit

## "People, Places, Environments"

### Conceptual Lens

**Geography**

Use of resources for needs
- Food
- Clothing

Middle Kingdom
- Technology and irrigation
- Location
- Natural land forms

**Economics**

Transportation
Natural resources
- Nile River
Land ownership
Trade
Grain storage (supply and demand)
Pyramids

**Culture**

Class system
Roles
Religion
Development of art, mathematics, science
Rosetta stone
Hieroglyphics
Death and dying; mummification
Afterlife; pyramids

**Government and Politics**

Lineage and rulers
Alliances

**History**

Upper, Lower Egypt
Old Kingdom
- Historical periods
- Slavery
- Dynasties

**Unit Title**

"Ancient Egypt and the Development of Culture"

### Culminating Performance Task

Investigate the development of ancient Egyptian culture in order to understand that cultures address human needs in similar and different ways.

As a cultural anthropologist, research the mummification beliefs related to other ancient religious beliefs. In an article for the *Religious Quarterly*, describe the mummification process and compare it to the "death/afterlife" process of other ancient cultures. Using their religious beliefs and culture as a base, explain the similarities and differences.

*(Continued)*

| Enduring Understandings (Generalizations) | Guiding Questions |
|---|---|
| 1. All cultures share basic elements such as food, shelter, clothing, and language. | 1. How did rivers play a vital role in the development of early civilizations? How did the Nile River affect the lives of the people of Egypt? How did alliances with other cultures enable the Egyptians to obtain resources? What impact did hieroglyphics have on the development of the Egyptian culture? In what ways did the geography of the region influence the development of Egyptian culture? |
| 2. Cultures develop and progress through the exchange of ideas and products. | 2. What influence did Egyptian culture have on other civilizations? What limitations in Egyptian resources led to far-reaching trade? How did trade develop based on internal and external needs? How did Egyptian conquests improve the standard of living? How did the development of mathematics, science, and art change the standard of living in Egypt? How does the exchange of ideas and products across cultures stimulate progress? |
| 3. Cultures address human needs in similar and different ways. | 3. How was land ownership a source of social, economic, and political power? In what way do societies assign power to individuals, groups, or institutions? What was the selection process for pharaohs? How did the structure of social classes in Egypt meet societal needs? What are the positive and negative effects of social classes? Should societies have social classes? |
| 4. Geographical and political unification affect the development of civilizations and cultures. | 4. What is meant by "unification"? How did unification affect the growth of Egyptian civilizations? In what ways did geography play a role in unification? How did unification impact the development of the class system in ancient Egypt? |

SOURCE: Wayne Zalaski, Jody Muldoon, Phil Mannarino, Frank Bogdan. Plainville Community School District, Plainville, Connecticut. Used with permission.

**Figure 5.2**   Transportation Unit

## "Motion and Energy"
### Conceptual Lens

**Literature**

*Sheep in a Jeep*
  (shared/guided)
*On the Go*
  (shared/guided)
*Wheels on the Bus*
  (read aloud)
*Dan the Flying Man*
  (shared)
*To Town*
  (shared)
*Trucks*
  (read aloud)
*What Makes Things Move*
  (shared)

**Field Trips**

Airport
Train station

**Social Studies**

Types of transportation
  • Boats, bus
  • Land, water, air
  • Airplane, walking
  • Trucks, bikes
  • Hot air balloons
  • Trains

**Mathematics**

Graphing          Speed
Estimation        Size
Sorting           Geometrical
Categorizing        shapes
Measurements      Counting
Patterns          Lengths

**Unit Title**
**"Transportation"**

**Culminating Performance Tasks**

What: Investigate, observe, and analyze
      three forms of transportation: land,
      sea, and air and determine
      how each mode of transportation
      moves.

Why:  . . . in order to prove that for
      something to move there must be
      a source of energy.

How:  Create three moving vehicles:
      land, sea, and air. Your vehicle
      designs must move from one place
      to another. Build and decorate your
      vehicle with materials found in the
      classroom. Demonstrate and
      explain how energy powers
      your vehicle.

**Grade Level: Kindergarten**

(Continued)

(Continued)

| Enduring Understandings (Generalizations) | Guiding Questions |
|---|---|
| 1. Energy causes objects to move. | 1. What things in your house use energy? What is energy? Do you have a toy that can move because of energy? How does the energy cause it to move? What is power? Where does power come from? |
| 2. Motion and power create energy. | 2. When a car moves is it in motion? When a river runs is it in motion? What is motion? Can you think of other things that show motion? Will more power create more motion? Can you think of something that would show how more power and motion create more energy? |
| 3. Friction produces power, which creates a push/pull movement | 3. Why do many forms of transportation use wheels? What makes wheels work? |
| 4. Different types of transportation move at different speeds. | 4. Why do airplanes move faster than cars? Which has greater energy? Which has the least energy: bicycles, trains, or cars? |
| 5. People depend on transportation to take them from place to place. | 5. Why is transportation important? Which form of transportation do you use most often? |

SOURCE: Southwood Elementary School, Orange County School District, Orlando, Florida. Used with permission.

**Figure 5.3** Unit Planner: Regions of the United States

# Unit Planner

**Unit Title: "Regions of the United States"**
**Conceptual Lens: "Government and Economic Systems"**

## Literature
Regional historical figures;
  biographies
  of leaders in government
  and the economy;
  inventors
Historical fiction

## Fine Art
Artists
State songs
Flags
Symbols

## Mathematics
Comparisons
  • Graphs/charts
Data analysis
Trends

## Science
Economic resources
Shelter; materials
Technology advances
  • Transportation
  • Communication
Population; impact on economy;
  resources

### Unit Title
**"Regions of the
United States"**

## Social Studies and Economics
Jobs/skills/adaptation (workforce,
  labor)
Technology; impact on economics
Transportation; how and why it varies
Communication systems
Workforce labor
Economic impact of environment
  trade

## History
Settlement
Assimilation
Statehood
Conflict within and
  between regions
Schooling
Civil rights

## Geography
Political maps
Locations
Landforms

### Unit Overview

This unit web is one of three templates for
studying regions of the United States. This
unit's focus is "Government and Economic
Systems." The other two units look at
regions through the lenses of "Cultural
Unity and Diversity" and "People, Places,
and Environments."

NOTE: The three unit templates are
applied to the study of each region and
allow comparisons of regional similarities
and differences.

**Grade Level: Fourth**

*(Continued)*

(Continued)

## Enduring Understandings (Generalizations)

1. Changing economic factors can create shifts in immigration patterns.

2. Economic need drives technological advances in transportation and communication.

3. Technological advances change the selection criteria of workers.

## Guiding Questions

1. How are all cultures similar in how they meet basic needs?
   How are they different?
   How does the exchange of ideas and innovations affect a culture?
   What are the economic factors that can cause shifts in immigration patterns?
   What are some of the specific population and economic issues of the _____ region?

2. How did economic need affect the development of transportation in the _____ region?
   Why is communication important to a region's economy?

3. How have jobs and industry changed over time in the _____ region?
   Why have jobs and industries changed?
   How has the selection criteria for workers changed?
   What skills do you think will be needed when you enter the workforce?

Mathematics

4. Graphs and charts can show economic trends.

5. Decimal placement determines place value in addition and subtraction.

Fine Art

6. Music and art help unify a people.

Literature

7. Biographies contribute to an historical record and show how individuals, groups, or institutions shape culture.

4. How are graphs and charts used to predict trends?

5. What is "place value"?
   Why does the location of a decimal determine its place value?
   Why is place value important in economic predictions?

6. Why do governments commission artists and musicians to create state or national symbols?
   What techniques or elements do artists employ to create patriotic feelings?
   When is a piece of music or art considered patriotic?

7. Why do authors write biographies?
   How do you think they select their subjects?
   What criteria must an author use when writing a biography?

*(Continued)*

● 113

(Continued)

# Critical Content and Skills

AC = Assessment Code:

Q-Quizzes     P-Prompts
T-Tests     O-Observations
WS-Work Samples     D-Dialogues
SA-Student Self-Assessment

| Students Will Know . . . | AC |
|---|---|
| 1. Key facts related to the government and economics of the Northeast, Southeast, Midwest, Northwest, and Southwest regions of the United States. | Q |
| 2. Geographical locations for each region | T |
| 3. Major landforms and resources contributing to the economics of each region | D |

**Key Skills . . .**

Social Studies

1. Identify and label
2. Use map key, compass rose, and distance scale
3. Use primary source documents to compare perspectives
4. Use the Internet to locate information

Language Arts

5. Read historical fiction and biographies to gain and compare information
6. Generate questions for study and interest
7. Organize and recall information
8. Use electronic sources and tools to research and communicate

Mathematics

9. _____

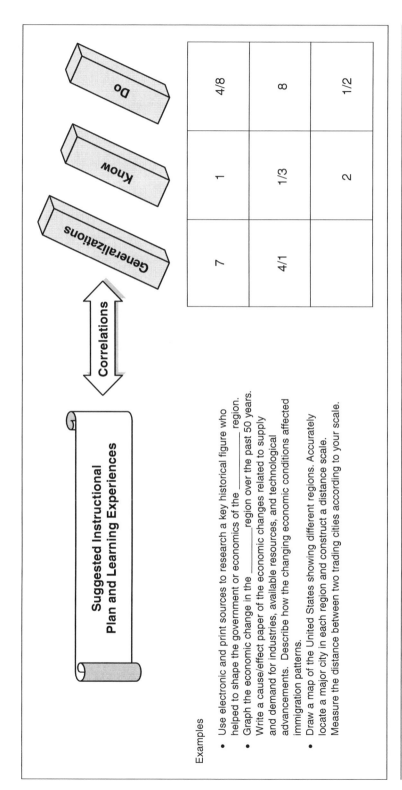

**Suggested Instructional Plan and Learning Experiences**

| Generalizations | Know | Do |
|---|---|---|
| 7 | 1 | 4/8 |
| 4/1 | 1/3 | 8 |
| | 2 | 1/2 |

Correlations

Examples

- Use electronic and print sources to research a key historical figure who helped to shape the government or economics of the _____ region.
- Graph the economic change in the _____ region over the past 50 years. Write a cause/effect paper of the economic changes related to supply and demand for industries, available resources, and technological advancements. Describe how the changing economic conditions affected immigration patterns.
- Draw a map of the United States showing different regions. Accurately locate a major city in each region and construct a distance scale. Measure the distance between two trading cities according to your scale.

SOURCE: Wayne Zalaski, Jody Muldoon, Phil Mannarino, Frank Bogdan. Plainville Community School District, Plainville, Connecticut. Used with permission.

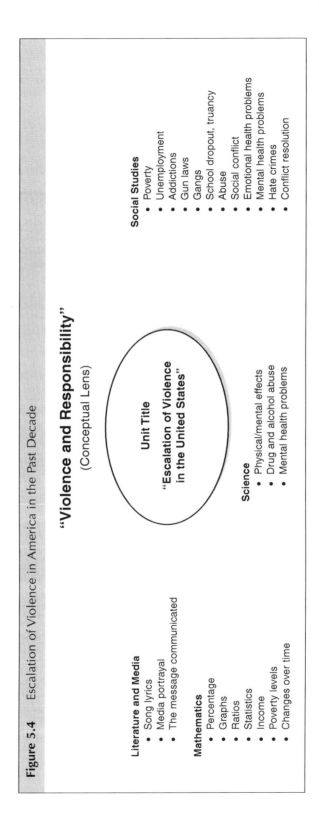

**Figure 5.4**   Escalation of Violence in America in the Past Decade

**"Violence and Responsibility"**
(Conceptual Lens)

**Unit Title**

**"Escalation of Violence
in the United States"**

**Literature and Media**
• Song lyrics
• Media portrayal
• The message communicated

**Mathematics**
• Percentage
• Graphs
• Ratios
• Statistics
• Income
• Poverty levels
• Changes over time

**Science**
• Physical/mental effects
• Drug and alcohol abuse
• Mental health problems

**Social Studies**
• Poverty
• Unemployment
• Addictions
• Gun laws
• Gangs
• School dropout, truancy
• Abuse
• Social conflict
• Emotional health problems
• Mental health problems
• Hate crimes
• Conflict resolution

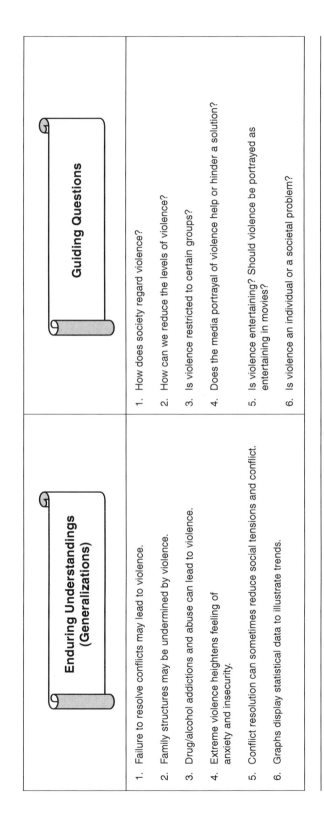

**Enduring Understandings (Generalizations)**

1. Failure to resolve conflicts may lead to violence.

2. Family structures may be undermined by violence.

3. Drug/alcohol addictions and abuse can lead to violence.

4. Extreme violence heightens feeling of anxiety and insecurity.

5. Conflict resolution can sometimes reduce social tensions and conflict.

6. Graphs display statistical data to illustrate trends.

**Guiding Questions**

1. How does society regard violence?

2. How can we reduce the levels of violence?

3. Is violence restricted to certain groups?

4. Does the media portrayal of violence help or hinder a solution?

5. Is violence entertaining? Should violence be portrayed as entertaining in movies?

6. Is violence an individual or a societal problem?

SOURCE: Angela Mills, Betty Hazel, Ellamae Washington, and Evelyn Workman. Toole Middle School, Charleston, South Carolina. Used with permission.

Figure 5.5   French Influence on North American Culture

# "Culture and Identity"
(Conceptual Lens)

**Exploration and Settlement**
- Regions
- Reasons
- Colonization

**Holidays and Traditions**
- Origins
- Clothing
- Food

**Education**
- Structure
- Subjects
- Attitudes

**The Arts and Leisure**
- Sports
- Dance
- Music
- Visual arts

**Government**
- Organization
- Laws
- Courts

**Unit Title**
"French Influence on North American Culture"

**Inventions**
- Health and vaccines
- Measurement

**Architecture**
- Commercial Style
- Residential Style
- Religious Style

**Technology**
- Aviation
- Scuba diving
- Medicines
- Computer

**Trade and Economy**
- Imports
- Exports

**Religion**
- Beliefs/values
- Structure
- Persecution
- History

**Language**
- Literature
- Vocabulary

**Occupations**
- Fashion
- Agriculture
- Health

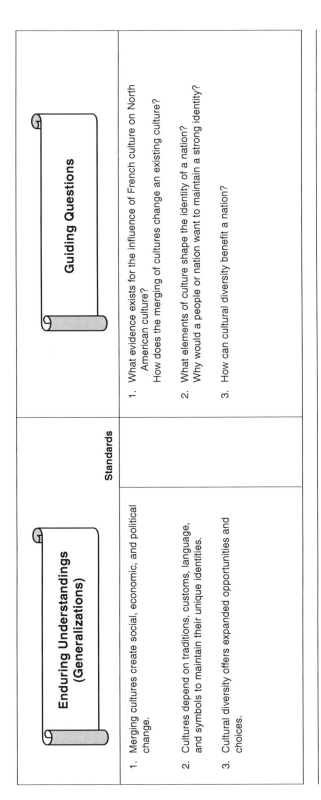

**Enduring Understandings (Generalizations)**

**Standards**

1. Merging cultures create social, economic, and political change.

2. Cultures depend on traditions, customs, language, and symbols to maintain their unique identities.

3. Cultural diversity offers expanded opportunities and choices.

**Guiding Questions**

1. What evidence exists for the influence of French culture on North American culture?
   How does the merging of cultures change an existing culture?

2. What elements of culture shape the identity of a nation?
   Why would a people or nation want to maintain a strong identity?

3. How can cultural diversity benefit a nation?

SOURCE: Adapted from the work of Sue Pasqualicchio (Dubose Middle School, Summerville, South Carolina) and Laura Childers and Camilla D. Groome (Alston Middle School, Summerville, South Carolina).

**Figure 5.6** My Family Unit Web

# Critical Content–Concept Web

# Unit Planner

## "Interdependence"
(Conceptual Lens)

### History
*Families* past and present
- *ancestors;how did families work together?*

*Changing roles over time:* mother, father, children

### Geography
Where families live
- *migration*
- influence of *jobs* on *living location*
- *living locations* of *extended family*
- effect of *distance* on *family relationships: transportation; communication*

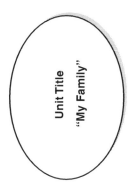

**Unit Title**
**"My Family"**

### Culture
*Education*
*Entertainment and influence on family*
*Holiday traditions*
*Families working together*
*Values and beliefs*

### Economics
*Budget and allowances*
*Jobs*
*Needs versus wants*
- *shelter, clothing, food*
- *goods families consume (consumption)*

*Money*
*Goods and services*

### Government
*Types of governments*
*Regulations*
- *influence on family life/structure*

*Right/responsibilities*
*Family rules*

NOTE: Concepts italicized.

---

### Unit Overview

Some families are large, some are small, but your family is very important to you. Your family takes care of you and helps you meet your needs and wants.

Have you ever wondered . . .
- Why families live in different cities?
- Why some of your relatives live in different locations?
- Why you have to follow rules?
- Why people use money?
- Why family members have to work together?
- What childhood was like for your parents and grandparents?

Let's find out!

**Grade Level: First**

| Enduring Understandings (Generalizations) | Guiding Questions |
|---|---|
| Culture | |
| 1. Values and beliefs guide the decisions in a family. | 1. When you say you believe something, what do you mean? What do you believe?<br>How are values different from beliefs?<br>What is a decision? How are your decisions influenced by your family's beliefs/values? |
| Economics | |
| 2. Family members work to meet needs and wants. | 2. What needs do you have in your family? Are there things you *want* but do not really *need*?<br>How does your family meet its needs? Wants? What can you do to meet your want? |
| 3. Families work together to make choices dependinig on their needs and wants. | 3. How do families work together to make choices for the good of the family?<br>Why is compromise a good way to make choices when family member cannot agree? |
| Geography | |
| 4. Families use money to purchase goods and services. | 4. Why is money sometimes coins and sometimes paper?<br>What are goods? Services?<br>Why must families pay money for goods and services? |
| 5. Occupations often determine the living location of a family. | 5. What jobs (occupations) do your family members have?<br>Why do people work at jobs?<br>Why did your family move to your present living location? |
| 6. Distance influences family communications. | 6. Do some of your family members live in different locations?<br>How often do you see these family members?<br>How do you communicate with them?<br>How does distance affect the way you communicate with family members? |

*(Continued)*

| Enduring Understandings (Generalizations) | Guiding Questions |
|---|---|
| Government | 1. Why do we have school rules?<br>What would our classroom be like if there were no rules?<br>Where else do you follow rules?<br>What rules do you have at home? |
| 1. Rules provide order in a family. | |
| 2. Rules and decisions made by families are intended for the good of the family. | 2. Do the rules in families ever affect their decisions?<br>Should rules affect family decisions?<br>When have family rules affected something you wanted to do?<br>Should families have rules? |
| History | 3. What chores do you have at home?<br>Do families sometimes share chores?<br>What chores did your parents have when they were children?<br>How have chores changed over time?<br>How have the way families work together at home changed over time? |
| 3. The way families work together at home changes over time. | |
| 4. Ancestors pass on family traditions to the next generation. | 4. Who are some of your ancestors?<br>What family traditions have been passed on from your ancestors?<br>Why are traditions important to a family?<br>Do different cultures celebrate different traditions?<br>Why are traditions important to a cultural group? |

# Critical Content and Skills

AC = Assessment Code:

Q-Quizzes
T-Tests
**WS**-Work Samples
**SA**-Student Self-Assessment

P-Prompts
O-Observations
D-Dialogues

### Students Will Know . . .

| Students Will Know . . . | AC |
|---|---|
| 1. The characteristics of a family. | SA |
| 2. The meaning of key concepts: role, money, goods, services . . . | D |
| 3. The difference between a need and a want. | D |
| 4. Examples of family and cultural traditions. | P |

### Key Skills . . .

| Key Skills . . . | AC |
|---|---|
| A. Express own ideas | D |
| B. Express ideas through different forms: writing, speaking, and visual art. | WS |
| C. Listen for specific information. | Q |
| D. Adjust behavior appropriately in cooperative work group. | O |

SOURCE: Meridian Joint School District No. 2, Meridian, Idaho. Used with permission.

*(Text continued from page 106)*

State standards require an in-depth knowledge of state history. Concept-based teachers teach important ideas in addition to teaching key facts about the state. Figure 5.7 is an example of a state unit on "Idaho in the Present."

### Intradisciplinary, Integrated Unit Examples

The unit shown in Figures 5.8 is an intradisciplinary high school unit for photography. Notice how the generalizations guide the unit study. Students will discover other enduring understandings in their search for knowledge.

Figure 5.9 is a chemistry web followed by the alternative unit design format found in Resource A. This unit has clear generalizations and supportive questions.

Physics classes teach to enduring principles and concepts to facilitate the transfer of knowledge and a deeper understanding of the discipline. The unit excerpt in Figure 5.10 illustrates how the generalizations and questions work together.

# MULTIAGE CLASSROOMS AND CONCEPT-BASED CURRICULUM

There is ongoing interest in multiage classrooms education. Multiage classrooms combine two and occasionally three levels to provide a broader age span for the learning environment. There are benefits to these arrangements as long as the teacher has a solid understanding of how to approach curriculum and instruction with the increased span of abilities and maturity levels.

One question that arises frequently is, "How do we handle the multiple levels of curriculum within the multiage structure?" For multiage classes, the use of major concepts in social studies allows teachers in multiage classrooms to use related unit titles each year. As long as the concept stays the same, different titles (usually referred to as grade level themes) can focus the content across age levels or grade spans. Teachers can have students working on different themes related to the concept in a classroom, or they can do a different theme each year (e.g., "Family," "Community," "State") for the same conceptual lens (e.g., "Interdependence," "Change and Continuity," "Culture").

A Washington State example demonstrates the use of concepts, themes, and generalizations as an effective way to articulate the content curriculum in a multiage or traditional grade level school setting. This promising plan to write a global social studies curriculum was started in Washington State a number of years ago. Unfortunately, like many curriculum projects, it was never completed because of administrative changes, but the design is worth sharing.

Realizing that students live in a globally interdependent world, the teachers developed a K–6 framework to address key concepts using examples from different cultural regions of the world. Three social studies integrated units were developed for each grade level with a conceptual focus that was developed through the grades.

*(Text continues on page 135)*

**Figure 5.7**  Idaho Unit Web

# Critical Content–Concept Web

## Unit Planner

**"Identity"**

(Conceptual Lens)

**Unit Title**

**"Idaho in the Present"**

### Culture
- Architecture
- Populations
- Migration; immigration
- Education
- Media
- Recreation
- Diversity/unity

### Economics
- Idaho economics
- Global trade
- Forestry
- Boise Cascade
- Agriculture
- Mining, water, salmon, tourism
- Technology; Micron
- Industries and resources
- Environmental issues

### History
- Frank Church
- Cecil Andrus
- JR Simplot
- The arts—Morrison; Simplot
- Development of agriculture; industry

### Geography
- Populations
- Northwest region and Idaho region
- Landforms—rivers mountains
- Agriculture and irrigation; dams

### Government
- Tribal rights
- County and state government
- Executive, judicial, and legislative branches
- Regulation of industry

NOTE: Concepts italicized.

### Unit Overview

We live in Idaho—a great state in the Pacific Northwest!

In this unit we will explore the "identity" of Idaho and its people.

- Who are the people of Idaho? Where do they come from?
- Who are the leaders and industries that have shaped the economy of this region?
- How has geography and location influenced our region?
- What makes Idaho unique as a state? What is our identity?

We learned about Idaho in the past. Now let's visit Idaho in the present, and project our future!

**Grade Level: Fourth**

*(Continued)*

| Enduring Understandings (Generalizations) | Guiding Questions |
|---|---|
| Culture | |
| 1. Differing values and economic concerns and/or interests can create tension and conflict between individuals, groups, or nations. | 1. Why are Idaho loggers and environmentalists in conflict? What interest do biologists, farmers, sportsmen, developers, and hydroelectric companies each have in Idaho's river systems? Why may differing interests create conflict among individuals and groups? How can people resolve conflicts? |
| 2. Cultural, state, and regional celebrations express the identity of a people. | 2. What celebrations do we have in Idaho that express the diversity, unity, and identity of our people? Why is cultural identity important to a people? Why is cultural diversity important to a community? |
| Economics | |
| 3. Economic systems are complex institutions that include families, workers, large and small businesses, and governments. | 3. What businesses and industries are important to the economy of Idaho? What factors have helped to develop these Idaho businesses? What is Idaho's role in the economy of the Pacific Northwest? What is an economic system? What makes an economic system strong? |
| 4. Incentives, values, traditions, and habits influence economic decisions. | 4. How are values formed? What are incentives? Does advertising suggest incentives for purchasing products? Are some products purchased through habit? Give examples of family economic decisions or purchases based on values and based on habit. |
| 5. The cost of goods and services relates to the supply and the demand. | 5. Why is it possible to produce certain goods at a reasonable cost in Idaho? What determines the cost of a good or service? Where do we buy goods that we cannot produce? |

Geography

1. The physical environment affects where and how people in a region live.

2. Land and resources can serve more than one purpose.

Government

3. Government is an organized institution for establishing order among people, groups, and institutions.

4. Citizenship carries responsibility as well as rights.

1. Where are Idaho's population centers?
   Why are they located in these areas?
   What recreational opportunities exist in Idaho and the Northwest region?
   How does the physical environment contribute to tourism and growth?

2. In what ways do we use the land and resources in Idaho . . . public use? . . . private use?
   What conflicts and concerns presently exist over the uses of land resources?
   How will people resolve these differences?

3. How is Idaho's state government organized?
   Who are the current government leaders in Idaho?
   How is Idaho represented at the federal level?
   What other government divisions exist in Idaho?
   What are the responsibilities of state government?
   Why do states establish governments?
   How can citizens influence government decisions?

4. What are the responsibilities of a citizen . . . by law? . . . by choice?
   Why do governments make laws?
   What happens when citizens do not follow the laws?
   What are some of the rights that you have as a citizen?

(Continued)

# Critical Content and Skills

**AC = Assessment Code:**

Q-Quizzes
T-Tests
**WS**-Work Samples
**SA**-Student Self-Assessment

P-Prompts
O-Observations
D-Dialogues

| Students Will Know . . . | AC |
|---|---|
| 1. Current environmental issues in Idaho | WS |
| 2. Important celebrations in Idaho and what they represent. | |
| 3. Information on Idaho businesses and industries. | WS |
| 4. Different cultural groups and populations in Idaho and their contributions. | |
| 5. The structure and function of Idaho government; current leaders. | T |
| 6. Factors that shape Idaho's identity. | P |

| Key Skills . . . | AC |
|---|---|
| A. Identify fact and opinion. | |
| B. Recognize point of view. | SA |
| C. Write a persuasive essay. | P |
| D. Locate current information from a variety of sources: newspaper, Internet, pamphlets, brochures. | |
| E. Conduct interviews. | |
| F. Read and interpret graphs and charts. | D |
| G. Express personal convictions. | T |

SOURCE: Meridian Mathematics Committee, Meridian Joint School District No. 2, Meridian, Idaho. Used with permission.

**Figure 5.8** High School Photography Conceptual Lens

### Communication and Control

*Conceptual Lens*

**Subconcepts**

| | | |
|---|---|---|
| Expression | Detail | Appropriation |
| Focus | Ethics | Culture |
| Contrast | Symbolism | Multiplicity |
| Light quality | Abstraction | Intent |
| Perspective | Integration | Limitation |

**Generalizations**

1. Art communicates a perspective.

2. Words and images combined can create powerful communications.

3. Light quality affects image.

4. Color and black-and-white imagery convey contrasting meaning.

5. Detail can inform or obstruct meaning.

6. Symbolism and abstraction can effectively evoke reality.

7. A visual communication can convey multiple messages.

8. Artists interpret and reflect the complexity of culture.

9. Art combined with technology can shape and reflect culture.

**Guiding Questions**

- How does a visual communication evolve?
- What makes a visual communication work?
- How does an artist evoke reality without recreating it?
- Are visual communications ever neutral?
- Why do both color and black-and-white images make sense to the viewer?
- How does human vision work?
- How do artists respond to technical limitations?
- How does the artist decide on the amount of detail to incorporate in the work?
- How does the quality of light affect the viewer's feelings toward an image?
- What techniques can the artist use to convey multiple, conflicting messages in an image?
- What is the relationship between art and culture?
- How can words be used to enhance a visual image?
- What role does ethics play in art?
- How do art and technology interact to shape culture?

*(Continued)*

(Continued)

---

**Processes and Skills**

1. Apply technical knowledge to creative problem solving:
   - Manipulate camera controls of a manual camera for special effects.
   - Use graphics software for photo-based communications.
   - Use photographic chemicals to create color images.

2. Apply theory to technique:
   - Manipulate film development for special effects.
   - Integrate computer and camera technologies to create images.
   - Use studio and natural lighting for special effects.

**Activities (Examples)**

- Create a visual communication with a manual camera.
- Create photographs that have a controlled depth of field to direct the viewer's attention to a specific area.
- Create photographs that have controlled blur to create visual metaphors.
- Manipulate and enhance photographs with graphics software.
- Create color photographs using photographic chemicals.
- Experiment with studio and natural lighting to create a special photographic effect.
- Use creative darkroom techniques to communicate mood.
- Create extreme candid photographs using pushed film to communicate hidden truths.
- Read and discuss the ethics of candid photography and paparazzi versus photojournalism to realize the sociological impact of the camera.
- Create color negatives and prints to communicate using the full spectrum of color.
- Tone black-and-white prints (blue, sepia) to communicate using a limited color palette.
- Integrate words into a photograph using transparent overlays to explore the use of photography in graphic design.
- Use appropriate images creatively to create an image with complex meaning.

**Culminating Performance Tasks**

Analyze and evaluate your own photographs to understand how a body of work in art communicates a clear style or message, or both. Create and present in a portfolio eight mounted 8 × 10 prints that communicate your style or message, or both. The prints are to be made from your own negatives and must be well printed and well composed with the style of intent clearly communicated.

As an art jurist, draw another artist's (student's) name and present a three-minute summary and critique of the message and style.

---

SOURCE: Rosamond Hyde, Gloucester Public Schools, Gloucester, Massachusetts. Used with permission.

TEACHER'S NOTE: As the designer of this unit, I worked from the activities to the concepts, generalizations, and essential questions. They evolved from an analysis of the activities' meanings, purposes, and intended learnings. This helped me organize the unit and integrate deeper levels of understanding into the material and instruction.

**Figure 5.9** Chemistry Unit

**"System and Interaction"**
(Conceptual Lens)

**Atomic Structures**
Valence electrons
Formation of ions
Electronegativity

**Electronegativity**
Periodic table trend
Ionic/covalent
   continuum

**Bond Types**
Covalent, ionic, metallic
Polar covalent
Orbital hybridization
Sigma and pi bonds

**Molecular Shape**
VSEPR theory
Valence-bond theory
Polarity

Unit Title
**"Chemical Bonding"**

**Intermolecular Forces**
London dispersion
Dipole-dipole
Hydrogen bonding

**Bond Energy**
Potential energy
Bond strength
Exothermic and endothermic bonds

**Modern Materials**
Liquid crystals
Polymers
Ceramics

**Compounds and Properties**
Amorphous solid
Crystalline solid
• Molecular, ionic, atomic (liquids)
• Molecules with strong intermolecular forces (gases)
• Molecules with weak intermolecular forces

(Continued)

(Continued)

Course: Chemistry
Unit Title: "Chemical Bonding"
Conceptual Lens: "System and Interaction"

Instructor: _____
Length of Unit: _____

| Key Topics and Concepts Subconcepts | Enduring Understandings (Generalizations) (Understand) | Guiding Questions | Critical Content and Key Facts (Know) | Instructional Activities and Resources | Skill Objectives (Able to Do) | Assessments |
|---|---|---|---|---|---|---|
| Electronegativity | The electronegativity of an atom determines the type of chemical bond that is formed in a chemical reaction | • How is electronegativity related to the periodic table?<br>• How can you predict the type of bond using the electronegativity?<br>• What are the types of bonds dependent on electronegativity?<br>• What types of compounds are produced from these bonds? | Concepts:<br>○ Electronegativity<br>○ Ionic bond<br>○ Covalent bonds<br>○ Polar covalent bond<br>○ Periodic trend | • 3D Periodic Table Lab<br>• Calculate the difference in electronegativity | Predict the bond type<br><br>Analyze the continuum between ionic and covalent bonds to determine the degree of bond character<br><br>Describe the periodic trend | Investigate chemical bonding in order to understand that the electronegativity of an atom determines the type of chemical bond that is formed in a chemical reaction<br><br>Analyze bonds in an organic compound, inorganic compound, and water to determine the bond type using electronegativity values.<br><br>Plot the differences in electronegativity on a bond character curve |
| Atomic Structure | The increased stability of a completed outer atomic energy level drives chemical bonding | • How does the element's electron configuration affect bonding?<br>• Why is a completed outer energy level more stable?<br>• Do all atoms need to form a completed outer energy level? | Electron configuration<br><br>Atomic energy levels | | Predict if bonding will occur<br>Predict if bonding will not occur | |

132  ●

| Bond Energy | Each chemical bond stores an amount of potential energy dependent on the atoms involved. | • How is potential energy stored in a chemical bond?<br>• Does every bond have the same amount of energy?<br>• What happens when the bond breaks?<br>• How is the energy transferred to new bonds? | Potential energy<br><br>Endothermic reactions<br><br>Exothermic reactions | • Research the values of bond energy.<br>• Describe the law of conservation of energy with respect to chemistry. |
|---|---|---|---|---|
| Molecular Shape | The shape of molecules is determined by the repulsion of electrons in the chemical bonds and pairs of valence electrons. | • Why do electrons repel each other?<br>• Why is the shape of a water molecule beat? | Electron repulse<br><br>PR theory | • Predict bond angles<br>• Describe the impact of different molecular geometries<br>• Determine polarity of molecules |

SOURCE: Jean Lummis, Washington Township High School, Washington Township School District, Sewell, New Jersey. Used with permission.

**Figure 5.10** Physics Unit

Course: Physics
Unit Title: "Electromagnetism"
Conceptual Lens: "Energy and Matter"

Instructor: _____
Length of Unit: _____

| Key Topics and Concepts Subconcepts | Enduring Understandings (Generalizations) (Understand) | Guiding Questions | Critical Content (Know) | Skill Objectives (Able to Do) | Resources and Materials | Assessments |
|---|---|---|---|---|---|---|
| Electromagnetic Force<br><br>• Electric<br>• Magnetic | Electricity and magnetism are two aspects of a single electromagnetic force.<br><br>Charge 1 bodies can attract or repel with a force that depends on the nature and distance between them.<br><br>Between any two charged particles the electro-magnetic force is vastly greater than the gravitational force. | • What happens when like charges are brought together?<br>• How does the distance between two charges affect the force they exert on each other?<br>• How is the EM force similar to the gravitational force?<br>• Which force, EM or gravitational, is greater when objects are closer together? When they are far apart?<br>• How do you produce a magnetic force?<br>• How are the electric and magnetic forces related?<br>• Why is the EM force considered a fundamental force? | How a magnetic force is produced.<br><br>The criteria for a fundamental force, and why the EM force fits the criteria. | Predict the repulsion and /or attraction of two particles.<br><br>Calculate the EM force using Coulomb's Law.<br><br>Use Newton's Law of Universal Gravitation to compare the EM force to the gravitational force.<br><br>Describe the production of the magnetic force.<br><br>Calculate the magnetic force. | Demonstration equipment<br>  o Glass/plastic rods<br>  o Silk/fur<br>  o Ring stand<br>  o Pith ball<br>  o Electroscope<br><br>Text resource<br><br>Instructor notes<br><br>Demonstrate the transfer of energy | Quiz<br><br>Lab report<br><br>Outside assignments<br><br>Performance task |

SOURCE: Amy Carpinelli, Washington Township High School, Washington Township School District, Sewell, New Jersey. Used with permission.

*(Text continued from page 124)*

Figure 5.11 shows in Unit I how the conceptual lens of "Diversity/ Commonality" is developed through different unit titles at each grade level. Examples of unit titles are "Diversity and Commonality in Self and Family" in kindergarten; "Diversity and Commonality in Family and Neighborhood" in Grade 1; and "Diversity and Commonality in Neighborhood and Community" in Grades 2. This model allows for developing sophistication in conceptual understanding as students deepen their thinking and knowledge about diversity and commonality using the expanding model of self and families in kindergarten and Grade 1 to the world in Grade 6. It is easy to see how the attachment of a conceptual focus to the traditional content takes thinking and learning to a higher level. The students participate in many learning experiences to understand the concept in relation to the unit title.

Unit II used the conceptual lens of "Interdependence" for the same grade-level themes (Unit III used the lens of "Change and Continuity"). Changing the lens essentially changes the units because understanding "Diversity and Commonality" is different from understanding the lessons to be learned about "Interdependence." Some of the enduring understandings that guided the learning activities for the conceptual lens of "Interdependence" through the grades included the following:

- Families work together to provide for needs and wants (Grades K–1).
- Nations work together to solve common problems (Grade 5).
- Advances in transportation and technology provide opportunities for developing nations to gain economic power (Grade 8).

Another interesting aspect of the Washington model is the use of geographical *biomes* (world geographic regions with similar climate and vegetation) to identify other cultures for study. Each grade level chooses cultures within a particular biome for in-depth study. The teachers reasoned that selecting cultures from different biomes allows students to learn how cultural groups interact with and use diverse environments for living. It also provides a representative sampling of cultures from around the world.

This social studies format allows for interdisciplinary curriculum as literature, art, music, drama, or other related subtopics and subconcepts are brought into the design. The progress toward interdisciplinary curriculum is slow (especially at the secondary school level); teachers and administrators learn as they go. It is important to move forward at a pace that allows for cognitive processing of what works and what doesn't. One approach that does not work is to jump too quickly from single-subject area curriculum designs into a seamless, interdisciplinary curriculum. If we lose the structure of the separate disciplines, we run the risk of losing many critical concepts and skills and of destroying a coherent educational plan. We first need to start with the articulation of the critical concepts, content, and skills for each discipline and then work toward a logically articulated, interdisciplinary curriculum format. Secondary schools should not expect to create more than one to three interdisciplinary units in a year unless they are allowed the

**Figure 5.11** Social Studies Excerpt

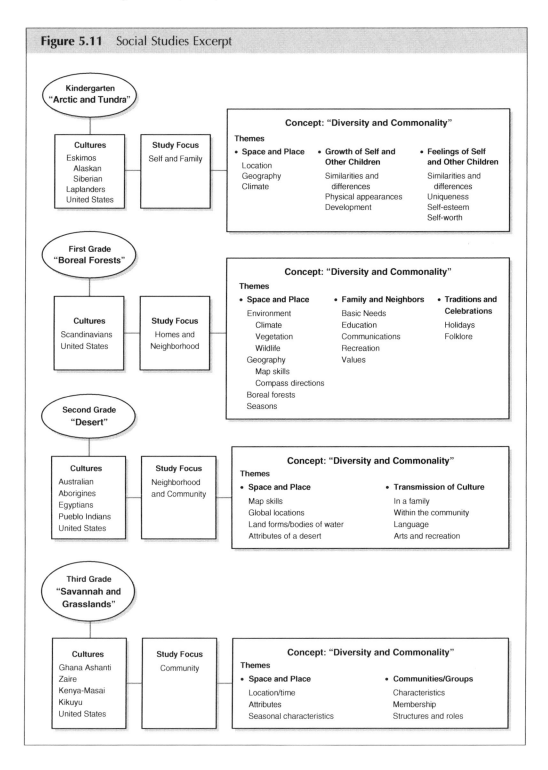

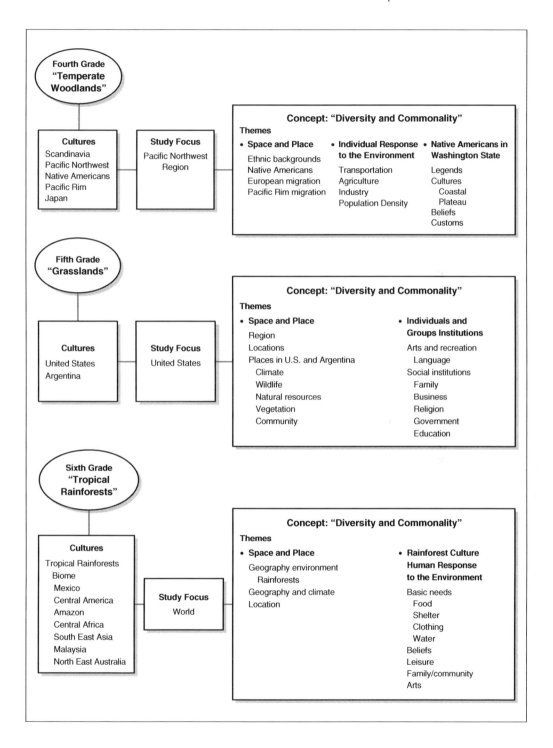

Fourth Grade "Temperate Woodlands"

**Cultures**
Scandinavia
Pacific Northwest
Native Americans
Pacific Rim
Japan

**Study Focus**
Pacific Northwest Region

**Concept: "Diversity and Commonality"**
Themes
- **Space and Place**
  Ethnic backgrounds
  Native Americans
  European migration
  Pacific Rim migration
- **Individual Response to the Environment**
  Transportation
  Agriculture
  Industry
  Population Density
- **Native Americans in Washington State**
  Legends
  Cultures
    Coastal
    Plateau
  Beliefs
  Customs

Fifth Grade "Grasslands"

**Cultures**
United States
Argentina

**Study Focus**
United States

**Concept: "Diversity and Commonality"**
Themes
- **Space and Place**
  Region
  Locations
  Places in U.S. and Argentina
    Climate
    Wildlife
    Natural resources
    Vegetation
    Community
- **Individuals and Groups Institutions**
  Arts and recreation
  Language
  Social institutions
    Family
    Business
    Religion
    Government
    Education

Sixth Grade "Tropical Rainforests"

**Cultures**
Tropical Rainforests
  Biome
  Mexico
  Central America
  Amazon
  Central Africa
  South East Asia
  Malaysia
  North East Australia

**Study Focus**
World

**Concept: "Diversity and Commonality"**
Themes
- **Space and Place**
  Geography environment
    Rainforests
  Geography and climate
  Location
- **Rainforest Culture Human Response to the Environment**
  Basic needs
    Food
    Shelter
    Clothing
    Water
  Beliefs
  Leisure
  Family/community
  Arts

SOURCE: Federal Way Public Schools, Federal Way, Washington. Used with permission.

flexibility to design innovative curricula. Discipline-based academic standards set tight parameters for most disciplines.

We don't want to lose depth and complexity in learning in the process of creating interdisciplinary units, so it is helpful to remember that the broader the unit title (e.g., "Patterns") the shallower the treatment. Depth and complexity require a focused unit title, and each discipline brought into the study has to contribute a relevant dimension not covered by the other subjects. Each discipline has to approach the unit focus through its unique content and concepts. This ensures depth and complexity. For instance, the "Patterns" unit would have greater depth and complexity if it were titled "Patterns in Nature."

## QUESTIONS AND ANSWERS: ELEMENTARY SCHOOLS

### 1. Why should interdisciplinary units have both a concept and a specific title?

**Answer:** A concept by itself does not provide enough focus to the study across disciplines. A specific unit title carries the idea of the concept into a form that is understandable and approachable for students and sets the parameters for the content study.

*Example:*

*Conceptual Lens:* "Culture"

*Unit Title:* "African and Japanese Art as Expressions of Culture"

The unit title brings focus and direction to the study of culture. The unit title also can be stated as a question to engage students in their search for knowledge: "Why are African and Japanese art considered culturally expressive?"

### 2. How does the concept-based unit design compare with the project approach and inquiry unit designs?

**Answer:** Both the project approach and inquiry design models are open-ended frameworks that allow the student to go on the search for knowledge and construct personal meaning. The emphasis is on investigation and collaborative inquiry around a major topic of interest to the students. Sometimes the inquiry may be around a concept alone such as "Innovation," and sometimes the disciplines serve as the viewing lens. For example, if the study revolved around the issue of "Global Warming," study might revolve around this question: "What generalizations, principles, or conclusions would a scientist want us to learn? . . . a psychologist? . . . a mathematician? . . . an artist?"

- Because the project approach and inquiry models value the process of open-ended knowledge construction emanating from the interests of children, they may not address the issue of K–12 curriculum articulation.
- The concept-based unit design presented in this chapter also sends students on a search for knowledge and a personal construction of meaning, but the search is focused beyond the facts to higher-level enduring understandings related to the concept and unit focus, as opposed to purely open-ended inquiry. This structure has two benefits:
  - o It facilitates the instruction of students' thinking so they can analyze, synthesize, and summarize factual information.
  - o It allows for an articulation of concepts and topics through the grades and protects a balance of process and content. The integrity of student construction of knowledge and responsibility for learning is still protected. Student insights and personally constructed generalizations, supported with facts, are definitely celebrated, however, because the ultimate goal is conceptual thinking supported by factual knowledge.

## 3. Can I use open-ended as well as structured unit designs in my classroom?

**Answer:** Certainly. Both forms have unique benefits in the learning environment. The task will be twofold:

- To lay out the units of instruction so that the standards for content and process development are met
- To provide opportunities for open-ended, experiential learning

## 4. How can I engage students in the planning of the units?

**Answer:** Once you are comfortable with the components of unit design, you can ask students to plan the unit overview with you. Find out what students know about the concept and unit topic. They can help define related subtopics to be studied and can assist in developing the guiding questions. Remember, though, that you need to make certain there are conceptual and provocative (essential) questions that will cause students to arrive at enduring understandings—those transferable lessons of life that help students make conceptual and real sense of their world.

## 5. How long should units last?

**Answer:** The time varies. A kindergarten or first-grade unit may last only a few days to a week; a secondary unit developed by an interdisciplinary team may last four to six weeks.

## 6. How should I begin moving toward interdisciplinary instruction?

**Answer:** Begin with a single unit. Learn from the steps for designing integrated, interdisciplinary units and then develop a second unit.

## 7. How many units might I introduce in a year?

**Answer:** For a district core curriculum, there are usually three to four social studies–based units and three to four science-based units per grade level in a year. Other subjects, such as art or mathematics, also have their respective curriculum documents, but they fuse concepts and skills into social studies or science core units when it is reasonable to do so. Content that will not fuse well into interdisciplinary units is taught within the discipline. We do not want to force-fit content and concepts just for the sake of interdisciplinarity.

## 8. How can I structure my day for direct and integrated instruction?

**Answer:** Teacher preference plays heavily into this question, but I prefer direct instruction of skills in the morning and interdisciplinary unit work in the afternoon. Teachers may also use learning centers and flexible skill groups to carry out some of the unit work in the morning. Teachers design the learning experience in different ways, but they ensure that skills receive direct instruction as well as application in interdisciplinary units or other contexts.

Direct instruction means teacher presentation of skills to develop reading, writing, and speaking abilities or teacher presentation of content critical to the unit work. The direct instruction of content usually establishes the foundation for the student search for knowledge.

## 9. I have difficulty finding a unit title that lends itself well to the study of interdisciplinary science and social studies.

**Answer:** Because social studies is oriented toward culture and humanity, it is sometimes difficult to bridge to the physical and nonhuman branches of science. You will find that environmental unit titles such as "Pollution as a Threat to Humanity" lend themselves well to social studies as well as science because they have strong ramifications for both domains. We should not stretch to try and make a subject fit into an interdisciplinary unit: this dilutes the integrity of the study as a whole. You will find that units with a science focus incorporate mathematics, health, vocations, and technology quite easily. Units with a social studies focus readily incorporate the arts, music, literature, and media. The focus of units can be alternated throughout a year. Mathematics and language process skills apply across all curricular areas, however.

## 10. Is it always necessary to design interdisciplinary units that relate to the content of the district curriculum frameworks?

**Answer:** Teachers need the latitude to design some units of interest and relevance to students that may not fall within the mandated frameworks. Some of the unit overview webs provided in this book are examples of teachers choosing to design a unit that deviated (e.g., "Escalation of Violence in America"). Teachers balance the professional responsibility to address the content mandated in academic standards with the need to explore issues of critical and meaningful social significance. Realize that discipline-based concepts can be taught through any number of unit titles, so we can meet the mandates for teaching some of the required concepts through units of choice.

# QUESTIONS AND ANSWERS: SECONDARY SCHOOLS

## 1. Some of our teachers do not see any need to change from the traditional approaches to curriculum and instruction. How can we bring them on board?

**Answer:** The first step in encouraging change is education. As a staff, share and discuss articles that address current and critical issues in education from leading journals and newspapers such as *Phi Delta Kappan*, *Educational Leadership,* and *Education Week*. Book studies on school initiatives for curriculum and instruction are also powerful tools for change.

Many teachers subscribe to field-specific journals, such as *Social Education,* the excellent publication from the National Council of Social Studies, to extend their professional thinking. Books and articles that share current information on economic, social, and political trends provide additional insight into change. Curriculum is largely shaped by these trends, and teachers need to be aware of the issues so that special interest groups do not take advantage of an awareness vacuum to install narrow interpretations into curricular materials.

Chapter 1 addressed the issues of staff change. It can take three or four years to change a person's mental paradigm. Teachers are more receptive to new ideas when they see that their content and skills will not be lost in the change. Spending time in staff meetings discussing educational trends and the need for change is an invaluable first step. It also helps to begin the move toward concept-based curriculum with one concept-based, intradisciplinary unit so that teachers learn the rationale and process of unit design in their own subject before they move to the interdisciplinary format. Schools that have more flexibility in their use of time and content will find it easier to create interdisciplinary units. Traditional school structures may be able to create one to three interdisciplinary units per year. It is easier to have two different subject area teachers work together than to have five or six different subject area teachers try to coordinate their work.

## 2. How do we organize as a staff for interdisciplinary teaching?

**Answer:** There are many different models—from a looser, multidisciplinary format with two teachers in different fields coordinating topics they are teaching (e.g., a literature teacher and a history teacher dealing with the Renaissance period at the same time in the year) to broader interdisciplinary teaching teams organized under theme-based (e.g., "Global Business and Marketing") and concept-based curriculum models.

There are many examples of schools around the United States that have altered their class schedules to facilitate interdisciplinary teaching. Two examples are block scheduling of two or three subjects and the "school within a school" concept that sets up interdisciplinary teams of teachers with a set number of students who design the minischool schedule according to the curricular and instructional plan. The degree to which a school decides to transform its curricular and instructional program is determined by the school and parent community, and by the school's ability to maintain adherence to required standards. District-level support is crucial.

## 3. What issues should we consider in determining our readiness to transform our curricular and instructional program?

**Answer:**

- How committed is the staff to making change? Do you need to start with education and discussion as first steps?
- What leadership resources do you have? How knowledgeable are leaders in
  - Current trends
  - Articulating the horizontal and vertical curriculum through curriculum mapping
  - Concept-based curriculum and instruction
  - Integrating curriculum
  - Teaching to standards
  - Scheduling
  - Teaming
  - Consensus building
  - Conflict resolution

The issues listed above will unfold as teachers learn by doing, but leaders need to have baseline knowledge or know where to find the resource help so that valuable time is not wasted in committees.

## 4. I am a mathematics teacher. I don't have time for participating in interdisciplinary curriculum because I have to prepare my students for the next level of mathematics, and it takes a full year.

**Answer:** The revised national mathematics standards, published by the National Council of Teachers of Mathematics (2000), stress the importance of mathematical reasoning and problem solving, as well as communicating and using mathematics in real-world applications. Because interdisciplinary units revolve around life problems, issues, and concepts, they provide a fertile context for the relevant application of mathematics.

Mathematics teachers realize that their job is not only to prepare students for the next level of mathematics, but also to prepare them for a life that makes use of mathematics. Because of the heavy emphasis in traditional instruction on the isolated drill and practice with algorithms, students often fail to see the relevance of their learning. Perhaps if students become personally engaged with the applications of the algorithm, they will need less drill and practice to gain understanding.

Mathematics teachers in the changing paradigm realize that their job is not only to prepare students to follow and solve equations perfunctorily, but also to provide students with the process tools of mathematics and to see that those tools are used to solve real-world problems. Progressive teachers of mathematics extend understanding of topics across subject areas. They help students reason mathematically. Mathematics is a process tool just as language is a process tool. And like language arts, mathematics is a form of both thought and communication.

## 5. What is the role of mathematics in interdisciplinary unit designs?

**Answer:** Mathematics serves as a process tool in interdisciplinary units. Interdisciplinary units show students how mathematics is applied in real-world contexts to explain phenomena and solve problems. Mathematics resembles the language arts in these units. It is applied across the disciplines as a thinking and process tool. For too long, we have allowed mathematics to work in a box—isolated from the rest of the curriculum. We would never think of working with the language arts areas of reading and writing without a context, yet we have been doing so for 100 years with mathematics instruction. It is true that mathematics must have a time for direct skill instruction, but the application of those skills flows naturally into interdisciplinary units of study. Where else can we find a context that brings so many different disciplines together to investigate an important problem, topic, or issue? Mathematics teachers should be overjoyed to have an opportunity to show how important mathematics is to the other disciplines. What a forum for demonstrating the power of mathematics in our everyday lives! And just as we say, "All teachers are language arts teachers," we should be saying, "All teachers are mathematics teachers," because both are process tools for thinking about and understanding content across the disciplines.

## 6. What is the role of the mathematics teacher on an interdisciplinary team?

**Answer:** Because mathematics teachers have to teach a sequence of skills and concepts, they may not spend three weeks doing mathematics around the unit focus, but they should work in two ways on the team:

- Provide suggestions to other subject area teachers for mathematics applications that they could use when studying particular topics in those subjects (history, science, or art).
- Use topics from other subject areas to teach current concepts and skills that are being taught in the mathematics class.

The mathematics teacher is an invaluable team member and should plan the unit with the interdisciplinary team and identify his or her own concepts, generalizations, guiding questions, and skills to teach toward as the unit is implemented.

## 7. How do I identify the topics for the mathematics category on the web?

**Answer:** Mathematics is the last subject to be webbed. Once the other disciplines have defined their topics and concepts for study, take mathematics out of the box and ask the question, "How can mathematics be applied to extend understanding of the items listed under history, economics, geography, music, art, media, science, and so on?" Brainstorm all of the possible applications of mathematics related to the different subject area topics. Do not list mathematics learning experiences on the web (e.g., "Estimate the dimensions of colonial ships")—just identify the mathematics processes and concepts at this time (estimation, percentage, etc.). The determination of specific learning experiences comes later in the planning process.

## 8. How should our interdisciplinary team decide on a focus for our unit?

**Answer:** As stated earlier, curriculum mapping is a useful tool for identifying critical content topics prior to designing integrated units. Social studies, as representative of culture and people; and science, as representative of the natural and physical world, often provide the base for identifying unit themes. The humanities—art, philosophy, music, literature, drama, and dance—usually fit well into culture-based units. Technology, mathematics, and health work well in the physical and natural world units, so unit titles can be drawn from the sociocultural world and the science world, or they may be drawn from contemporary or persistent issues in our world.

## 9. How are concepts used in integrated units?

**Answer:** There are one and sometimes two broader concepts (but never more than two) that serve as a conceptual lens for a unit. The conceptual lens integrates and focuses the study beyond the facts. Realize, however, that many other subconcepts are listed as content to study under each strand around the web. Concepts are used in three ways in units:

1. To draw thinking above the topic; to conceptually integrate thinking so knowledge can be transferred

2. To help students understand the attributes of concepts by experiencing myriad concrete examples

3. To help students learn how to understand and articulate the enduring understandings (i.e., generalizations and principles) that emerge out of the unit study

To maintain the integrity of the different disciplines, some interdisciplinary teams choose a focus concept (e.g., "Systems") and then let each team "do its own thing" in their curriculum as long as the content ties to the focus concept. This approach may help students understand the attributes of a concept across a variety of examples, but it does nothing to help students integrate their thinking around a common theme, problem, issue, or question by drawing on the offerings of each discipline. Without discipline coherence—all subjects focusing on developing different facets of the unit topic and lens—there is no interdisciplinarity, and the disciplines do not work together to facilitate understanding of the ideas that transcend the unit title and facts.

## 10. How do we maintain the integrity of disciplines in interdisciplinary units?

**Answer:** Many secondary teachers express concern that their discipline is merely a handmaiden to either social studies or science because interdisciplinary units often come from these areas. The key to maintaining the integrity of different disciplines in the design process is for each subject area to identify and teach to its own discipline-based concepts. The identification of subject area concepts is accomplished during the webbing process. Figure 5.12 shows a secondary web for a unit on "The Revolutionary Period" in American history that illustrates how subtopics should be identified for each subject. Sometimes, the topic listed for a subject will actually be a general concept, such as "Independence," but at other times the topic will be very specific, such as a book title (e.g., *The American Revolution*, by Edward Dolan). In the case of specific topics, it is helpful to list the related concepts to the right of the topic on the web. For Dolan's book, the related concepts might be "Heroes, Ideals, and Characterization." Please note that even though you are teaching the concepts of each discipline, your unit remains integrated and interdisciplinary because of the focus on the common unit title and, directly or indirectly, on the conceptual lens.

**Figure 5.12** The Revolutionary Period

# Unit Planner

## Critical Content–Concept Web

### Unit Title: "The Revolutionary Period"
### Conceptual Lens: "Conflict/ Independence"

**Unit Overview**

Should colonies be independent of mother countries?

The Early American colonists thought so . . . and today citizens of the United Stated are free and independent of British rule.

Why did the colonists want to be free?

Are there places in the world today where people want their freedom from a mother country?

What does it mean to be free?

How do you think freedom affects the economic life of a people? The social life?

How do you think music and art express the feelings of people who are oppressed?

**Grade Level: Fifth**

**History**
*Colonies*
*Taxation*
*Revolt*
• Boston
• Tea Party

**Literature/Media**
*The American Revolution, by Edward Dolan (heroes, ideals, characterization)*
*The Boston Tea Party, by Laurie O'Neill (oppression, revolt)*
*Changes for Felicity, by Valerie Tripp (war, friendship, plot, theme)*

NOTE: Concepts italicized.

**Unit Title
"The Revolutionary Period"**

**Music**
"History of the American Revolution"
"American History Through Folk Song" *(rhythm, pattern, pitch, tone, timbre)*

**Art**
"Portrait of Washington by Peale"
"Washington Crossing the Delaware"
"Winter at Valley Forge" *(realism, line, color)*

**Math**
*Timelines*
*Estimation*
*Graphs*
*Probability*

*Independence and Revolution*
*Forming a government*

**Figure 5.13** Revolutionary Period Generalizations/Questions

## Enduring Understandings (Generalizations)

Standards

1. Social, political, or economic oppression can lead to revolution.

2. Music and art express the mood of a culture.

3. Realistic art conveys a sense of authenticity.

4. Timelines can be used to track the sequence of events for determining causes and effects.

5. Political power can be a positive or corrupting influence.

## Guiding Questions

1. Why did the colonists in early America resist British control? What is economic oppression? How do people react to oppression?

2. How did the music of the Revolutionary era convey the mood of the people? How does the timbre in music convey mood?

3. How did the artist use line and color to convey authenticity in "Winter at Valley Forge"?

4. Why would historians want to use timelines in the analysis of historical events?

5. In the story "The American Revolution," how did _____ use his political power? What was the effect?

## 11. Why is discipline integrity important?

**Answer:** If we cannot maintain the integrity of disciplines (i.e., conceptual integrity), then we should not design interdisciplinary units. Disregarding the conceptual base of the different disciplines leads to the handmaiden phenomenon. In a handmaiden design, all of the enduring understandings from the unit of study relate to the unit title, which is usually based in the social or physical world (social studies or science). In a concept-based model, the enduring understandings for each discipline show a balance: some understandings relate to the unit title, and some understandings express the enduring understandings of the different disciplines. Figure 5.13 shows enduring understandings that represent different subject areas and the guiding questions that tie the ideas to the unit focus expressed in the title.

## 12. Will my subject area (physical education, health, anatomy and physiology, mathematics) be the main focus of an integrated unit? Do I always have to work under a social studies or science focus?

**Answer:** The answer to the first question is, "Of course," and to the second, "No." A strong unit can be designed around a physical education or health concept. An example would be a unit on "Fitness." As a content field, health has many concepts that would serve to organize a relevant interdisciplinary study: disease, organism, cycle, wellness, and so on. Because social studies and science are broader fields, however, they contain a greater range of concepts and focus topics. It is easier for the elective subjects to fit into the broader frames than the converse. Elective subjects do need to design their own articulated curriculums prior to interdisciplinary integration. They can then select appropriate content and concepts for interdisciplinary units. The remainder would be taught within their own integrated, intradisciplinary units.

Physical education, health, and consumer science teachers can team to design powerfully relevant units for students based on personal, family, and community issues. It is effective to have flexible team structures. It doesn't work to force physical education into a science-based unit, for example, if the unit focus and conceptual lens are not appropriate. It is better to form the interdisciplinary team with members who can contribute broadened perspectives to the question under study.

## 13. I teach world languages. How does that fit in?

**Answer:** World languages are based in culture and will fit into any social studies unit that organizes around a culture-based concept. They will also fit into science units. The language, people, and land of the culture under study will provide the setting. World language teachers by necessity have a strong emphasis on skill development in their courses, as do English and language arts teachers, but world language teachers should use the concepts of "Culture" and "Communication" to engage student thinking and interest.

## 14. How about technology? How does that fit in?

**Answer:** Technology is a tool to access, ponder, and portray information. Like mathematics, it is applied across the fields of study to access information, extend understanding, and display learning. The uses of technology in society often fit into both social studies–based and science-based units. Technology is a powerful communication tool allowing visual, auditory, and written forms for making meaning. And certainly, with the increasing importance of technology in science and society, it is a key player in unit design across the disciplines.

## 15. If I take time for interdisciplinary units, I won't be able to cover the material in my textbook.

**Answer:** If you compare the thickness and size of a textbook today with a textbook from 1980, you will likely see a significant increase in size. One publisher is now sending out two volumes of world history for one course. If you look at the depth of treatment related to critical issues in history, you will find abbreviated summaries of key events compared to a 1980 text. If you feel compelled to "cover the book," you are essentially skimming over surface data, losing many students along the way, and sacrificing the development of intellectual sophistication and deeper understanding.

Belief in the new paradigm that "less is more" challenges you to focus curriculum and instruction around significant concepts and topics. Your textbook will be one of many resources that students will use as they search for knowledge. The classroom is characterized by cooperative group and individual activity, and process activities such as drama, debates, dialogues, artistic renderings, and music. Students will have greater retention of the key concepts and critical issues because of their personal involvement in learning. By participating in integrated, interdisciplinary units, the students will have the benefit of multiple perspectives and greater depth of understanding. You are correct, though: you must not sacrifice the integrity of your core concepts and content just for the sake of being interdisciplinary. Interdisciplinary units are best designed around relevant issues that require a variety of disciplinary perspectives, such as "Global Warming" or "Health and Fitness," to gain deep understanding. Perhaps you will want to consider one to three interdisciplinary units a year with colleagues.

## 16. Does interdisciplinary integration require that all subjects be included in the study?

**Answer:** No. You should bring only those subjects into the study that deepen understanding of the unit focus in relation to the conceptual lens. The following are two considerations as to how subjects and their topics of study should be selected to complete the webbing:

• You should not force both social studies and science into every unit. Although the conceptual lens can be treated by subtopics in both disciplines, the content may be so disparate that students would experience cognitive dissonance. I would not want to deal with cycles of human history in the same unit that I am dealing with cycles in the animal world. This unit would lack coherence and could not be considered in an interdisciplinary way even though the conceptual lens of cycles is shared in common. This topic dissonance is a common error in unit development today. On the flip side, however, science and social studies do fit well together in some units. If the theme has both physical world and social world implications, then science and social studies can work together; otherwise, they should remain independent. "Environmental Issues" or "Technology and Society" themes work well with the duality of subjects.

• When you are deciding on subtopics and subconcepts for each of the discipline strands, ask the following question: "Which subtopics and subconcepts would best develop understanding of this theme with this conceptual lens?" Remember that different conceptual lenses affect the choice of subtopics and subconcepts under the discipline strands.

## THE INTERNATIONAL BACCALAUREATE PROGRAMME

The International Baccalaureate (IB) Programme (International Baccalaureate Organization, 2007) deserves special mention because it keeps the child, rather than test scores, as the center focus of curriculum and instruction. It closely mirrors the philosophy and beliefs expressed in this book. The IB Program consists of three levels: the Primary Years Programme, the Middle Years Programme, and the Diploma Programme. These programs have been in development since 1994 under the auspices of the International Baccalaureate Organization, a nonprofit, international educational foundation, which was established in 1968, and is registered in Switzerland.

The IB Programme is gaining new schools internationally at a rapid rate. It offers an educational philosophy and direction that I believe benefits all children. Three basic tenets underlie the IB Programme philosophy:

• *Holistic Learning.* Using student construction of knowledge and deeper understanding; using metacognition and prior knowledge in consciously learning how to learn

• *Intercultural Awareness.* Developing attitudes, knowledge, and skills that reflect internationally minded knowledge and understanding; knowing one's own and other cultures; focusing on global issues; becoming informed about and sensitive to the experiences of others; and providing service to local, national, and international communities

- *Communication.* Developing a strong command of verbal and nonverbal communication, to include proficiency in one or more additional languages; understanding and appreciating the arts and information technologies as other modes of communication

As an example, in the Middle Years Programme the IB curriculum provides a framework of concepts and skills for eight subject groups that sets a direction, yet has enough flexibility to allow for the development of specific curricula in each school according to local mandates. The framework provides adequate parameters to achieve a sense of commonality among the Middle Years Programme schools worldwide. The nonnegotiables in the IB Programmes are the adherence to the basic aims and tenets. I would consider the IB Programmes concept based because a major goal is deeper, conceptual understanding.

# CAREER AND TECHNICAL EDUCATION PROGRAMS

We cannot leave this chapter on interdisciplinary curricula without also looking at some of the secondary school models that integrate academics with career and technical education. It is important to study these career and technical education (CTE) models because they provide a relevant context for learning and problem solving.

Just as concepts and interesting unit titles provide a rich context for focused, higher-level learning in the regular classrooms, an organizing theme such as "Production and Technology" can provide focus and relevance for interdisciplinary work between science, career and technology, economics, and mathematics. CTE models, such as career pathways and CTE academies, provide a meaningful, future-oriented framework for learning. Content is applied in a purposeful context, and the relevancy question, "So what?" has an answer. Work still needs to be done in the area of articulating critical concepts and content to design quality interdisciplinary units within the CTE programs, but it is vital work. Traditional academic classes alone cannot address all of the work skills that are required to keep our economy humming.

## CTE Curriculum Design

The blending of a traditional liberal arts college preparation program in high schools and a CTE model present important curricular design questions:

- How can we preserve the integrity of a liberal arts philosophy, while at the same time providing a school program that prepares students for work as well as for further education?

- How can we blend academic and CTE curricula to develop the high-level performance skills outlined years ago in the Secretary's Commission on Achieving Necessary Skills Report (SCANS) (1991, Appendix C) and the more recent calls for upgrading performance abilities, such as the report *Learning for the 21st Century: A Report and Mile Guide for 21st Century Skills* (Partnership for 21st Century Skills, 2002) sponsored by major industries and organizations such as Microsoft, AOL, Dell, Cisco, and the National Education Association; and the 2007 report by the National Center on Education and the Economy, *Tough Choices or Tough Times: The Report of the New Commission on the Skills of the American Workforce* (NCEE, 2007).

Our high school curriculum is delivered as if all students will graduate from a four-year college, a mind-set that appears to be even more pronounced since the advent of state academic content standards. The statistics, however, show that even though 60 percent to 70 percent of students may begin university programs, only about 30 percent complete the four years. And will there be jobs in the designated fields for those graduates? Most students have traditionally had little experience with the kinds of skills outlined in SCANS and the executive function skills, yet the continuing vitality of our economic system, and the student's ability to compete for jobs in the global labor market depend on these broadened, generalizable skills and abilities.

We need to support blended models for high schools, such as the career pathway models, career academies, and the CTE-funded small learning communities. Outcomes for these programs reflect at least five sources:

1. SCANS, to meet the needs of a quality workforce (see Resource C)

2. Executive function skills, to make students creative and innovative, self-disciplined, well organized, comfortable with ideas and abstractions; and to make students able to learn quickly, to analyze and synthesize complex data, to work well both independently and as a team member, and to adapt quickly to frequent changes in the workplace (NCEE, 2007, p. xix)

3. Liberal arts curricula, to preserve the lessons of discourse, culture, and humanity

4. Core academic content from mathematics, language arts skills, and science

5. Higher-level life skill curricula, to prepare students for daily life with everything from money management, to civic responsibility, to character development

Two different approaches to curriculum design seem appropriate. In one approach, key concepts are identified that relate to the subject areas supporting the particular CTE pathway. In a career pathway titled "Manufacturing Production and Processes," examples of key concepts might be

- "Functionality, Producability, Prototype, Tooling, and Data Sets" when teaching product design in CTE
- "Raw Material Properties," "Heat Processes," or "Stress Analysis" for science

- "Measurement" (related to tooling, for example), "Estimation," "Scale" (related to digitized data sets and tooling, for example), and "The Computation of Stress Analysis" for mathematics

The focus topic for each subject area is "Manufacturing Production and Processes," but the disciplinary concepts bring breadth and depth to student understanding. The concepts support each other, creating the interdisciplinarity for the study. Additional concepts would be added to increase the depth and complexity of the curriculum.

The fusion of appropriate core skills and knowledge from the state academic content standards can be designed into the CTE curricula. As process subjects, English and mathematics are applied across the interdisciplinary fields of study. All teachers are teachers of language, and mathematics extends understanding across disciplines. Both subjects communicate meaning. The skills of English and mathematics can be taught in single-subject study, but they gain meaning and practicality in authentic work contexts.

The second method for designing curricula for CTE programs encourages core subject area teachers to make connections to career fields and career content. I would call this a coordinated curriculum approach, however, rather than an interdisciplinary approach because the curriculum depends on connections rather than on fusion of academic and CTE expectations under common or related concepts and unit titles.

Blended academic and CTE programs will require extensive dialogue among the teachers involved, administrators, parents, and the business community. It will be important for all parties to see the perceived need and to agree that things must change. How that change occurs will require teamwork, the ability to leave the familiar in curriculum and instruction, and the willingness to take some risks. Teachers will need to feel that the risks are supported by administrators and parents. The business community must take a partnership role in helping to suggest and design authentic experiences or simulations for students. Schools can gain suggestions for classroom simulations by surveying local businesses for a list of employee activities that require the use of the CTE and academic competencies. The survey describes the competencies and leaves room for the employer (or employees) to fill in related job responsibilities and tasks. These can then be transformed into classroom simulations by the teachers.

The current political pressure to meet the academic standards of traditional content areas makes progress more difficult for CTE programs. I hope we don't jettison this valuable movement just because the curriculum design task is daunting. It is critical that our traditional high school structure, organization, and pedagogical practices involve all students in meaningful, applied curricula that develop their life skills, motivate their minds, and engage their spirits. A broadened approach to educating the diverse needs and learning styles of students can fix the problems of "slip in, slide through, or shoved out."

The programs that effectively blend CTE and academic curricula when reasonable, and that structure learning toward high-level performance outcomes offer promising models for secondary schools. At the same time, we have to balance a curriculum that prepares students for work, citizenship, and family life, with a curriculum that

- Ensures success in further schooling
- Develops aesthetic knowledge and appreciation
- Develops healthy self-esteem, values, and ethics

It is for this reason that I advocate defining the major concepts and critical content that underlie the separate academic, as well as career and technology subject areas prior to making interdisciplinary connections and blends. Concepts that cut across disciplines can then serve to integrate the content. The focus of content can be defined through the unit titles. Areas of study are drawn from all contexts of life such as work; family; aesthetics; sport, health and well-being; and political, economic, and sociocultural issues. Even if a school has a CTE focus, the areas of study need to include the range of life issues to develop a balanced foundation of knowledge, skills, attitudes, and values.

## The Arizona Model for Career and Technical Education

The Arizona Department of Education (2007), CTE division, has worked diligently through the years to develop one of the many strong programs in the United States. Figure 5.14 shows the Arizona CTE delivery system from career awareness in grade levels K–6, to postsecondary expectations. Note the inclusion of the academic foundations in the secondary programs.

Arizona, like most states, is developing its CTE program based on the 16-career clusters and their pathways that were adopted and supported by the National Association of State Directors for Career and Technical Education in 2002 (Ruffing, n.d.).

The Arizona CTE Web site provides a sample program for a career pathway called "Industrial Manufacturing" with student options for developing different strands of technical skills (see Figure 5.15).

Addressing national concerns that students in career preparation programs were not required to master core academic competencies, the Arizona CTE programs developed standards for their career clusters. They also developed a competency crosswalk to the Arizona academic standards. These documents align the Arizona CTE program standards with the language arts and mathematics expectations outlined in the Arizona academic standards. SCANS was a catalyst for the initial CTE work, but they expanded on the original vision to include other workplace competencies: the abilities to manage resources, to work collaboratively and productively with others, to acquire and use information, to master complex systems, and to work with a variety of technologies.

**Figure 5.14**   Arizona CTE Delivery System

**Vision:** Ensure a dynamic workforce by fully developing each student's career and academic potential.

**Mission:** Prepare Arizona students for workforce success and continuous learning.

**Career Management**

Students will manage their careers for workforce success by

    Transitioning to higher education
    Using labor market information for career selection
    Obtaining postsecondary occupational certificates and degrees
    Completing on-the-job training
    Updating technical skills

**Career Preparation: Grades 10–12**

Students[1] will have an opportunity to prepare for careers by

    Enrolling in CTE programs reflecting current labor market projections in Arizona
    Achieving academic standards including reading, writing, mathematics, and science that are
        embedded in CTE programs
    Attaining industry-validated competencies
    Completing technical assessment options identified for CTE programs
    Enrolling in CTE programs with curricular flow articulation to the postsecondary level

**Career Exploration: Grades 7–9**

Students will explore careers and attain academic and technical skills in the following foundation areas:[2]

    Academic foundations
    Communications
    Problem solving and critical thinking
    Information technology
    Organizational systems
    Safety, health, and environment
    Leadership and teamwork
    Ethics and legal responsibilities
    Employability and career development
    Technical foundations

**Career Awareness: Grades K–6**

Students will demonstrate proficiency at appropriate levels in the Arizona Workplace Standards:[3]

    Communication skills
    Computation skills and data analysis techniques
    Critical and creative thinking skills
    Teamwork skills
    Marketable skills development
    Social, organizational, and technological systems
    Technological literacy
    Personal and professional resource management

SOURCE: Arizona Department of Education, Career and Technical Education. http://www.ade.az.gov/cte/CTEdeliverysystem/6-KeyConcepts3-28-05.pdf.

NOTES

1. Some ninth-grade Career Exploration may include Career Preparation when the curriculum is designed to be delivered in Grades 9–12.
2. Career Clusters on the web at http://www.careerclusters.org/16clusters.htm.
3. Arizona Workplace Standards on the Web at http://www.ade.az.gov/standards/workplace/default.asp.

| **Figure 5.15** Sample CTE Program: Industrial Manufacturing | |
|---|---|
| *Career Preparation (Grades 10–12)* | *Sample Program Core Industrial Manufacturing* |
| **Sample CTE Program: Industrial Manufacturing**<br><br>Students will have the skills for workforce success and continuous learning. They will attain academic and occupational knowledge and skills for employment and transitioning to continued higher education in the industrial manufacturing cluster.<br><br>This program will also prepare students for professional certification in the program area (if available) for industry-approved program assessments. | Apply mathematical processes to problems in industrial manufacturing.<br><br>Apply measurement techniques to problems in industrial manufacturing.<br><br>Interpret schematics, blueprints, and technical drawings.<br><br>Apply manufacturing technology.<br><br>Evaluate methods of energy applications.<br><br>Develop a plan for a career in program area.<br><br>Prepare for employment.<br><br>Participate in work-based learning experiences.<br><br>Demonstrate oral communication skills.<br><br>Demonstrate written communication skills.<br><br>Demonstrate business and financial management practices needed in program area.<br><br>Evaluate leadership styles appropriate for the workplace.<br><br>Participate in leadership activities such as those supported by career and technical student organizations.<br><br>Program-specific technical and occupational skills. |

| **Options for Technical and Occupational Skills in Industrial Manufacturing** | | |
|---|---|---|
| *Option A*<br>Metals Manufacturing | *Option B*<br>Plastics Manufacturing | *Option C*<br>Principles of Engineering |

SOURCE: Arizona Department of Education, Career and Technical Education. http://www.ade.az.gov/cte/CTEdeliverysystem/6-KeyConcepts3-28-05.pdf.

# SUMMARY

Transforming instructional units from topic based to concept based is a relatively easy process when teachers use a conceptual lens to integrate students' thinking. This chapter looks at different examples of concept-based units from interdisciplinary to intradisciplinary, and reinforces the idea that both forms can be concept based and integrated if a conceptual lens is used to focus the thinking to the integration level. Questions and answers related to the design and implementation of concept-based, integrated units help teachers with their planning.

The IB Programmes are gaining ground as a powerful model for education. The programs reflect most of the tenets outlined in this book and deserve to be mentioned.

Finally, I believe we need to support the blending of academic and career and technical education not only because it provides a relevant context for academic applications and provides future work skills, but also because it provides a powerful platform for engaging the hearts and minds of young people. CTE programs are active and require student self-direction. When each student can personally "take charge," his intellect and emotions are tapped.

## EXTENDING THOUGHT

1. What value does concept-based curriculum design have over topically based curriculum design in terms of the following?
   - Reducing the overloaded content curriculum
   - Focusing instruction to develop higher-level thinking
   - Creating interdisciplinary connections
   - Facilitating the transfer of knowledge
   - Sharing the commonality as well as the diversity of culture and humanity
   - Highlighting the lessons of history through time

2. How can teachers transform a topic-based unit into a concept-based unit?

3. How can teachers involve students in the design of interdisciplinary units?

4. React to this statement: "Teachers do not need to know all of the specific content information of a unit prior to student engagement. They learn along with the students who search out and construct knowledge. Teachers do, however, need to think through the anticipated interplay of concepts and topics to determine some of the enduring understandings that they expect students to derive from the study."

5. Discuss the dilemma at the high school level between providing a traditional college preparatory curriculum and a CTE curriculum. How can both aims be accommodated through an interdisciplinary model?

# Assessing and Reporting Student Progress

Assessment experts and teachers work diligently to design assessments aimed at improving learning and reporting progress at the classroom level. Subject area committees at the national and state levels have outlined content and performance standards. In most cases, the standards are being implemented with *high-stakes legislation:* students will be denied a high school diploma if the standards are not met as demonstrated through state assessments.

Policy makers appear with the persuasive argument that if we just test for what we want, the product will emerge, and the testing machine will magically transform instruction to the identified ends. It is true that defining the targets for curriculum and instruction in the assessment instruments will assist in making changes in the classroom, but to assume that an instructional change to meet higher standards will occur without systematic staff development is short-circuit thinking.

We can and should set performance standards, as well as monitor and adjust curriculum and instruction, from elementary through secondary schools to ensure that children reach appropriate graduating standards. But we are in a race with irrational expectations in many states, including high-stakes cognitive and performance standards applied to bulging curricula, with inadequate attention to the need for teacher and administrator training, professional dialogue, and student support. Without this focus at the teaching level, the testing mandates are going to swing around and knock the policy makers off their feet.

Parents will not stand for their students being held back from graduation. The resulting dialogue will highlight the conditions of inequity and the needs for instructional and student support. Why wait for this hailstorm to occur? Why not develop a reasonable systems approach for addressing the desired student standards? Rather than a simplistic, top-down "test is best" mentality, we should evaluate the foundation for learning at the classroom level and weigh instructional practices and student needs against the desired graduation standards.

Each component of the school system—curriculum, instruction, evaluation and assessment, decision making, leadership, roles, communication, human resource development, parents, and community—should be evaluated and aligned toward the achievement of success, as defined by desired standards, for all students. Although some school districts are taking such a systems approach to restructuring, too many districts are simply doing what we have always done—writing low-level content objectives at the district level that match the topics of state standards. Practice changes little in the classroom because the curriculum design reinforces coverage rather than deeper, intellectual engagement, and the design problem is inherent in the way objectives are written—tacking a verb onto a topic with an assumption that a deeper understanding will be reached.

In this chapter, we will focus on the component of evaluation and assessment, beginning with a brief comparison of standardized, criterion-referenced, and performance-based measures. Then we will take a closer look at process and **performance assessments** by studying specific classroom examples. Key to the discussion will be the critical importance of student self-assessment. The value of authentic assessment as a means of relating learning to real-life contexts and situations will be displayed through selected examples. Steps for designing performance assessments to evaluate what students know, understand, and can do will lead to a summary discussion on the value of performance-based measurement.

## A BRIEF REVIEW: FORM AND FUNCTION

### Normative-Referenced Tests

Normative-referenced tests are designed to assess and compare mass populations on specific items of knowledge or skill. These tests can be multiple-choice, machine-scored instruments. When these tests are used to place a student or a group of students in rank order compared with other test takers in the same grade or age population, the test is normatively referenced. Normative-referenced, standardized tests were influenced heavily by the use of a multiple-choice format on the Army Alpha Examination during World War I. The Alpha format efficiently and effectively sorted nearly 2 million military personnel to determine aptitude for officer status (Popham, 2006, pp. 15–16).

### Criterion-Referenced Tests

Criterion-referenced tests became especially popular in the late 1970s and 1980s as an attempt to identify clearly and specifically what knowledge and skills students are to master. Criterion-referenced tests measure the objectives taught in the classroom. They intend to highlight a student's strengths and weaknesses. According to James Popham (2006, p. 37), both norm-referenced and criterion-referenced interpretations are needed to accomplish educational ends.

Popham (2006, p. 38) suggests three steps for determining what should be measured:

1. Identify the decision to be influenced by the students' test performances.

2. Choose the appropriate type of inference—either a relative (normative) or absolute (criterion-referenced) interpretation of measurement results.

3. Determine the appropriate source of item content—the place or places for locating suitable items or exercises to use in the assessments.

## Alternative Assessments

The term "alternative assessments" is a catchphrase for forms of assessment that depart from the traditional multiple-choice, normatively referenced tests. During the late 1980s, educators raised questions with the testing establishment concerning the usefulness of standardized tests in sharing information on what students are actually capable of doing. In response to the many questions and to meet the changing emphases in assessment, alternative forms of assessment have been designed. Each form emphasizes a specific focus for assessment:

- *Standards-based assessment* is concerned with measuring the benchmark progress toward grade-level academic standards identified by states and school districts.
- *Performance assessments* combine content and process into a format that shows what students know—and what they can do with what they know. Performance assessments take knowledge to the doing level. The assessments may be authentic, as defined below, but are not always so. Traditional performance assessments take subject area content, such as information on the American Civil War, and engage students in a performance task calling on their knowledge and skills. The performance task might take the form of an essay, a play, a debate, or a visual representation related to an aspect or issue of the Civil War.

In concept-based curriculum models, a performance assessment also requires demonstration of conceptual understanding in addition to demonstration of content knowledge.

- *Portfolio assessment* emphasizes student self-assessment. A portfolio is a collection of student work that tells a story through time. It shows growth and development related to established criteria. The purpose of a portfolio is to facilitate classroom learning and instruction.
- *Authentic assessment* is a form of assessment based on students' performances of tasks drawn from real-world contexts. The performances are simulations of problems, issues, or challenges that a professional worker or adult might face in his or her life.

Alternative assessments support the recognized need to develop the internal process or lifelong learning skills of each unique child. These assessments struggle to survive in the present test-heavy environment of standards-based education, though, because they require more time—and time is a premium in classrooms today.

### Developmental Process Assessments

The alternative assessments discussed in the preceding section measure both process and content, but they are only snapshots of a student's performance in time.

To effectively monitor a student's continuous development within each process area from elementary grades through high school we need to identify the developmental characteristics or indicators for each developmental stage. The developmental stages may be defined by grade bands, such as kindergarten through Grade 3, or by individual grade designations with a range of indicators. The developmental indicators are grouped under organizing categories. For example, the process area of writing can be defined by the categories of organization, conventions, word usage, and fluency.

Specific indicators for different levels of performance provide teachers with a developmental road map for helping students celebrate how far they have come, and for showing the teachers the next steps. Table 6.1, which comes from the Northwest Regional Educational Laboratory (NWREL) (2000), provides a quality example of a developmental continuum for K–3 reading These indicators can be used by teachers in an ongoing assessment of reading ability for six distinct traits and five levels of performance. The NWREL's indicators of six traits are supported by significant research. If districts wish to write indicators with language from their state standards, there is a wealth of material available from NWREL to help guide the process.

## THE IMPLICATIONS OF PROCESS ASSESSMENT

Process and content are two different entities: *process* develops over time within each child; *content* is inert and exists outside of the child. Because of these differences, we should teach and assess process and content in different ways, but traditionally we have treated them alike. We have called the processes of reading and writing "subjects." We have graded students in these "subjects" using a deficit model—emphasizing what they cannot yet do, rather than celebrating accomplishments and encouraging them along the path to the next stage of development. This deficit approach to process development is one reason why so many children feel defeated by the time they reach the third grade. The NWREL material avoids this problem and addresses what the child is able to do at each level of performance: emerging, beginning, developing, expanding, and bridging.

If we believe that the ability to collaborate is a developmental process, then we have to wonder why we assess the student's progress as if she should have already arrived—no matter what the age or developmental level. Would we use such a deficit model to encourage a one-year-old to walk or a two-year-old to talk?

**Table 6.1** K–3 Developmental Reading Curriculum

| 1 EMERGING | 2 BEGINNING | 3 DEVELOPING | 4 EXPANDING | 5 BRIDGING |
|---|---|---|---|---|
| Decoding Conventions | Decoding Conventions | Decoding Conventions | Decoding Conventions | Decoding Conventions |
| • Choosing reading material independently<br>• Seeing self as a "reader"<br>• Recognizing familiar words in print<br>• Locating title and author on book cover | • Beginning to self-correct when reading orally<br>• Using letter sound cues when reading orally<br>• Using basic punctuation when reading orally<br>• Using sentence structure cues with guidance<br>• Identifying basic literary genres (poetry, story, play) | • Beginning to read aloud with expression<br>• Beginning to read aloud with fluency on familiar stories<br>• Identifying chapter titles, table of contents (text organizers)<br>• Identifying genres with ease | • Reading aloud with expressive fluency in self-chosen genres<br>• Identifying more test organizers—captions, unit headings<br>• Identifying subgenres—mysteries, histories, autobiographies, fantasies, etc.<br>• Identifying elements of punctuation and grammar | • Reading aloud fluently in more than one genre<br>• Identifying text organizers—index, glossary,content area titles<br>• Identifying genres and subgenres independently<br>• Identifying complex punctuation and sentence structures with guidance |
| Establishing Comprehension | Establishing Comprehension | Establishing Comprehension | Establishing Comprehension | Establishing Comprehension |
| • Making meaningful predictions based on illustrations<br>• Identifying characters in a story<br>• Relying on illustrations more heavily than on print for meaning | • Using sentence strategies with modeling and guidance<br>• Finding the "main character" in a story<br>• Retelling beginning, middle, and end with guidance<br>• Relying on illustrations and print | • Using prereading, during reading, and postreading strategies with deliberation<br>• Distinguishing between obvious major and minor characters<br>• Retelling beginning, middle, and end by self<br>• Summarizing with references to single parts of stories—characters, plot, and setting | • Using reading strategies consistently<br>• Learning that a detail is used to describe an element of a story<br>• Summarizing whole stories in addition to their parts<br>• Summarizing a literary purpose (explaining the moral of a fable, for example) with guidance<br>• Relying primarily on print to establish understanding | • Actively seeking print to gain understanding (wanting to read to find out)<br>• Beginning to distinguish between significant and supporting details<br>• Summarizing whole stories and parts of stories with ease |

(Continued)

(Continued)

| Realizing Context | Realizing Context | Realizing Context | Realizing Context | Realizing Context |
|---|---|---|---|---|
| • Recognizing familiar places and words<br>• Expressing interest in common events discussed in literature<br>• Assigning characteristics to characters in stories (angry, sad, happy) | • Beginning to recognize high-frequency words<br>• Making initial attempts at inferring meaning<br>• Identifying point of view with modeling and guidance<br>• Beginning to use meaning cues to increase vocabulary | • Beginning to use contextual vocabulary<br>• Inferring meaning with practice<br>• Identifying point of view by self<br>• Using meaning clues consistently<br>• Identifying tone and voice with guidance | • Experimenting with contextual vocabulary<br>• Gaining deeper meaning by "reading between the lines" with guidance<br>• Articulating difference in stories—race, class, gender—with guidance<br>• Identifying the tone of the author or story with guidance<br>• Making good guesses at the time period of the story with guidance | • Using contextual vocabulary with confidence<br>• Seeking deeper meaning by "reading between the lines"<br>• Articulating difference in stories—race, class, gender<br>• Identifying the tone of the author or story with confidence<br>• Making good guesses based on textual clues<br>• Beginning to see relationships between time, history, culture, society, and stories, with guidance |
| *Developing Interpretation* | *Developing Interpretation* | *Developing Interpretation* | *Developing Interpretation* | *Developing Interpretation* |
| • Participating in literature discussions<br>• Voicing a problem in a story<br>• Expressing concern over story conflict | • Participating and understanding the need for literature discussions<br>• Attempting to orally grapple with a problem in a story<br>• Responding to facts, characters, and situations in stories | • Generating thoughtful oral and written responses to stories, based on discussion questions<br>• Accurately identifying major conflict or problem of story<br>• Connecting facts and situations in stories to conflicts | • Confidently developing an extended response to questions<br>• Attempting to resolve a problem in story through analysis<br>• Distinguishing between fact and opinion with modeling, guidance, and examples<br>• Beginning to see a bigger picture | • Generating in-depth responses orally and in writing<br>• Recognizing the resolution of a problem in story thorough analysis as part of reading<br>• Distinguishing between fact and opinion with a degree of success<br>• Making conscious connections between analysis and reading |

## Integrating for Synthesis

- Connecting read-aloud books to own experience
- Learning information from stories and sharing with others
- Locating beginning, middle, and end of story visually

## Critiquing for Evaluation

- Explaining why he liked or disliked story using own words
- Explaining why she thought a story was good, asking questions about a story

---

## Integrating for Synthesis

- Comparing and contrasting story with own experience
- Finding explicit similarities and differences in characters
- Retelling story events in a sequential order with guidance

## Critiquing for Evaluation

- Explaining why story is liked or disliked by citing a scene, character trait, or problem in story
- Questioning why something happens in a story
- Identifying particular reading strategies and setting goals with guidance

---

## Integrating for Synthesis

- Understanding the concept of "Cause and Effect" with guidance
- Beginning to use other resources to gain information (encyclopedia and nonfiction texts)
- Putting story in chronological order even if not originally that way
- Using charts, graphs, tables, and maps with guidance to depict story information

## Critiquing for Evaluation

- Explaining why a story is good based on reason combined with story elements
- Questioning by asking why characters act in a certain way or why a story ends
- Setting goals and identifying ways to improve own reading with guidance
- Seeking out challenging reading material with guidance

---

## Integrating for Synthesis

- Understanding cause and effect and finding it in a story
- Using resources (other than stories) to locate information independently
- Integrating nonfiction information to develop an understanding with guidance
- Using charts, graphs, tables, and maps to depict story lines and information
- Finding information using alphabetical order

## Critiquing for Evaluation

- Responding to issues and ideas in literature as well as facts or story events
- Posing alternative scenarios with guidance
- Beginning to think of reading as a critical skill: recognizing the use of reading to learn
- Actively identifying reading strengths and challenges, and setting goals
- Actively seeking out challenging reading material by self

---

## Integrating for Synthesis

- Comparing and contrasting two stories with guidance
- Reading for information and to solve problems with ease
- Adding depth to responses by connecting to other reading and experiences
- Integrating multiple perspectives to form a thoughtful response

## Critiquing for Evaluation

- Responding to issues and ideas in literature as well as facts or story events
- Posing alternative scenarios with success
- Thinking of reading as a critical skill
- Actively identifying reading strengths and setting goals
- Actively seeking out reading materials across content areas
- Critiquing literature's quality with reasons and examples that illustrate use of story elements

SOURCE: Used with permission. Northwest Regional Educational Laboratory © 2000.

Teaching for process development in the school-age child requires the same kind of praise, encouragement, and support that we provide the preschool child who is learning to talk, walk, think, and speak. Assessment scales need to be supportive of learning at all levels, rather than negatively evaluative of students at the beginning levels.

The deficit model of assessment is apparent in most performance-based rubrics even today. Are we really measuring progress toward a standard if we give no credit at the beginning levels for what students can do in relation to the standard? What effect does negative feedback have on the developing processes that are so sensitively related to the child's ego and personal being? Highly successful coaches set and clarify the standard for athletes—then they positively celebrate small advancements toward the goal. Corrections are made, but expressed belief in the individual and support through the different levels of development are the main strategies for training.

## REPORTING PROCESS DEVELOPMENT

As a result of the renewed perspective that language is a developing process, many schools have revised their elementary report card. Student progress in writing is placed along a developmental continuum at the beginning, intermediate, or advanced level in kindergarten through sixth grade. The goal is to place all language skills on a developmental continuum on the report card and remove the meaningless letter grades. Each parent receives a booklet showing all of the writing indicators, K–12, when a child enters school. Parents are encouraged to follow these indicators and assist their children's progress along the continuum.

Report cards that give a letter grade for reading, writing, oral communication, or any other developing process skill do not provide a helpful profile for what the child has actually accomplished. Narrative reports that detail the child's progress through descriptive indicators of actual performance are far more meaningful to both parents and children. These reports become even more valuable when the child has self-assessed his own work according to defined performance indicators. Figure 6.1 from Southwood Elementary School in Orlando, Florida, shows excerpts from a Grade 1 report card based on descriptive indicators.

## ASSESSING CRITICAL THINKING DEVELOPMENTALLY

Critical thinking is one of the most challenging areas to assess developmentally. It is challenging because there are few, if any, models that define indicators of developing sophistication for this area. There have been some benchmark snapshots that describe critical thinking in a general way as applied to a specific task, but we need a more complete picture to assist teachers.

There is no question that the development of sophisticated thinking abilities is required for individual success in the 21st century. National, state, and district

**Figure 6.1**    Southwood Elementary Report Card

| | Quarter | | | |
|---|---|---|---|---|
| | 1 | 2 | 3 | 4 |
| *Reading/Language* | | | | |
| Recognizes high-frequency words | | | | |
| Identifies and uses letters and sounds in reading | | | | |
| Can retell, discuss, summarize, and supply information from stories | | | | |
| Identifies main ideas from text | | | | |
| Identifies supporting information | | | | |
| Uses strategies to identify words and construct meaning | | | | |
| Selects appropriate materials to read | | | | |
| Recognizes rhyme, rhythm, and patterned structures | | | | |
| Distinguishes between fiction and nonfiction | | | | |
| Can formulate questions | | | | |
| Recognizes standard language patterns (questions, statements) | | | | |
| *Writing* | | | | |
| Composes simple sentences and stories | | | | |
| Develops a purpose and plan for writing | | | | |
| Uses basic sentence structure with punctuation | | | | |
| Uses correct spacing between words | | | | |
| Writes legibly | | | | |
| Applies simple editing skills | | | | |

*(Continued)*

(Continued)

Key

| | | |
|---|---|---|
| Mastery | + | Applies knowledge/skill in different ways; transfers and extends knowledge |
| Developing | ✓ | Shows progress toward mastery; applies knowledge and skills with developing proficiency |
| Needs improvement | – | Applies knowledge/skills with limited proficiency |
| Introduced/not yet assessed | I | Introduced but not assessed at this time |

**Reading Development**

☐ *Emergent Reader.* The child is not yet reading but is developing concepts of "Print." This reader may know several high-frequency words and pretend to read familiar texts. Occurs at approximately ages five to six.

☐ *Early Reader.* The child is in the stage when true reading is beginning to occur. This reader is developing strategies for reading and self-correction. Occurs at approximately ages six to eight.

☐ *Fluent Reader.* The child is gaining control of reading so that self-correction is becoming automatic. Silent reading is becoming part of the child's behavior. Occurs at approximately ages seven to 10.

**Writing Development**

☐ *Emergent Writer.* The child uses scribbling and letter-like approximations to convey meaning. Many words are represented by the first letter sound of the word. Occurs at approximately ages five to six.

☐ *Early Writer.* The child uses beginning sounds, ending sounds, and vowels. More words are spelled correctly than approximated. Occurs at approximately ages six to eight.

☐ *Fluent Writer.* The child is expressing more complex ideas with greater ease. These writers are using some editing and proofreading skills to improve the message. Occurs at approximately ages seven to 10.

SOURCE: Southwood Elementary School, Orange County School District, Orlando, Florida. Used with permission.

learning standards specify the ability to think critically, problem solve, and reason as key goals for education. But teachers have had little training in how to teach for and assess thinking abilities. This is a more serious problem than most policy makers recognize. Teachers, however, know that this is a critical area of need for staff development.

In addition to the limited emphasis on this area in teacher training programs, our traditional curriculum fosters the antithesis of higher-order thinking. A primary focus on isolated mathematical algorithms, grammar drills, and the memorization of isolated facts hinders the pursuit of higher-order understandings. Lower-order memory work should not be the end of instruction. Instead, it should be viewed as a necessary tool to support effective higher-order thinking.

Today, the trend is away from isolated thinking skill instruction to embedded thinking as a natural part of the teaching and learning process. So the question remains, "How can we identify the developmental indicators of critical thinking to facilitate the progress of each child as he moves through the grades?"

## STANDARDS FOR THINKING

We can find help in answering the question by starting with the standards for critical thinking that have been identified by Richard Paul and Linda Elder in *Critical Thinking*: *Tools for Taking Charge of Your Learning and Your Life* (2006, pp. 87–99), which state, and rightly so, that we cannot assume that we are reasoning well. Rather, we must apply a set of standards to assess the quality of our reasoning.

Paul and Elder (2006, p. 87) identify nine basic intellectual standards, although they caution there are others as well:

| | | |
|---|---|---|
| Clarity | Relevance | Logic |
| Accuracy | Depth | Significance |
| Precision | Breadth | Fairness |

Paul and Elder (2006, p. 99; see Table 6.2) suggest using questions to help develop the intellectual standards.

To help students learn how to think critically, we need to define the indicators for each of these standards. What does clarity "look like" at Grades K to 2, 3 to 5, 6 to 8, and 9 to 12? We might say that "clarity is clarity" no matter what the grade level. This is true. Clarity is a concept with the attributes of clearness and lucidity, no matter what the grade level, so when we begin to assess what the critical thinking standards look like at each grade band we have to go beyond the simple, generalizable attributes.

**Table 6.2**    Questions to Develop Intellectual Standards

| Clarity | Logic |
|---|---|
| • Could you elaborate?<br>• Could you illustrate what you mean?<br>• Could you give me an example? | • Does all of this make sense together?<br>• Does your first paragraph fit in with your last one?<br>• Does what you say follow from the evidence? |
| Accuracy | Significance |
| • How could we check on that?<br>• How could we find out if that is true?<br>• How could we verify or test that? | • Is this the most important problem to consider?<br>• Is this the central idea to focus on?<br>• Which of these facts are most important? |
| Precision | Breadth |
| • Could you be more specific?<br>• Could you give more details?<br>• Could you be more exact? | • Do we need to look at this from another perspective?<br>• Do we need to consider another point of view?<br>• Do we need to look at this in other ways? |
| Depth | Fairness |
| • What factors make this difficult?<br>• What are some of the complexities in this question?<br>• What are some of the difficulties we need to deal with? | • Is my thinking justifiable in context?<br>• Am I taking into account the thinking of others?<br>• Is my purpose fair given the situation?<br>• Am I using my concepts in keeping with educated usage, or am I distorting them to get what I want? |
| Relevance | |
| • How does that relate to the problem?<br>• How does that bear on the question?<br>• How does that help us with the issue? | |

SOURCE: Richard Paul and Linda Elder, Center for Critical Thinking, www.criticalthinking.org. Used with permission.

We need to consider how clarity will be expressed as applied to particular content. The expression of clarity as a developmental performance is dependent on a number of factors:

- The sophistication of the content in terms of depth and complexity of ideas
- The cognitive processing of the students—their ability to analyze, synthesize, and organize content and ideas
- The communication ability of the students—their skill in conveying ideas so that others clearly understand the message

Let's examine a specific case in which increasing sophistication of content provides a framework for assessing developing sophistication in critical thinking processes.

In Chapter 5, I discussed the idea of organizing a social studies curriculum according to a limited number of organizing concepts that cut through Grades K to 6. The unit titles at each grade level are considered in relation to the conceptual lens of "Interdependence." The unit on "Families and Interdependence" at Grade 1 leads to expanded conceptual understanding: units on "Communities and Interdependence," "States and Interdependence," "Interdependence in Our Nation," and "Interdependence in Our World." Content is nested within these increasingly sophisticated conceptual units.

As students participate in many learning experiences related to the unit of study, they come to understand universal generalizations to parallel the depth of the content study. Remember that a universal generalization is two or more concepts stated in a relationship. A child arrives inductively at increasingly sophisticated generalizations related to the concept of "Interdependence" at the various grade levels:

Grade 1: A family cares for its members.

Grade 3: A community provides for needs and wants.

Grade 5: A nation develops trade relationships with other nations to meet economic needs.

Grade 6: Social, economic, and political interdependence among nations can lead to complex relationships of conflict and cooperation.

A teacher might provide students with one or more generalizations at the end of a unit of study and ask the students to give examples and defend or refute the generalization based on the unit study and additional student-generated examples. The teacher states that "clarity" will be one of the standards by which the presentation is judged. The product can be oral, written, or visual, but all of the expected criteria for assessment are made clear to the student at the beginning of the unit work.

How will we let first graders know what clear examples look like? How about giving fifth or sixth graders clarity? Students can be invited to participate in developing the indicators for a trait. Along with a discussion of the trait, students need to see and discuss actual examples of clear examples and presentations. They need to self-assess their own work for clarity (metacognition).

As learners progress through the grades, the standard for clarity challenges the student because they have to organize and express increasingly sophisticated content and ideas. They also have to explain in a self-assessment why their work has met or is developing toward the standard.

Helping students to define performance expectations and challenging students to reach the intellectual standards with increasingly complex material would go a long way toward the development of reasoned thinkers.

## The Elements of Reasoning

Paul and Elder (2006) discuss the importance of knowing the elements of reasoning when developing thinking to meet intellectual standards. Figure 6.2 shows the relationship between the intellectual standards, the elements of reasoning, and the desired intellectual traits (Paul and Elder, 2006, p. 54).

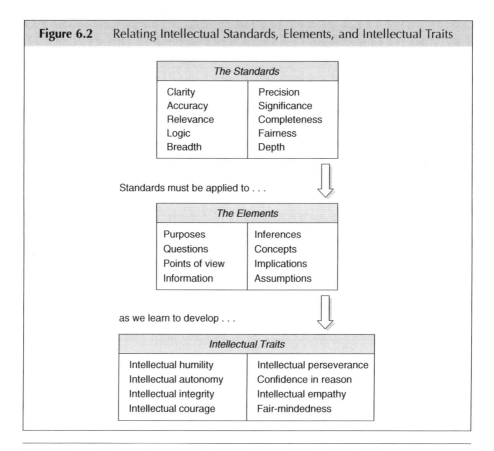

**Figure 6.2** Relating Intellectual Standards, Elements, and Intellectual Traits

The Standards

| | |
|---|---|
| Clarity | Precision |
| Accuracy | Significance |
| Relevance | Completeness |
| Logic | Fairness |
| Breadth | Depth |

Standards must be applied to . . .

The Elements

| | |
|---|---|
| Purposes | Inferences |
| Questions | Concepts |
| Points of view | Implications |
| Information | Assumptions |

as we learn to develop . . .

Intellectual Traits

| | |
|---|---|
| Intellectual humility | Intellectual perseverance |
| Intellectual autonomy | Confidence in reason |
| Intellectual integrity | Intellectual empathy |
| Intellectual courage | Fair-mindedness |

SOURCE: Used with permission. www.criticalthinking.org and Paul and Elder, 2006.

Paul and Elder (2006) define reasoning as "making sense of something by giving it some meaning in one's mind" (p. 57), and effectively summarize the interrelatedness of the elements of thought:

> Whenever you are *reasoning,* you are trying to accomplish some *purpose,* within a *point of view,* using *concepts* or *ideas.* You are focused on some *question, issue,* or *problem,* using *information* to come to *conclusions,* based on *assumptions,* all of which have *implications.* (p. 57; emphasis in original)

They go on to describe the significance of this interrelatedness:

- our purpose affects the manner in which we ask *questions;*
- the manner in which we ask *questions* affects the *information* we gather;
- the *information* we gather affects the way we *interpret* it;
- the way we *interpret* information affects the way we *conceptualize* it;
- the way we *conceptualize* information affects the *assumptions* we make;
- the *assumptions* we make affect the *implications* that follow from our thinking;
- the *implications* that follow from our thinking affect the way we see things—our *point of view.* (p. 62; emphasis in original)

Reasoning involves a set of skills that students can be taught. The goal would be students who know the intellectual standards and elements of reasoning, and who can metacognitively evaluate and guide the quality of their own thinking. They develop these abilities to the point of intuitive use. Questions become sharper over time, allowing the student to gather and clarify information to be used in conceptualizing, making assumptions, determining implications, and creating a reasoned point of view. Reasoning is a critical ability for the 21st century. We have a lot of work to do in this area.

## Generalizability

An issue of concern in performance assessment relates to the generalizability of test results related to the content under scrutiny. Just because a student demonstrates content knowledge related to the Westward Movement, for example, does not ensure that she will demonstrate content knowledge related to any other topic in American history. Generalizability of knowledge is not guaranteed.

I believe we have a problem with generalizability of content because we too often focus our assessment on the lower-level topic. We would find assessment results related to content to be far more reliable in relation to generalizability if we assessed for the students' understanding of the generalizations arising out of the content and concepts. The generalizations must be supported by specific fact-based examples that allow us to assess conceptual understanding, specific supporting content, and sophistication in the use of the process skills involved in the task. We assess, therefore, the three components of the tripartite curriculum model described in Chapter 3 (see Figure 3.1).

As an example, if we use a generalization related to the concept of "Interdependence"—"Trade is dependent on supply and demand"—secondary school students could be required to do the following:

- Analyze and support the generalization, "Trade is dependent on supply and demand," using specific examples from in-class learning and other current world examples.
- Relate the concepts of "Dependence" and "Interdependence" to the concepts of "Trade," and "Supply and Demand."

This assessment places the focus on generalizable knowledge and skills—the process skill of analysis and understanding of a generalization that encompasses many examples across cultures and through time.

The generalizability of the process of analysis is dependent on the conceptual ability (concepts), prior knowledge (critical content), and process skill (application). We can generalize a student's ability to use a process skill, such as critical thinking, when the performance tasks are matched to the student's developmental level. We can generalize performance to the point that the variables of a task (conceptual, prior knowledge, and process applications) are congruent with other tasks.

# SCORING GUIDES FOR PERFORMANCE TASKS

Chapter 4 outlined a formula for writing a culminating performance task for intra- and interdisciplinary units of instruction. The culminating task provides a high-level performance showing what the student knows, understands, and can do as a result of the unit study. Although units will use a variety of assessment formats, the performance task(s) will carry significant weight in assessment. For this reason, it is important to design a quality scoring guide or set of criteria and a standard to direct, define, and assess the quality of work.

## Scoring Guides: General Development

There are four common elements included in a scoring guide:

### 1. One or More Traits That Serve as a Basis for Judging

Traits can be identified as the broad categories to be assessed, such as content knowledge or oral presentation. Traits can also be presented as a set of criteria that the student is expected to fulfill. For example, assessment criteria for a unit on "Media as a Persuasive Force in American Society" might be the following:

- Evaluate the forms and techniques of media in American society.
- Analyze the characteristics of persuasion as a force.
- Design a persuasive advertisement (using any medium) for your new product. Incorporate at least three elements of persuasive advertising.

*2. A Definition and Examples to Clarify the Meaning of Each Trait*

The definition and examples answer the question, "What are the attributes of the trait to be assessed?" How do we define oral presentation, for example? Attributes might include the following:

- *Clarity.* A clear and lucid message
- *Voice.* Tone, volume, projection, confidence
- *Stance.* Shoulders back, head up, relaxed posture, avoidance of distracting mannerisms and distracting speech habits
- *Audience Awareness.* Presentation self-monitored and adjusted according to audience reactions

When criteria are set for a culminating performance, they need to be explained clearly to students: What are the expectations for evaluation, analysis, and design in the unit titled "Media as a Persuasive Force in American Society?"

*3. A Scale of Value (or Counting System)*
*on Which to Rate Each Trait (Examples)*

- *Qualitative Scale.* Excellent; highly competent; competent; developing
- *Numerical Scale.* 4 (high quality) to 1 (developing)

The qualitative and numerical scales are often combined in performance scoring guides.

*4. Standards of Excellence for Performance*
*Levels With Models or Examples for Each*

4 = *Excellent.* The oral presentation is well organized and focused. The presenter makes eye contact with the audience and speaks clearly; she does not display distracting mannerisms. The audience is engaged with an appropriate feeling tone. Audience reaction is monitored as the presentation proceeds, and appropriate adjustments are made to reengage the audience when necessary.

3 = *Highly Competent*

2 = *Competent*

1 = *Developing.* The oral presentation has a topic focus. Eye contact is made twice with an audience member. Voice tone is audible, but variability in feeling tone is yet to be developed. Presentation stance is appropriate.

I have taken the liberty of using the term "developing" at the base level in the previous scoring guide to support the philosophy of developing growth toward a standard and to avoid a deficit model of viewing progress. Students should view assessments as evidence of their progress toward the standard. The teacher should also counsel them as to the next stages of development and should show models of the standard expectations for the work.

## Scoring Guide Examples

Figure 6.3a provides a reproducible typical scoring guide model for teachers to use in constructing a task, trait, or generic scoring tool, while Figure 6.3b shows an example of a completed guide.

Table 6.3 shares a scoring guide by Jacqueline Kapp, a visual arts teacher in Gloucester, Massachusetts—a pen-and-ink line collage composition creating movement with a curvilinear, organic line.

**Table 6.3**    Pen-and-Ink Scoring Guide

| Criteria | Apprentice | Practitioner | Expert |
|---|---|---|---|
| Variety of line | Variety of three to five different organic lines in a variety of thickness | Variety of more than five distinct organic lines of various lengths and thickness | Neat and deliberate execution of organic lines of multiple variety, length, and thickness |
| Quality of line | Occasional line control | Control of line apparent; neat work | Professional-quality line; consistent, deliberate start and stop; flawless, neat work |
| Use of materials | Uses two different pen nibs to create line variety; uses the pen in a proper upright position | Uses two different pen nibs to create line variety; uses pen in upright and upside-down position for line variety | Uses several different pen nibs to create line variety; uses the pen in proper positions for predetermined effect; does not spill ink |
| Craftsmanship | Lines vary between clear and messy; collage not yet well constructed | Lines are neat and collage is well constructed | Lines are crisp and clean; collage is professionally constructed and presented |
| Understanding of the concept of "Movement" | Movement can be weakly detected | Movement is clearly created by the placement of the lines | Movement is clearly accomplished by the placement of the squares in the composition; secondary movement is also created to present an exciting presentation |

SOURCE: Courtesy of Jacqueline Underwood, Gloucester Public Schools, Massachusetts. Used by permission.

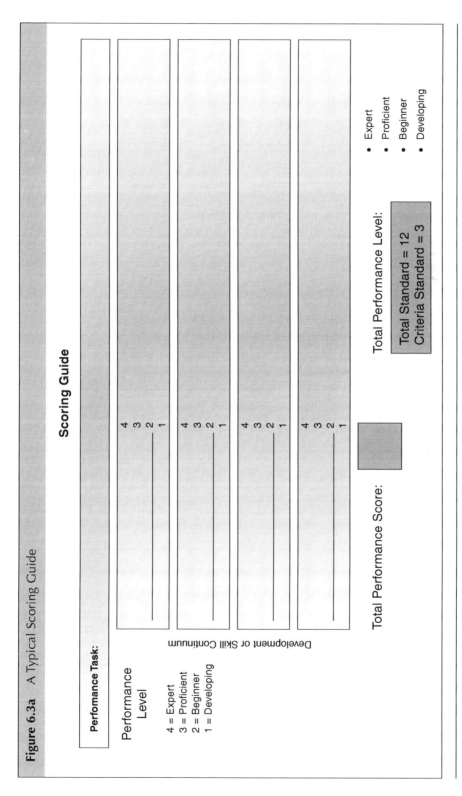

**Figure 6.3a** A Typical Scoring Guide

## Scoring Guide

Perfomance Task:

Performance
Level

4 = Expert
3 = Proficient
2 = Beginner
1 = Developing

Development or Skill Continuum

| 4 3 2 1 | 4 3 2 1 | 4 3 2 1 | 4 3 2 1 |

Total Performance Score:

Total Performance Level:

Total Standard = 12
Criteria Standard = 3

- Expert
- Proficient
- Beginner
- Developing

**Figure 6.3b** A Typical Scoring Guide: An Example

## Scoring Guide

**Performance Task:** As an investigative reporter for a news magazine, analyze the continuing problems with race relations in American society in order to illuminate key issues to be addressed. Write a clear and **insightful report** for American readers highlighting key issues and multiple perspectives. Suggest a reasonable course of action for addressing key issues.

Performance Level

4 = Expert
3 = Proficient
2 = Beginner
1 = Developing

Development or Skill Continuum

### Content Validity

4 Precise and accurate detailing of significant race relation examples
3 Accurate detailing of prominent race relation examples
2 Generally accurate description of selected race relation examples
1 Partial description of a single race relation example

### Insight

4 Thoughtful; perception of significant causes and effects based on evaluation of multiple perspectives and evidence; reasonable and justified course of action proposed
3 Recognition of important causes and effects based on consideration of multiple perspectives and events; reasonable course of action
2 Recognition of causes and effects and limited reference to multiple perspectives; course of action proposed, but not linked to data.
1 Biased presentation of causes and effects; biases course of action

### Writing Clarity

4 Order, structures, and presentation of information purposefully crafted to guide the reader's comprehension
3 Order, structures, and presentation of information accurate and coherent
2 Order, structures, and presentation of information shows direction but lacks coherence and sense of purpose
1 Order, structures, and presentation of information attempted, but fragmented

### Impact

4 Generates a personal, thoughtful, and emotional response in the reader
3 Generates thoughtful reflection and reaction on the part of the reader
2 Engages reader's interest and reaction sporadically
1 Shares information, but lacks a compelling and engaging message

Total Performance Score:

Total Performance Level:

Total Standard = 12
Criteria Standard = 3

- Expert
- Proficient
- Beginner
- Developing

## Criteria for Quality Scoring Guides

Grant Wiggins (1998, pp. 184–185) sums up the criteria for evaluating rubric designs in *Educative Assessment*. Figures 6.4 and 6.5 share Wiggins's helpful insights.

# QUESTIONS AND ANSWERS

## 1. What is a scoring guide?

**Answer:** A set of criteria and a scale of value to assess work or performance. The scoring guide specifies the criteria for judging, traits and indicators of developmental performance, and a standard of excellence.

---

**Figure 6.4**   Quality Rubrics

1. Are sufficiently generic to relate to general goals beyond an individual performance task but specific enough to enable useful and sound inferences about the task.

2. Discriminate among performances validly, not arbitrarily, by assessing the central features of performance, not those that are easiest to see, count, or score.

3. Do not combine independent criteria in one rubric.

4. Are based on analysis of many work samples and on the widest possible range of work samples, including valid exemplars.

5. Rely on descriptive language (what quality or its absence looks like) as opposed to merely comparative or evaluative language, such as "not as thorough as" or "excellent product" to make a discrimination.

6. Provide useful and apt discrimination that enables sufficiently fine judgments but do not use so many points on the scale (typically more than 6) that reliability is threatened.

7. Use descriptors that are sufficiently rich to enable student performers to verify their scores, accurately self-assess, and self-correct. (Use of indicators makes description less ambiguous and hence more reliable by providing examples of what to recognize in each level of performance. However, even though indicators are useful, concrete signs of criteria being met, specific indicators may not be reliable or appropriate in every context.)

8. Highlight judging the impact of performance (the effect, given the purposes) rather than overreward process, formats, content, or the good-faith effort made.

---

SOURCE: Wiggins, G. (1998). *Educative Assessment: Designing Assessments to Inform and Improve Student Performance.* Copyright © 1998. Reprinted with permission of John Wiley & Sons, Inc.

**Figure 6.5    Technical Requirements of Rubrics**

1.  *Continuous.* The change in quality from score point to score point is equal: The degree of difference between five and four is the same as between two and one. The descriptors reflect this continuity.

2.  *Parallel.* Each descriptor parallels all the others in terms of the criteria language used in each sentence.

3.  *Coherent.* The rubric focuses on the same criteria throughout. Although the descriptor for each scale point is different from the ones before and after, the changes concern variance of quality for the (fixed) criteria, not language that explicitly or implicitly introduces new criteria or shifts the importance of the various criteria.

4.  *Aptly Weighted.* When multiple rubrics are used to assess one event, there is an apt, not arbitrary, weighting of each criterion in reference to the others.

5.  *Valid.* The rubric permits valid inferences about performance to the degree that what is scored is what is central to performance, not what is merely easy to see and score. The proposed differences in quality should reflect task analysis and be based on samples of work across the full range of performance; describe qualitative, not quantitative, differences in performance, and do not confuse merely correlative behaviors with actual authentic criteria.

6.  *Reliable.* The rubric enables consistent scoring across judges and time. Rubrics allow reliable scoring to the degree that evaluative language (*excellent, poor*) and comparative language (*better than, worse than*) is transformed into highly descriptive language that helps judges to recognize the salient and distinctive features of each level of performance.

SOURCE: Wiggins, G. (1998). *Educative Assessment: Designing Assessments to Inform and Improve Student Performance.* Copyright © 1998. Reprinted with permission of John Wiley & Sons, Inc.

## 2. What is a standard?

**Answer:** A set point for quality (not minimal) performance against which student growth can be measured developmentally and over time. In a four-point scale, the standard is set at three to allow room for exceptional performance.

## 3. How should teachers view standards?

**Answer:** Teachers should view standards as goals for each student. This means that the teacher needs to develop and implement support strategies to help each child progress along the continuum of progress. It also means refusing to accept work that has shown no effort. It means expecting the best effort and providing support to ensure success.

## 4. How do we grade learning disability or slower-achieving students?

**Answer:** I would rather we assess than grade. Assessment of developmental process skills such as writing or speaking should be based on how much growth the student has made over time toward the standard. Conveying an assessment of this growth to the child and parent through the use of work samples, scales of growth, or developmental indicators is preferable to trying to do so with a letter grade. If the teacher is required to give letter grades, the grade should be based on the evident growth, but there also needs to be a narrative description or method for showing the developmental level (beginning, intermediate, or advanced).

## 5. How do we assess mastery of content?

**Answer:** Because content is not a personal, developmental process like learning how to read, content mastery can be assessed more quantitatively through criterion-referenced tests. Letter grades are more appropriate for indicating levels of content mastery than they are for indicating developmental growth in reading or writing processes.

## 6. Why is there so much emphasis today on the design of scoring guides?

**Answer:** There is increasing emphasis on the design of scoring guides because they help clarify our performance expectations for students. Teachers often find, as they design the guides, that their assessment does not really address the critical outcomes they wish to measure. Quality scoring guides clarify the assessment criteria and standards for process performance and content knowledge. Teachers often adjust their assessment task after developing the scoring guide. They strive to align the task with the expected outcomes as defined by the criteria and standards.

# SUMMARY

In the frenzy to meet the economic, social, and political demands of an interdependent world, government and business have teamed to set an agenda for schools. National and state governmental bodies legislate academic standards, and subject area committees work to define what students must know and be able to do by the time they graduate from high school.

This movement can be helpful to schools if the issues of time and funding for training and technology are addressed. If the assessments that accompany the national and state standards are high stakes, and issues such as training and inequitability of resources and opportunity have not been addressed, the plans will fail. States that address the classroom issues related to the attainment of standards will have the greatest chance of success.

Demands for higher levels of performance in what students know and can do are causing a tidal wave in the testing community. Old paradigms of bell-shaped curves; normative or standardized testing; and reliability, validity, and generalizability have been shaken up.

States now purchase or develop standards-based assessments to measure how well students are meeting expectations. Some states have embraced the notion that assessments must reflect conceptual understanding as well as core knowledge and skills. This is a positive step on the assessment end—except that these state leaders usually fail to realize that the teachers have not been trained on how to teach for conceptual understanding or even to differentiate between standards that are factual, conceptual, or skill driven. This is no small matter when it comes to raising standards.

Other states have fallen back on the traditional standardized tests from publishers. In some cases, these standardized purchases have poor alignment with the state standards. You can imagine the frustration of teachers and students at test time! And even if there is alignment, we are reinforcing an outdated factory mentality for our intellectual age.

Despite the political heat from standards, alternative assessments are claiming their authentic role in meeting the new educational demands. Teachers attend workshops and conferences, and feel the pressure to understand the talk of portfolios and performance assessments. Performance assessments are carried out in classrooms. Concept-based performance tasks measure what students know, understand and can do through complex tasks that combine content and process skills. A scoring guide sets the criteria and standard for the performance. What used to be a letter grade with a few subjective comments now appears as a numeric or qualitative scale of performance descriptors or indicators.

New forms of assessment squeeze in beside the old, at times bumping against each other. The fit is not comfortable. Teachers prefer the newer forms, and the public prefers the old. But the two must share space until educators develop the newer forms to a level that satisfies public questions and concerns, and until educators align those forms to state-required academic standards.

## EXTENDING THOUGHT

1. How do traditional report cards need to change to reflect process development and content knowledge?

2. If you were the public relations director for your school, how would you help parents see the value of performance assessment? How would you address their concerns with standardized test scores?

3. What is a performance assessment?

4. How can performance assessment assist you in meeting the educational needs of your students?

5. How does self-assessment contribute to the development of independent learners?

6. What is the teacher's responsibility to each child when teaching to academic standards?

# Concept-Based Instruction

There are three basic components in transitioning to a concept-based model of instruction: The first is an understanding of how concept-based curriculum design differs from the traditional fact-based model. The second is access to a concept-based curriculum, or knowing how to adapt traditional curriculum for oneself. And the third, which this chapter looks at, is the actual implementation component—concept-based instruction.

Fact-based instruction differs from concept-based instruction in a significant way:

- *Fact-based instruction* places the instructional emphasis on learning the facts related to specific topics. Knowledge related to the facts is the end goal.
- *Concept-based instruction* places the instructional emphasis on understanding the concepts, principles, and transferable ideas that arise from the study of significant topics and facts. Deeper conceptual understanding supported by specific facts is the end goal.

Because the instructional emphasis shifts to the deeper understanding of concepts and ideas, both student and teacher are required to use higher levels of thinking. Students and teachers consider and apply facts in the context of the related concepts and generalizations. This ability to think beyond the facts and link specific information to abstract ideas is a skill that can and must be taught.

Previous chapters in this book outlined the theory and practice of designing concept-based curriculum; this chapter discusses how concept-based instruction differs from traditional instruction, then describes some of the popular initiatives in education today that can support concept-based instruction. Though there are many initiatives that work well with concept-based instruction, this chapter will concentrate on the following: describing and illustrating how instructional strategies, learning experiences, and assessments can be enhanced using a concept-based focus:

*Instructional Strategies*

- Cooperative learning
- Essential questions and guiding questions
- Differentiation of curriculum and instruction
- Use of graphic organizers
- Use of technology

*Learning Experiences*

- Teachers design for learning
  o Inquiry
  o Projects or problem-based learning
- Adapting instructional materials and lessons

# INSTRUCTIONAL STRATEGIES

## Cooperative Learning

Cooperative learning as an instructional strategy has been in use for many decades. It is also one of the most researched and supported techniques for maximizing student learning. Johnson, Johnson, and Stanne from the University of Minnesota (2000) published a meta-analysis of 164 research studies investigating eight different cooperative learning methods. The researchers found that all eight methods had a significant positive impact on student achievement.

Cooperative learning can take different forms, but generally class members are organized into small groups to work through an assigned task together. In their book *Cooperation in the Classroom* (1993), Johnson, Johnson, and Holubec cite five essential components for the group work:

1. Positive interdependence
2. Face to face interactions to promote each member's learning
3. Individual and group accountability for achieving the task goals
4. Interpersonal and small-group skills for effective functioning
5. Group processing of how well members are working together, and how the group effectiveness can be improved

Of all the teaching strategies, cooperative learning has the greatest potential for reaching the greatest number of students. First, it is inclusive. All group members are expected to participate actively, and indeed the success of the group work depends on each member taking individual responsibility for their contribution to the work. Members are often assigned roles such as Presenter, Recorder, Timer, and so on, to help them learn group skills.

Second, with cooperative learning, students are not sitting in straight rows with the teacher doing all of the important talking and only a handful of students answering a question here and there. No—all students are thinking and working, and the many minds on task generate piggyback extension of thoughts and ideas. When teachers in my workshops are working in their cooperative groups to learn how to link factual content to concepts and enduring understandings, they often remark, "It is much easier to do this kind of work when I have the group to help clarify and extend my thinking!" Believe me—students feel the same way.

There is a third reason why cooperative learning reaches more students. Most classrooms today are multicultural in makeup. Many students are still learning the English language. Cooperative learning groups give them the opportunity to use and practice the language in a social setting. Straight rows mean they dialogue very little with others. How can they internalize the English language if they hear it but have limited opportunity to use it?

Cooperative learning is used more in elementary than in secondary classrooms. They have more flexibility in their day if they keep the same students from beginning to end so it is easier. The higher we go in the grade levels, however, the less use we see of cooperative groups. Secondary teachers complain that with 150 students rotating through every day it is difficult to plan for this kind of student interaction. They also fear that they won't be able to reach their academic standards if there is more group work. I am sympathetic to their concerns, but when we weigh the loss of deeper intellectual engagement, deeper understanding of content and concepts, and decreased motivation for learning, it appears that we need a better balance of pedagogical practices. Perhaps some classes during a day could use cooperative learning processes while others are engaged in whole class or independent work. The learning processes would be switched on another day. In any case, when we walk in a student's shoes through a day of school and find ourselves sitting in straight rows just listening to the delivery of information, followed by paperwork at our desk, we know why their eyes lack sparkle.

Another reason that many teachers resist cooperative learning is that they fear "losing control" of the class, or they may have an administrator that believes "a quiet class is a well-behaved class." Both of these ideas are irrational. Noise in a classroom does not necessarily mean a loss of control or bad behavior. A class that is humming with enthusiastic, on-task learners, who excitedly share their thoughts and findings with group members can be easily discerned from a class with an aimless, loud, and rowdy bunch of hooligans. The aimless bunch most likely did not have an interesting and well-directed group task. I hope that administrators support the teachers who dare to break out of rows and encourage cooperative work. After all, isn't cooperative effort the way most people solve the major issues of life? Where will our students learn these skills if not at school?

## Essential Questions and Guiding Questions

Essential questions and guiding questions are critical drivers for concept-based instruction. They serve three main purposes:

1. To encourage students to think deeply about a significant question that cannot be easily answered

2. To help students develop and explore a foundation of factual knowledge

3. To guide students' thinking beyond the facts to the generalizations and principles that form the deep and transferable understandings of a discipline

First let's look at the use of essential questions. The term "essential question" has been used widely over the years (e.g., Wiggins & McTighe 1999, 2005; Hayes-Jacobs 1997, 2004) to describe questions that require deep reflection or research; questions that cannot be answered with a simple response; and questions that probe the deeper meaning of life events and issues. Essential questions support inductive teaching—guiding students to discover meaning—rather than relying only on deductive lecture methods. Essential questions pique the students' curiosity because the answers are not at once apparent. They invite the students to search for answers, and require more complex thinking.

Essential and guiding questions have far greater power in the instructional process than do our traditional "objectives." Read these objectives, then read the questions that follow:

---

*Objectives*

1. Identify the early Native American tribes in America.

2. Describe their housing.

3. Evaluate how nature influenced their beliefs.

4. Match the cultural artifacts in the illustration with the correct tribe.

*Questions*

1. Why were indigenous tribes referred to as Native Americans?

2. How do people meet their basic needs? Are some needs more basic than others?

3. In what situations does nature have the greatest influence on the beliefs of a people?

4. Can people ever ignore nature?

5. How can cultural artifacts tell a story? Would it be possible to wrongly interpret the story?

What did you notice as you read the questions that differed from what you noticed as you read the objectives? Did you find that your mind was "on autopilot" as you read the objectives, but that you were thinking as you read the questions? Did the questions pique your interest because you wanted to answer the questions based on your own knowledge and perspectives? Why do so many curriculum documents attempt to drive teaching through the use of objectives when they obviously create so little passion for thinking and learning? Could it be that objectives are easier to test and score? Do we need objectives if we have identified clearly the critical content topics (without verbs) that students are to study, the enduring understandings (generalizations) to be drawn from content, and the key processes (complex performances) and skills?

Essential questions are difficult for many people to write because we are so comfortable with writing the easy fact-based questions. I have found in my workshops that teachers develop strong, provocative essential questions after they have written some of the conceptual understandings that reflect the deeper enduring ideas for the unit. These enduring understandings and the related guiding questions that lead student thinking from the factual to the conceptual level set the stage for writing one or two powerful essential questions for the unit. In this respect, my process for designing the essential question for a unit differs from my colleagues' process. It is a difference in design preference, but we achieve the same goal.

Now let's take a look at guiding questions. The purpose of guiding questions is to lead a student's thinking from the factual level to the conceptual level of thinking. This is a learned skill. It is not that we want all students to arrive at only the generalizations we have developed, but we do want them to learn the skill of bridging from facts to conceptual, enduring understandings. We also have some deep understandings that give meaning to why we are instructing specific content. But at the same time, we are looking for students who bridge to ideas we may not have thought of—and we celebrate when they do. Our goal is students who think.

Here is a tip for writing guiding questions: after you have written the enduring understandings for your unit as discussed earlier in this book, turn the generalizations into a question as a first step. For example, if I have a generalization in Grade 2 social studies that states, "Community members have roles," then I might turn it into the question, "Why do community members have roles?

If I have a generalization in mathematics and science that states, "The mass of any object increases with its velocity," then I would turn it into the question, "Why does the mass of any object increase with its velocity?" Answering the question leads to a more sophisticated generalization, "Velocity generates energy, which converts to mass." The answer uses more specific conceptual terminology and this gives the student greater clarity and depth in her understanding.

As a rule of thumb, each generalization in a unit needs a set of three to five questions in the design process that are a mix of factual and conceptual questions. We can't just ask open-ended, provocative essential questions all the time. We don't have the time to debate all day, and we do have content that needs to be addressed. These guiding questions are to help the teachers, who need to use them wisely. For example, we should not just stand in front of the class and deliver the questions in a rote fashion as if we were shooting volleys from a cannon. We would want to creatively and wisely use the questions. Perhaps we would give different cooperative groups a question or two to work on, then use a jigsaw strategy to have students share their findings with other groups. And certainly the strategy of having students develop their own questions around major unit topics is a sound strategy. If I were going to do this I would teach them the difference between a fact-based question and a conceptual question (one of them transfers through time and across situations—guess which one) so that they can write various kinds of questions. It would also be wonderful to have the students come up with a debatable, essential question for the unit after they became comfortable with writing guiding questions.

We want to post essential questions and guiding questions for an instructional sequence. Students read and think about these questions when they are in clear view. (Posting academic standards is of dubious value because they do little to engage the mind or heart.)

## Differentiation of Curriculum and Instruction

It seems awkward to even have to discuss the idea of differentiating curriculum and instruction to meet the needs of different kinds of learners, but the reality is that too many classrooms are still teaching with the focus of "one for all and all for one." No one would deny that children learn in different ways and with different amounts of time on task, but traditional school structures, pressures of content coverage for standardized tests, and limited budgets for staff development make the idea of differentiating to maximize learning a mountain still to be climbed. But we must—just as we must raise the intellectual bar for curriculum and instruction through concept-based models.

Carol Ann Tomlinson, international presenter, author, and expert on differentiation of curriculum and instruction, reminds us that the United States is a multicultural society that needs to master a high-quality curriculum for an increasingly complex society (Tomlinson & Strickland, 2005, p. 1). Add to this realization the fact that schools will deny students high school diplomas if they do not master this curriculum. Tomlinson and Strickland suggest five classroom elements that teachers can differentiate to meet the various learning needs of students (2005, paraphrased from p. 6):

- *Content.* What students will learn
- *Process.* How students will connect personally to the learning
- *Products.* What evidence students will produce from their learning
- *Affect.* The interactive nature of mind and emotions
- *Learning Environment.* The learning climate and operational structures

If you have not yet reflected on the writings of Carol Ann Tomlinson and her colleagues Eidson and Strickland, I encourage you to find a bookstore post haste. In addition to *Differentiation in Practice: A Resource Guide for Differentiating Curriculum, Grades 9–12,* by Tomlinson and Strickland, there are two other books in the series for Grades K–5 and Grades 5–9 by Tomlinson and Eidson (2003a, 2003b).

To give you an idea of the kinds of support you can find in Tomlinson and Strickland's book (2005) Table 7.1 shares some of their suggested strategies for differentiating process work in Grades 9 through 12.

**Table 7.1**    Strategies for Differentiating Process

| Student Characteristic | Strategy |
| --- | --- |
| Readiness | • Use tiered activities (activities at different levels of difficulty, but focused on the same key learning goals).<br>• Make task directions more detailed and specific for some learners and more open for others.<br>• Provide resource materials at varied levels of readability and sophistication.<br>• Provide small-group discussions at varied levels of complexity and focused on a variety of skills.<br>• Use both like-readiness and mixed-readiness work groups.<br>• Use a variety of criteria for success, based on whole-class requirements as well as individual student readiness needs.<br>• Provide materials in the primary language of second language learners.<br>• Provide readiness-based homework assignments.<br>• Vary the pacing of student work. |
| Interest | • Use interest-based work groups and discussion groups.<br>• Use both like-interest and mixed-interest work groups.<br>• Allow students to specialize in aspects of a topic that they find interesting and to share their findings with others.<br>• Design tasks that require multiple interests for successful completion.<br>• Encourage students to design or participate in the design of some tasks. |
| Learning Profile | • Allow multiple options for how students express learning.<br>• Encourage students to work together or independently.<br>• Balance competitive, collegial, and independent work arrangements.<br>• Develop activities that seek multiple perspectives on topics and issues. |

SOURCE: From *Differentiation in Practice: A Resource Guide for Differentiating Curriculum, Grades 9–12* by Carol Ann Tomlinson & Cindy Strickland, Figure 2 (p. 10). Alexandria, VA: ASCD, 2005. Used with permission. The Association for Supervision and Curriculum Development is a worldwide community of educators advocating sound policies and sharing best practices to achieve the success of each learner. To learn more, visit ASCD at www.ascd.org.

For practice, select one of the activities you will be using in your class in the near future. Using Table 7.1 as a guide, plan ways to differentiate the processes to meet the various needs of the students in your class. The more you practice planning for differentiation, the easier it will become. Eventually you will internalize the differentiation strategies to the point that they become automatic in your planning.

I agree with Tomlinson that differentiation does not mean we dumb down the curriculum when students have trouble learning. All students need to attain critical knowledge, understandings, and skills. Nevertheless, we can differentiate how we get them to the goals, and that means we need to know our individual students as learners. How can we plan for effective learning for all students? It does not mean individualized teaching for each student—we can differentiate for groups as well as for individuals—but one size will surely not fit all.

## Use of Graphic Organizers

Graphic organizers are a powerful tool for helping students visualize and organize data. With slight adaptations, they also make powerful tools for developing conceptual thinking. In *Concept-Based Curriculum and Instruction for the Thinking Classroom* (Erickson, 2007) I provide a number of examples showing how graphic organizers can be adapted to make them concept-based, so I will provide just one example here. We are all familiar with historical timelines. A typical graphic organizer might look like the one in Figure 7.1.

This timeline presents only dates and events; it is a record of factual information. To adapt this graphic organizer to a concept-based model requires the introduction of conceptual thinking—seeing the patterns and connections of information through time.

Figure 7.2 shows the adapted timeline, which would be suitable for a high school history class. Now the students must start with a major event in history and work backward, identifying the causative factors that led up to the major event.

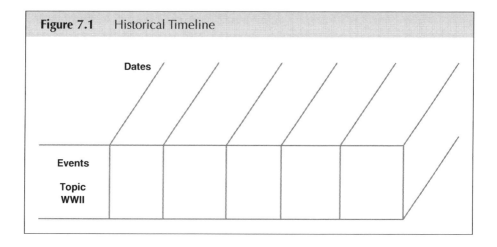

**Figure 7.1    Historical Timeline**

Dates

Events

Topic
WWII

They identify the effects of each event and develop a deeper understanding of the complex relationships leading to war. Below the timeline, students write a paragraph explaining a transferable lesson of history drawn from and supported by the analysis and events on their timeline. This would be a wonderful cooperative learning exercise because of the discussion involved.

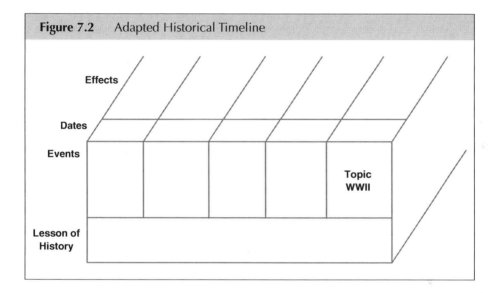

**Figure 7.2**   Adapted Historical Timeline

## Use of Technology

Technology is an integral tool for instruction in today's classrooms because it engages the mind and motivates the student. For instance, students use the Internet and other resources to gather information on an ocean animal of their choice. They research concepts such as breathing, propulsion, reproduction, diet, and predators.

One group may create a home page on the whale, complete with links to each of the researched concepts. In their oral presentations, students can project their information onto a screen, perhaps including video clips of whales and a discussion with Jacques Cousteau of great white whales as an endangered species. Then students can use the Internet to visit and ask questions of the underwater researchers. The class may even decide to hold an online forum on the dangers that ocean animals and humans pose to each other, with participation by students from other countries.

It is easy to see why students who use technology show greater interest and motivation in their learning. Technology allows students to become personally and intellectually engaged as they direct their own learning. The teacher is a facilitator, and a learner along with the students. The concept-based teacher would identify key concepts and generalizations to guide learning, but students would search for knowledge and understanding and creatively share their insights.

## LEARNING EXPERIENCES

Across the country today, teachers and administrators realize that the ability to think critically and creatively is paramount; and that learning experiences must support this higher cognitive standard. Teacher by teacher, school by school, and district by district educators are working to learn, design, and implement concept–process curriculum models. They realize that to teach students how to think requires continual development of the teacher's own thinking ability. Designing curriculum to develop thinking is hard work; teaching students to think is even harder work.

Following are some descriptions and reflections on concept–process lesson design and instruction from teachers around the country. The section opens with a letter written by Scott Hendrickson, when he was a high school mathematics teacher. He shows clearly the understanding of concept–process curriculum planning. He uses the content and applications of mathematics to develop key concepts and the conceptual, transferable understandings for mathematics. He teaches to the conceptual idea through focused, engaging, and relevant applications. Also evident in this letter is Scott Henrickson's enthusiasm for instruction. Bringing his own intellectual creativity, thought, and planning to the design for learning makes the engagement and progress of his students personally rewarding for him.

---

Since our meeting I have been thinking about the teaching of concepts in secondary mathematics. I realized that many math teachers seldom, if ever, teach mathematical conceptual understanding. For some reason the teaching of skills and symbolic manipulation has become the exclusive activity of many math classrooms, while teaching students to think mathematically, and to use mathematics to describe and model the world around them, has been almost totally ignored. For many years I was one of those who perfected the teaching of math skills and avoided teaching students the deeper thinking involved with mathematics. Fortunately, the National Council of Teachers of Mathematics Standards reawakened in me the joy that I had felt exploring mathematical ideas as a child. I remember cutting graph paper into various shapes and discovering the concept of "Area." I remember exploring "Patterns" in logarithmic tables and making the connection between those self-discovered patterns and an understanding of how my slide rule worked. It was the patterns, the themes, the beauty and the art of mathematics that drew me to it, not the symbols and the rote practicing of procedures. As tools of technology replace the manipulative skills of mathematics, there is even greater need to focus on the applications of mathematics.

The concept of "Mathematical Modeling" should be prevalent in our classes. The language of algebra, with its symbolic manipulations and procedures, is one way that we can model physical phenomena and make predictions about the world around us. But there are also graphical and numerical ways to perform the same types of analysis. The themes of algebraic, numerical, and graphical modeling form a powerful triad for allowing students to probe the world around them.

One of the most powerful tools of mathematics is the concept of "Slope." When data is portrayed graphically, patterns emerge. One of the simplest patterns occurs when the data is linear. On the first day of my math classes I have my students walk in front of a motion detector, a device that measures their distance from the detector as a function of time. As the students walk away from, or toward, the detector they see a graph plotted of their distance from the detector at each instant in time. If they walk at a steady pace, the graph is a line. The line slopes up when they move away from the detector and down when they move toward it. The faster they move, the steeper the line. It is the measure of the steepness of the line that we call "slope." Students clearly understand the generalization that the "slope of the line is a mathematical model of speed." When students vary their pace the graphs become even more interesting. If they are walking away from the motion detector at an increasing rate, the graph curves upward. If they are slowing down the graph curves a different way. They soon recognize that the graphical display contains all of the information they need to analyze the motion of the person who created the graph. They can predict the direction of the motion, the velocity of the motion, and whether the person was speeding up or slowing down.

*The slope of a graph at a particular point is a measure of the instantaneous rate of change.* This conceptual understanding transfers to the study of all types of rates of change: velocity, typing rate, reaction rate, etc. Whenever we use terms like miles per hour, feet per second, miles per gallon, words per minute, vibrations per second, revolutions per minute, moles per liter, we are treading on the concept of "Instantaneous Rate of Change." This is the concept which is referred to as the *derivative* in calculus.

This one simple activity has led us deep into a fundamental concept underlying differential calculus. I have found that other concepts of mathematics can be introduced in just such a visual and intuitive way. My students actively explore the concepts of mathematics (and skills). Though the skills are essential to quality performance, I also value interdisciplinary curriculum to help my students apply and experience the power of mathematics in authentic, real-world situations offered by the other disciplines.

SOURCE: Scott Hendrickson, Department of Mathematics Education, Brigham Young University. (Formerly a teacher with the Alpine School District, American Fork, Utah.) Used with permission.

Another letter, this one from a second-grade teacher shows the power of conceptual teaching in the elementary grades:

---

My students are making many connections with the "big ideas" that we have created from in-depth studies. Since September, we have been learning about, discussing and finding examples of the concept of "Perspectives" in our literature. A comparison chart helps the children understand the concept. We have read many books and record our thoughts on the chart under the heading of "Title, Issue, Characters, Perspectives, Outcome and Analysis." The children refer to the chart often and identify the *perspectives* of different characters. They also transfer the idea and use the word appropriately across the curriculum in other class discussions. I see deep understanding occurring for most students. For example, after reading a biography about Benjamin Franklin that told of the conflict between Franklin and his son William over loyalty to the colonies, a student made a connection for our perspective chart, "Different perspectives can cause conflict." Another boy concluded that "people have different perspectives on death" after he read the story *Annie and the Old One*.

I also see my students asking more intelligent questions:

- Could the colonists have gone back to live in England if they had wanted to?
- What benefit were the colonists getting for the taxes they paid the British? (We had learned about the concept of "Benefit" when we studied one of our units explaining why the Spanish kept coming to the New World while the Vikings didn't.)
- Why were the French going to help the colonists in the Revolutionary War when they had fought against them in the French and Indian War?

Our discussions are lively, and the conceptual focus to our curriculum really challenges my students to think.

---

SOURCE: Marianne Kroll, Palos Park School District, Palos Park, Illinois. Used with permission.

## The Law and Society

Teachers at all levels are thoughtfully planning their lessons to engage the minds and hearts of their students. Greg Isaacson, an exemplary high school teacher in Orlando, Florida, teaches a comprehensive law class for 24 students in Grades 10 to 12. He works in a school with a "four by four" schedule: students take four classes each semester and attend four 110-minute classes each day.

Greg wrote his thoughts and reflections on his instructional plan and the students' grasp of key concepts. As you read the following excerpt, can you identify the teaching strategies that motivate and engage the interest of Greg's students and that facilitate deeper levels of understanding?

All of the students in my class are in the Law Magnet Program, an honor's-level program for college-bound students. The class is ethnically diverse. The majority of students have been in other classes with me in previous years. In the middle of our "Law and Society" unit, I was teaching to the broad generalization that "law can shape society's values." I also wanted them to understand that "tort laws can shape, reflect, and enforce society's values." More specifically, I wanted them to recognize and objectively analyze how product liability suits can regulate industries that the legislature cannot, to recognize and analyze how "unreasonably dangerous products" are eliminated from the marketplace through product liability lawsuits, and to recognize and analyze how class action suits can be an effective litigation tool against manufacturers of unreasonably dangerous products.

I asked students to write a paper explaining how law affects their lives on a daily basis in order to assess their prior knowledge and genuine understanding from previous classes and discussions. Then we examined in greater detail cases mentioned during a class discussion—specifically, the cigarette and gun manufacturing lawsuits. We then did two assignments applying concepts learned. The first was an interpretive prediction of the outcome of the cigarette and gun lawsuits in the future. The second was an analytical discussion presented as a persuasive memo following a small group project, which asked students to identify potential targets of litigation from the vast array of potentially dangerous consumer products on the market.

Because, in my experience, students respond better to specific details when they can approach them from a broader, more identifiable context, I began this lesson with an open discussion on socially related topics and gradually focused the discussion and their thought processes on increasingly specific legal concepts.

Going into the transition between general discussion and our focused discussion on cigarette manufacturers' liability, I anticipated that students would make the stock arguments against banning cigarettes. I had hoped to illustrate how litigation could accomplish the same goal through the product liability lawsuit. The key concept for them to grasp was the difference between some beneficial aspects of alcohol when used as intended, as voiced by one student, and no benefits with cigarettes when used as intended, which was noted by two other students. This discussion effectively illustrated the "unreasonably dangerous product" principle.

Besides using the "general to specific" approach whenever a new concept or topic was introduced, I also allowed students to discuss peripheral issues as a means of "fleshing out" a concept before adding depth to the idea. For example, when I moved from the general concept of "Liability" to the more specific concept of "Tort Law," I asked a student to explain the difference between civil and criminal trials, drawing on their prior knowledge and understanding. I also encouraged students to apply concepts under study to their own life experiences.

I modeled thinking strategies when appropriate. At one point in the lesson, I made the statement, "I know this because. . . ." when applying what I knew about black-market guns to a future of black-market cigarettes. This models the thinking strategy of conceptual transfer of knowledge.

The use of humor and current events engages student emotions and interest, which helps them retain knowledge. Political cartoons provide an effective springboard for discussions on perspective.

Students know that I expect them to explain and defend their thinking with supporting data and sources. I look for evidence in class discussions that students have an enduring understanding of the complex legal concepts. When Jerry was able to clearly and concisely articulate the difference between a criminal and a civil case, he made the transition between the general concept of "Liability" and the more specific concept of "Tort Law." When Sarah brought up the second-hand smoke argument as an additional way cigarettes were unreasonably dangerous, she also asked a particularly insightful question, "What is the intent of cigarettes?" She was aware that no logical benefits derive from cigarettes and therefore met the test of an unreasonably dangerous product.

## Fairy Tales and Archetypes

Another outstanding middle school teacher, Louise Hamilton, from Greenville, North Carolina, developed a literature unit based on the play *Into the Woods,* by Stephen Sondheim and James Lapine. *Into the Woods* weaves four well-known fairy tales into a coherent whole through the use of an original quest story in which Rapunzel's older brother, a baker, attempts to remove the witch's curse of barrenness by gathering for her a cow as white as milk (Jack's from a "Jack and the Beanstalk"), a cape as red as blood (Red Riding Hood's), hair as yellow as corn (Rapunzel's), and a slipper as pure as gold (Cinderella's in the Grimm version of her story).

Hamilton used the dual conceptual lens of "Archetypes and Conflict" for the unit to help students realize that stories can survive centuries of oral transmission into a variety of media formats because they portray conflicts that are timeless. The conflicts that develop the theme of "Into the Woods" are those of adolescents struggling to grow up. All of the main characters go "into the woods" and struggle to resolve conflicts before moving on to the next stage in their lives: Jack must make his way in the world, although even his doting mother finds him ill equipped to do so; Little Red Riding Hood must learn to take care of herself even in the presence of the wolf; Cinderella must find a husband who will accept her for what she truly is; Rapunzel must escape from the clutches of her overprotective "mother"; and the baker and his wife must learn to work together if they are to conceive, much less parent, a child. This initiation into maturity is one of the archetypal human experiences.

To help students abstract their thinking from the specifics of the play to the deeper significance, Mrs. Hamilton provided a number of activities, including the following:

- Complete the chart [see Table 7.2] comparing characteristics from your own childhood role to the expectations for an adult role. Identify what kind of changes you will need to make to meet your adult role. Identify a fairytale character with a similar challenge.
- Identify archetypal characters in the play such as the "good mother," the "terrible mother," the "good father," the "absent father," or the "kindly grandparent."
- Choose a character to follow through Act I. Note what the character is like at the beginning of the play, what happens to him or her during the first act as he or she goes into the woods, and any changes that take place in the character.
- Form cooperative groups around your particular character and discuss the character's family background and the conflict faced in the adolescent woods experience. Use a handout to record how your character's past prepared him or her to handle the communal and personal crisis that will be faced in ever after (in Act II). Report and justify to the class your group's hypotheses on the future success of your character in handling his or her crisis.
- Synthesize what you have learned about archetypal conflicts, characters, and settings to create a fairy tale of your own that reflects your own life as an adolescent or another point of view (environmentalist, peace advocate, etc.). Take the part of the protagonist in your tale and represent the "real world" by identifying the conflict, describing the human emotions felt by the protagonist and antagonist, and using symbols to convey story concepts (e.g., giant [powerful], beans [poverty], gold hen [wealth]).

**Table 7.2**    Changing Roles

| Childhood Role | Changes From Childhood to Adulthood | Adult Role | Fairy-Tale Character |
|---|---|---|---|
| Economically dependent | Learns to earn own way in the world using talents | Wage earner who can support self and family | Jack |
| Vulnerable | Learns to protect self from the dangers of the world | World-wise and competent | Little Red Riding Hood |

SOURCE: Louise Hamilton, Pitt County School District, Greenville, North Carolina. Used with permission.

## Project or Problem-Based Learning Experiences

*Building Houses*

A letter from a kindergarten teacher shows how she combines elements of the popular project approach with the structure of concept–process curriculum design:

I just completed a unit on "Houses" with my kindergarten class. Concept–process curriculum design fits nicely into the three phases of this project. By engaging students with a project, in phases, I am able to help them understand the generalizations that frame the unit:

- Houses are built with different kinds of materials.
- Houses come in many shapes and sizes.
- Climate affects the type of house that is built.
- Building a house requires many job skills.
- Design and materials affect the quality of houses.

As each phase of the project progresses, the study takes on more seriousness for students.

We begin by relating stories of the subject matter—in this case, houses. Since the children have a good background in what a house is and why we have houses this can be done rather quickly. I have them draw pictures of a house and use this as a "pretest." They draw pictures of houses periodically throughout the unit. I compare the drawings to see what new knowledge they have added. The children ask questions which I write down. When we answer them in our research I write that down also. I bring in many nonfiction books about houses around the world, building houses, and families around the world. I use all the versions of the Three Little Pigs. A newer version has high-tech houses! Our purpose for reading them changes as we are evaluating the choices of home building materials. I also read lots of books about families. These books, along with the discussions and activities, answer many of the generalizations. I also bring in as many experts as I can find. This year one of my student's fathers owns a window business. He brought in samples of windows and brochures for the children. He told them how glass was made and the process for making windows. The children turned the rice table into a glass factory. Another father is a plumber. Students were building water systems and drawing diagrams of their creations. We looked at blueprints and they made their own. These children also experienced a local firestorm and many lost their homes and had to rebuild. I think that makes housebuilding even more important to these students. We also discussed what makes a "house" a "home."

We went for a walk and looked at houses in the neighborhood. I call this our field study. I give the students clipboards and assign groups specific things to look for on the walk. Roof types, window shapes, garages, siding types, etc. They draw pictures and when we get back we share the findings. Through these activities the children realize the importance of the various concepts in curricular areas because they need them to work on the project. If your job is to describe window shapes you had better know them! I get more comments from parents about this. Their children bug them to learn at home, because they need the information and skills to help them build the class house.

The actual building of the house happens many weeks after the beginning of the unit. The children sign up for a construction job. They look at books and ask the professionals how to do the job. I give them real saws, tape measures, paint brushes, pipes, etc. I make it as real as I can and still maintain safety. We had wiring, fuse boxes, outlets, hot water tank, wallpaper, tile roof, shingle roof, raingutter and windowboxes. Sometimes you had to use your imagination to really see it, but it was there.

We had a piece of carpeting, but it was too big for the house. The "carpet layers" tried to measure the floor with a yardstick, but the stick was too big. I asked them to think about the things in our room which could be used to measure. They looked around and finally found the Unifix Cubes (which is what I had hoped they would find). They hooked the cubes together into two lines for width and depth. They laid them out onto the carpet and drew the lines (I cut the carpet!). They counted each row of cubes and wrote them down so they could report back to the class. As you can see they used several mathematical concepts and also met some of the essential understandings.

For the generalization "Design and materials affect the quality of houses" I had them make houses out of marshmallows and toothpicks. We had interesting designs but alas—only certain houses remained standing. We analyzed why, and tried the same theories with block houses.

The preceding activities completed phases one and two of the unit. Phase three was sharing and playing. We shared with parents and other classes. Playing in the house is the reward for all the hard work. You asked me about any insights I might have about helping students understand the importance of concepts. I think it is the connection to real life. You can find real life applications of concepts within any theme. Connect students with the real world applications and let them play the required roles. This is especially true for primary children. Any time a child takes on an adult role it is important to him or her. Making the project big in size helps also. I observed the sixth graders looking at our house. They immediately got in and wanted to play. I began to think about the kind of house they would make and the details they could achieve. I almost wanted to move up a few grades! Teachers need to keep the learning as hands-on as possible. Children will naturally read, write, use mathematics skills, etc., if teachers demand they show their understanding of concepts and generalizations in different ways as they work on a big project.

SOURCE: Mary Russell, Ponderosa Elementary School, Spokane Valley, Washington. Used with permission.

*Brownies for Sale*

Two teachers from Palos Park School District, Palos Park, Illinois—Deanna Jackson and Deborah Pope—developed an economics unit for Grade 4 titled "Brownies for Sale." This unit teaches the students valuable lessons and concepts in economics. In a class letter they requested their parents' help, explaining that students were going to hold a bake sale to learn about economics concepts such as consumers, producers, supply and demand, and profit. Parents and student decided on the item they would make, purchased the ingredients to allow 12 individually wrapped items, and recorded the cost. They prepared the baked good and noted the time required for preparation. Then they set the price (no more than 50 cents) so that the student could make a profit.

Students made advertisements to be placed around the school, and the sale was on. The day after the bake sale, the students figured out the profit they made by completing this form:

---

*Bake Sale Cost and Profit Worksheet*

Kind of baked good _____

List of materials and ingredients purchased _____

Total cost of materials _____

Total amount of time for preparation and packaging _____

Price per bag _____

12 – _____ number of bags left = _____ number of bags sold

_____ number of bags sold × _____ price per bag

= _____ gross profit – _____ total cost

= _____ net profit

---

The students used an economics vocabulary sheet and this economics study guide to answer to prepare for a test:

---

*Economics Study Guide*

1. Review the definitions of the economic words. Use your economic vocabulary sheet or your social studies book.

2. Be able to answer the following questions about the bake sale (concepts are italicized):

---

- Who were the *producers*?
- Who were the *consumers*?
- What was the *profit*?
- Why did you need to know the *total cost* of your materials?
- How did *supply* and *demand* affect the amount of baked *goods* that were sold at different times during the day?
- Even though each person made his or her own baked good, were they really *self-sufficient*? Why or why not?

From the video, we learned the term *opportunity costs*.

- How does this idea relate to the bake *sale*?
- How did the bake *sale* demonstrate *interdependence*?
- What factors helped the *consumers* decide what to *buy*?
- What would you do differently for the next bake *sale* to increase *profits*?

Students discussed the successes and failures of the sale. For example, did some baked goods sell better than others? Was it price, advertising, or appearance? Then the students decided how to use all the money earned from the bake sale to benefit all the students of the school.

## Concept Maps

*Mind Maps for Kids: Max Your Memory and Concentration,* by Tony Buzan (2002), explains clearly the strategy of concept–content mapping. This strategy is useful in helping students understand the idea of related concepts and ideas. Buzan explains that mind maps use color and pictorial images in addition to words to engage personal creativity and emotions. These personal mind maps help students make more connections. Buzan provides a wealth of suggestions for helping students maximize memory and concentration.

Figure 7.3 shares the mind map of Ron Reddock, a teacher and educational consultant, as he listened to a presentation on concept-based curriculum design.

Figure 7.4 is a word mind map for the concept of "Wellness."

Try creating a word mind map for one of the concepts below. The idea is to help students see how specific concepts nest under broader concepts as you move away from the core. Notice also that the concepts become more specific (micro-concepts) as you move outward.

How is depth of understanding developed for a core concept based on your mind map for

- Color
- Fitness
- Energy
- Culture
- ??

**Figure 7.3**   Conceptual Mind Map

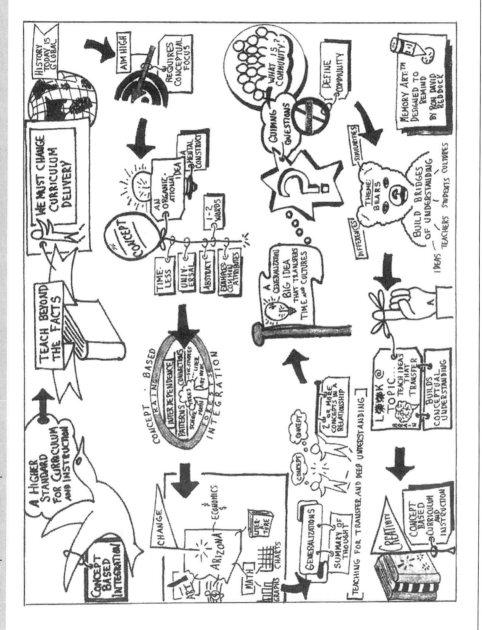

SOURCE: Ron David Reddock, Memory Art. Educator and consultant. Used with permission.

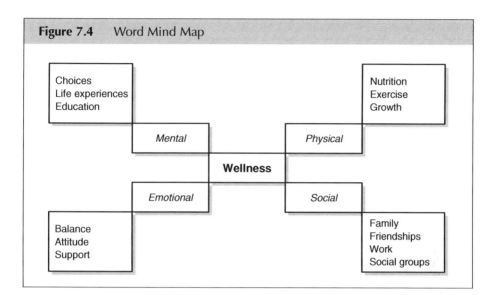

**Figure 7.4** Word Mind Map

Choices
Life experiences
Education

*Mental*

Nutrition
Exercise
Growth

*Physical*

**Wellness**

*Emotional*

*Social*

Balance
Attitude
Support

Family
Friendships
Work
Social groups

Students in Mrs. Vrchota's fifth-grade class at Southwood Elementary School in Orlando, Florida, read *The Missing 'Gator of Gumbo Limbo,* by Jean Craighead George. Mrs. Vrchota used a variety of strategies to help students think about their learning. Students created concept maps, such as the one shown in Figure 7.5 by fifth-grade student, Cristina Oliveras.

When students mind-map a concept or topic before and after a unit of study, they can see their personal growth in the depth and breadth of their knowledge and understanding.

Other strategies used by Mrs. Vrchota include Venn diagrams comparing *The Missing Gator of Gumbo Limbo* with another piece of literature, as well as a prediction chart, which asks students to predict the events of each chapter before reading it, then to write whether their predictions were accurate following reading. Another strategy, called multiple effects, asks students to take an event in the story and predict the various effects that the event might produce. All of these strategies force students to become intellectually engaged with the study and reinforce deep understanding and retention of knowledge.

Students must also be able to relate the facts they are studying to the enduring ideas—the generalizations—that will transfer to new specific examples. Below are suggested activities to help students bridge their thinking from factual examples to enduring understandings.

## Visual Metaphors

Students draw a visual representation of a generalization. Teachers give them the "generalization," and students decide on a specific example that can be drawn

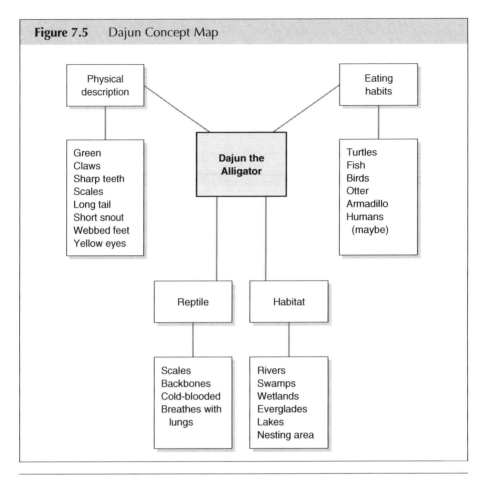

**Figure 7.5    Dajun Concept Map**

SOURCE: Christina Oliver, Southwood Elementary School, Orange County Public Schools, Orlando, Florida. Used with permission.

to represent the idea. They must understand the conceptual idea to convert it into a specific representation (Table 7.3).

## Card Games

Instead of having students draw a visual representation of an idea, the teacher can make a set of cards to have students play a matching game. The cards are composed of pairs—a generalization with its matching example, which can be in the form of a picture or a set of written examples. The student who gets the most pairs in each group is the winner of the game. Three to four students per group with six to eight generalizations and their matches is workable. There will be a total of 12 to 16 cards in a deck.

**Table 7.3**  Generalizations and Visual Representations

*Science*

| *Generalizations* | *Possible Examples* |
| --- | --- |
| Organisms adapt to changing environments. | Animal that changes color to match the environment (e.g., snowshoe rabbit, chameleon) |

*Fine Arts*

| *Generalizations* | *Possible Examples* |
| --- | --- |
| A visual communication can convey multiple messages. | An advertisement that conveys a mood and a message<br>A dance that tells a story and demonstrates artistic interpretation<br>A painting that conveys conflicting emotions (e.g., joy and sadness) |

*Social Studies*

| *Generalizations* | *Possible Examples* |
| --- | --- |
| Community members have roles. | Pictures of community members in their different roles |

## Big Ideas Through Time

Another technique to help students understand the enduring quality of generalizations is to have them find different historical examples of a significant enduring idea, such as "Revolutions create social, economic, and political change." Students can make a booklet comparing the social, economic, and political changes driven by three well-known revolutions. They summarize the comparison by addressing a series of guiding questions such as the following:

- What is a revolution?
- Why do people reach the point of revolution?
- What kinds of changes occur in society as a result of political revolutions?
- Do all revolutions lead to social, economic, and political change?
- How did the American Revolution shape the political, social, and economic directions of our country?
- What factors influence the kinds of changes that occur?
- Are revolutionary changes always positive for a society?
- Do revolutions affect other nations? How?
- In addition to political revolutions, are there other kinds of revolutions?
- What do they have in common with political revolutions?
- What role do leaders play in revolutions?

## Reflecting

Vaughn and Estes (1986) developed a comprehension strategy called "Insert," which asks students to use a marking system in the margins to react to text. Marianne Kroll and Ann Paziotopoulos, two outstanding teachers from Palos Park, Illinois, adapted and updated the comprehension strategy and called it "Reflecting."

Reflecting is a coding technique that allows students to identify their thoughts and feelings as they react to different pages of text. Kroll and Paziotopoulos (1995) developed two rubber stamps with coded reactions to use on small sticky notes. The stamped sticky notes require students to reflect and consciously interact with text. Students circle their reactions to specific pages of text as they read, using the following:

---

*SHARP*

  S = Makes me Sad

  H = Makes me Happy

  A = Anticipate something

  R = Reminds me of something

  P = See a Problem

*LEARN*

  L = Learned new and important information

  E = Explored the cause and effect

  A = Arrived at a conclusion

  R = Recognized different perspectives

  N = Noticed character traits

---

SOURCE: ©1995 Kroll and Paziotopoulos.

---

The Reflection notes focus students on the meaning of text and invite their reactions. Students are free to use blank notes to record additional or different reactions. Reflection notes also mark locations so that students can refer to specific pages in discussions or written analyses. The notes also allow the students to support their thoughts and feelings with specific references from the text. Reflection is essential for deeper comprehension. (Note: *Guided Reading That Improves Comprehension,* by Lois Lanning [in press], outlines "The Big Four" comprehension strategies with clear and specific guidelines to help teachers instruct and scaffold student comprehension.)

Modeling is a critical instructional strategy when students are learning the Reflecting procedure. Using an overhead projector or a big book, the teacher reads a page of text and then self-reflects aloud, "What thoughts or feelings cross my mind when I read this page?" The teacher talks through the critical text on the page to model the thinking process for students and then circles a letter or letters that reflect his or her thoughts and feelings.

When modeling, the teacher is careful to identify metacognitively the various steps for thinking about the relationship between specific text and the selections on the Reflection notes, and to share those connections with students. For example, on the SHARP note, if the teacher circled A = Anticipates something, she or he would think aloud and share the text clues that created the feeling of anticipation. After the coding lesson and student practice, the teacher models the use of Reflection notes as a way to keep track of thoughts and feelings in reading a book. The teacher helps students understand that thoughts and feelings are reinforced or may change as new information comes into the story.

Reflection notes can be used at all grade levels across different types of reading material, from content specific to literature based. Reflection notes can be used by individual students to record their reactions to text, and can then be used in cooperative groups to stimulate discussion and raise awareness of different perspectives on issues. Students develop a deeper understanding when they are required to defend, explain, or elaborate on a position.

Reflection notes allow students at different reading levels to read suitable books on a common theme. They can share their thoughts and feelings on the theme in cooperative groups or literature circles by referring to their particular book selection and notes. Reflection notes help differentiate curriculum and instruction without isolating students.

Reflection notes can be used at home as an enjoyable sharing activity between parent and child. The student takes home a book and 10 prestamped sticky notes. Five sticky notes are in one color for the student; the other five notes are in a different color for the parent. As the parent and child read the book together, they each ask, "What am I thinking about on this page?" They circle their codes independently and compare and discuss their reflections at the end of the book. One third-grade student shares her reflections on *The Enormous Crocodile,* by Roald Dahl, based on her sticky note thoughts:

---

*The Enormous Crocodile*

There are many ideas to think about from the book, *The Enormous Crocodile*. First I was sad on page 7 when the crocodile said he was going to eat the children because I wouldn't want to get eaten by a crocodile.

---

*(Continued)*

(Continued)

> Next I was sad again on page 8 when the crocodile bit Trunky the Elephant because Trunky was a nice elephant and there was no reason for the crocodile to bite him.
>
> Then I anticipated something on page 18. I anticipated that the crocodile was going to eat the children because the children wanted to collect coconuts and the crocodile had coconuts on him.
>
> Finally, I anticipated something on page 39. I anticipated that the elephant would let go of the crocodile and the crocodile would go flying into space.
>
> SOURCE: Lauren Nelson, third-grade student, Palos Park School District, Palos Park, Illinois. Used with permission.

Teachers do not assume that students know how to recognize or evaluate their own thinking. Students are taught specific procedures for thinking about text—and the Reflection notes provide critical support. Students are responsible for identifying and supporting their own reactions to text material.

Reflection notes can be adapted to help students bridge their thinking from facts to the conceptual, enduring understandings. Teachers may give students Reflection notes containing several of the enduring understandings that were developed throughout a unit of study. Students are asked to find specific factual examples from a variety of resources and communicate why they think the examples support the deeper understanding. When students can support an idea with more than one specific example, they demonstrate a more sophisticated grasp of the idea.

Paula Light, an enthusiastic kindergarten teacher in Channelview Independent School District, Channelview, Texas, shared a story about a child in her class who not only bridged from the factual to the conceptual level—but also transferred the concept.

> I was reading *Animals Nobody Loves,* by Seymour Simon, to my students to settle them after lunch. The book explained how roaches like to hide in the darkness. After reading a few pages, I shifted the focus to the start of our "Energy Unit." I asked the question: "What would happen if the lights never went off?" The children began throwing out answers: "You turn off the light switch." "Take out the bulb."
>
> I thought, "Oh dear, they don't understand the question." Then Christa raised her hand, "You wouldn't be able to go to sleep."
>
> "Good thinking, Christa," I replied. Then Dalen raised his hand.
>
> "The roaches wouldn't come out!" For a second I was puzzled. "Roaches? Where did that come from?" And then I remembered the after-lunch story. "Go Dalen!"

# ADAPTING ACTIVITIES

*Active Learning: 101 Strategies to Teach Any Subject,* by Mel Silberman (1996), is an older publication, but it offers timeless tips for teachers on how to actively engage students in learning. The 101 activities can be adapted to help students bridge from facts to concepts and big ideas. These are general activities that can be used with a wide variety of content to create viable learning experiences for students. I will provide just a few examples showing how teachers can adapt these activities to create concept-based learning experiences. Concept-based teachers evaluate their teaching materials and activities to make certain they engage the conceptual mind.

## Trading Places (Silberman, 1996, p. 35)

This activity helps students understand that concepts can be categorized and ordered from broader to more specific.

---

*Procedure*

1. Divide class into three teams.

2. Give three students on each team a blue sticky note naming a macroconcept under study (e.g., migration, government, energy).

3. Give the other students on each team a yellow sticky note with a related subconcept for one of the blue concepts on their team (e.g., "rules" or "roles" for government).

4. Students with yellow notes gravitate to their macroconcept.

5. Then each group organizes its concepts from the blue macroconcept (broadest concept) to the microconcept (most specific). The first group to line up its concepts correctly from macro to micro provides the rationale for their ordering of concepts and is applauded.

---

## Rotating Trio Exchange (Silberman, 1996, p. 59)

This is a way to allow students to share what they know and understand based on a unit of study. It could be used at the end of a unit to summarize learning. The questions you pose will become more complex as the rounds proceed. Your goal is to engage the mind of each student as they share the depth of their knowledge.

*Procedure*

1. Develop a set of questions for your students representing the factual, conceptual, and provocative levels. For example, with a unit on the American Revolution, the following questions could be included:
   - *Factual.* What were some of the causes of the American Revolution?
   - *Conceptual.* How do revolutions create change in a society?
   - *Provocative.* Should governments support revolutions in foreign countries?

2. Divide the students into trios. Arrange the trios in a circular pattern.

3. Give each trio the same opening question. Select the least challenging question for this round. Have students share their answers within their trio.

4. After a suitable period of discussion, ask the trio to assign a number—0, 1, or 2—to each member. For the next question, direct students with number 1 to rotate one trio clockwise. Ask the students with number 2 to rotate two trios clockwise. Students with the number 0 remain seated at the trio site and raise their hands so they can be located by rotaters.

5. Start a new round of trio exchange with a more difficult question.

6. You can rotate trios as many times as you wish.

## Lecture Bingo (Silberman, 1996, p. 75)

There are times when a lecture on content is in order as the most efficient way to impart critical information to students. The following adapted activity will help keep students "minds-on."

*Procedure*

1. Create a lecture-based lesson with up to nine key points.

2. Develop a bingo card that contains these key points in a $3 \times 3$ grid. Place a different point in each box.

3. Create several cards with the same points located in different boxes on the card.

4. Distribute a card to each student along with a strip of nine self-sticking colored dots.

5. Instruct students to place a dot on their cards for each point that you discuss.

6. Students call out "Bingo!" when they have three vertical, horizontal, or diagonal dots in a row.

7. As an advanced variation on this game, extend the card with three rows and print one enduring idea in each row. To call out "Bingo!" a student must also identify and place a dot beside the enduring understanding that best reflects the big idea for the lecture.

SOURCE: Cartoon by David Ford, davidford4@comcast.net.

## TEACHER REFLECTIONS ON CONCEPT-BASED INSTRUCTION

And finally, some general comments from teachers' initial training and implementation efforts in concept–process curriculum and instruction:

As I walked into class, I thought, "I know all there is to know about writing a unit." (I had learned all the latest in planning and developing interdisciplinary curriculum.) This will be an easy credit. Was I surprised! I realized that even though I had been making the connections with my "themes," my students had not. I was missing a key element by not presenting the concept and making certain my students were making the connections. I was teaching facts for the sake of knowing facts. I now know I must go back and redevelop my own way of thinking and revise my lessons. This class was a real eye-opener. I think it is not only going to make my students more excited about learning, but will make me more excited about teaching.

SOURCE: Doris Madden, Lake Washington School District, Redmond, Washington. Used with permission.

There is no doubt in my mind . . . that content must be tied directly to a concept or to concepts in order for students to assimilate the essential information and skills. At the workshop, our sixth-grade team was able to breathe life into our somewhat undefined unit on "Ancient Civilizations" by identifying a conceptual lens that would give greater purpose to our students' learning. With "Interconnections" as the lens on our theme of "Ancient Civilizations: Cairo to Canton to King County," our students will be able to relate the past to the present. The introduction of the concept has changed my social studies unit from teaching facts to teaching valuable knowledge that will benefit my students for a lifetime. If this sounds a little overly dramatic or a bit overstated, it is only because I am truly excited about the entirely new perspective I have on relevant and meaningful learning. Students need the basics and a balance in curriculum, but they also need the concept or "big picture"; these can make learning truly exciting for them.

SOURCE: Jodi Stueckle, Lake Washington School District, Kirkland, Washington. Used with permission.

## SUMMARY

Designing concept-based units is teachers' first step as they learn what concept-based curriculum is—and how it changes classroom pedagogy. When the teacher implements a concept-based unit, the real challenge begins. Teaching concept-based curriculum is an intellectual model that takes the thinking of both students and teacher through the facts to the level of conceptual, transferable understanding. This chapter provides valuable insights into the thinking of teachers such as Greg Isaacson, Louise Hamilton, and the Palos Park School District teachers as they plan for concept-based instruction.

When students become intellectually engaged in school on a personal level, they experience love of learning. In the final chapter, we continue to explore how teachers can stir the head, hearts, and souls of their students.

### EXTENDING THOUGHT

1. What is your understanding of the difference between topic-based instruction and concept-based instruction?

2. Why is it difficult at first to shift to concept-based instruction?

3. Can you think of an instructional activity that could be adapted to develop conceptual understanding? What adaptation would you make?

4. If you were observing a teacher in a concept-based classroom, what would you see and hear?

5. Why is it important for principals to understand concept-based curriculum and instruction?

6. What do parents need to understand about concept-based classrooms?

# Stirring the Head, Heart, and Soul

## Creating a Love of Learning

*8*

The classroom buzzes with activity. Children work in small groups, intent on discovering mysteries of life: How do birds fly? Just what is in those owl pellets? How do caterpillars change into butterflies? Why don't animals talk like humans? What would happen if the desert suddenly gained rivers? The teacher circulates from group to group—listening, asking probing questions, suggesting resources, and encouraging the efforts. Some students express ideas, some question and extend the thinking. New ideas emerge.

The room is rich with material. Student work lines the walls, and books, art prints, science materials, and mathematics manipulatives are evident in the plentiful workspace. Students use desktop computers and build reports on their findings. They access databases to find relevant material to the theme under study and compare notes on global pollution with students around the world. They design PowerPoint programs to display their knowledge and scan in pictures to enhance the graphic appeal. These are the students of the computer age.

Down the hall in another classroom, students sit in rows and stare at their social studies textbook while child after child reads a paragraph. The teacher perches on a stool in the front of the room and asks questions about the facts just read. Some posters hang on the wall, and books sit in tidy position on the shelves, sorted by size. The room is quiet except for the bored drone of the student reading and a bee that works furiously to escape through a window.

## STIRRING THE HEAD

### Brain-Based Learning

Teachers are the architects for learning. They design the environments for developing minds. Caine and Caine (1991), in their seminal book *Teaching and the Human Brain,* differentiate between surface knowledge and meaningful knowledge. *Surface knowledge* is the traditional memorization of facts and procedures. To acquire *meaningful knowledge,* however, students must be able to perceive relationships and patterns to make sense of information. Students make sense of information by relating it to their unique past experiences and the current environmental context and interactions (Caine & Caine, 1991).

A key point in the Caine and Caine (1991) text involves the ideas of disequilibrium and self-reorganization. *Disequilibrium* is "when the original state of equilibrium is disturbed." When a learner meets new information that is confusing or disturbing, he or she enters a mental state of disequilibrium. This state is reconciled when "the learner moves to a broader or more inclusive notion—a more sophisticated schema or [mental] map" (p. 129).

In their latest book, *12 Brain/Mind Learning Principles in Action: The Fieldbook for Making Connections, Teaching, and the Human Brain* (Caine, Caine, McClintic, & Klimek, 2005), the authors provide teachers and administrators with flexible field-based strategies for brain-based teaching and leadership. This is a must read for all educators. Drawing on their wealth of knowledge and experience the authors address principles associated with "Relaxed Alertness," "Orchestrated Immersion in Complex Experience," and "Active Processing" to expand our learning and knowledge, and to illuminate the path for quality teaching.

In *How the Brain Learns,* David Sousa (2006) differentiates between rate of learning and rate of retrieval (of information). He suggests that these rates are independent of each other (p. 108), and posits that the rate of retrieval is a learned skill. Sousa offers teaching strategies for helping students efficiently retrieve information from long-term memory storage.

Sousa (2006) states that the rate of retrieval determines how quickly transfer (of knowledge) occurs during a learning situation. He describes transfer *during* learning as "the effect of past learning on the processing and acquisition of new knowledge." He describes transfer *of* learning as "the degree to which new learning is applied by the learner in new situations" (p. 136).

Transfer of learning and the development of the intellect are the most important reasons for designing concept-based curriculum and instruction models. It just makes sense, besides the support provided by brain research, that teaching to concepts, generalizations, and principles creates structures in the brain for making connections, and for seeing patterns and relationships. The systematic development of these conceptual neural networks, as children progress through the grade levels, supports efficient retrieval and transfer of knowledge on both the factual and conceptual levels.

Sousa (2006) calls transfer of learning "the most powerful principle of learning. . . . Transfer is the core of problem solving, creative thinking, and all other higher mental processes, inventions, and artistic products" (p. 135).

## Thinking Teachers for Thinking Students

It is common talk today that students who take responsibility for their learning are more interested and engaged with the subject at hand. The same holds true for teachers. Teachers who take responsibility for the design, delivery, and assessment of curriculum and instruction show greater interest and engagement with the learning process. Districts that encourage teachers to design quality lessons to use in their classrooms stimulate higher levels of thoughtfulness in teaching.

Teachers who depend on textbooks to tell them what and how to teach are not thinking. Thinking teachers work within the required curricular structure, but they personalize the design for student learning by thinking deeply and creatively about students, outcomes, and their plans for curriculum and instruction.

Effective teachers hold a clear vision of student success and challenge themselves to draw out the best efforts. They differentiate curriculum and instruction to meet the diverse learning needs of students. They think on their feet and watch for opportunities to pop provocative questions. They listen and probe for the students' thoughtful rationale.

As architects for learning, teachers realize that a classroom built on traditional, control-oriented structures is antithetical to the engagement of reasoning, creative minds. As teachers move from old models of instruction, they develop new insights:

● *Teachers need some wisdom, not all wisdom.* In the newer models of instruction, teachers have enough wisdom to know key lessons to be learned from content instruction, but they look forward to learning more lessons along with their students as they discover and share new knowledge.

● *The textbook is only one tool for gaining information.* The learning environment is resource rich, with computers, magazines, videos, books, and dialogue corners for exploring ideas among friends. The community is an extension of the classroom, and students give service to learn social responsibility and the application of knowledge to life.

● *Tight control is replaced by purposeful enthusiasm.* The teacher recognizes that a purposeful, enthusiastic search for knowledge engages the student's self-direction; the teacher becomes a structural design engineer and facilitator rather than a maintenance engineer and controller.

● *Collaborative learning allows students to participate more actively,* expands their opportunities to use and develop language, and enhances teamwork skills.

## Student Engagement and Constructivism

Although the **constructivist** terminology is popular today, the philosophical basis for the ideas has been around since the days of educators and philosophers such as Pestalozzi, Froebel, Herbart, Dewey, and James. As with most trends in education, the term "constructivist" has a continuum of interpretations.

Jacqueline Grennon Brooks and Martin G. Brooks (1993), in a booklet titled *The Case for Constructivist Classrooms,* provide a set of teaching behaviors that they believe can be used to frame the constructivist methodology. The first behavior is at the heart of a purist, constructivist philosophy, so I have provided a short extension of the thought. This is followed by the remaining teaching behaviors identified by the authors.

*Constructivist Teachers Encourage and Accept Student Autonomy*

Students take responsibility for learning by posing questions and issues and searching for answers, connections, and possible new problems. The teacher's frame for an assignment affects the degree of autonomy and student initiative for learning. Heavy lecture and overcontrol of student work robs students of opportunities to be self-reliant thinkers. According to Brooks and Brooks (1993), constructivist teachers

- Encourage and accept student autonomy and initiative
- Use raw data and primary sources, along with manipulative, interactive, and physical materials
- Use cognitive terminology such as "classify," "analyze," "predict," and "create" when framing tasks
- Allow student responses to drive lessons, shift instructional strategies, and alter content
- Inquire about students' understandings of concepts before sharing their own understanding of those concepts
- Encourage students to engage in dialogue, both with the teacher and with one another
- Encourage student inquiry by asking thoughtful, open-ended questions and encouraging students to ask questions of each other
- Seek elaboration of students' initial responses
- Engage students in experiences that might engender contradictions to their initial hypotheses and then encourage discussion
- Allow wait time after posing questions
- Provide time for students to construct relationships and create metaphors
- Nurture students' natural curiosity through frequent use of the learning cycle model (pp. 103–118)

The authors end the discussion on teaching descriptors with the following statement: "These descriptors can serve as guides that may help other educators forge personal interpretations of what it means to become a constructivist teacher" (Brooks & Brooks, 1993, p. 118).

My own interpretation of the constructivist ideas supports all of the teaching behaviors outlined in the Brooks and Brooks listing, but deviates from a purist belief system on one significant point: I believe it is possible to have students initiate the search for knowledge, discover connections, and construct personal conceptual frameworks within the context of an articulated core content curriculum. The key, as the Brooks and Brooks booklet states, is how the teacher frames the assignments. Is the area under study framed by different kinds of guiding questions that engage the students' interest and intellect?

Students do not always need to decide on the issues for study, though they should have opportunities to do so. The currently popular project approach is an example of the purist constructivist philosophy in action. An assignment of a problem, issue, concept, or topic to pursue is selected by the students or assigned by the teacher. The questions for study are open-ended and engage students in the search and construction of knowledge. My problem with using this open project approach is that it fails to address the need for a developmental core content curriculum. The articulation of a core content curriculum and expected learnings appears antithetical, in the purist perspective, to the processes of constructing and creating knowledge. The requirement today to meet defined content standards at each grade level makes the purist approaches to constructivism and project-based learning almost a moot point. We are probably tied in more tightly than we would like to be to required academic standards, so we design for learning within the required structures. But that doesn't mean we can't still use quality designs for curriculum and pedagogy.

Teachers, for example, need to know some of the key generalizations that students will discover as they work with units of study. If teachers do not have these enduring understandings in mind as they facilitate the students' search for knowledge, then how can they know which questions to ask to stimulate deeper thought and understanding?

Suppose that Mr. Jackson has engaged his high school students in a unit on the concept of "Persuasion." The theme of the unit is "Media as a Persuasive Force in American Society." Students have brainstormed many questions to guide their search for knowledge: Is the media a positive or negative force in society? How do the media affect public opinion? Who or what controls the media? What is the role of the media in a society? How do the media affect me?

Mr. Jackson begins the unit by finding out the students' prior understanding of the concept of "Persuasion." As they begin searching for answers and debating positions, Mr. Jackson uses guiding questions to challenge the students to conceptually rise above the specific examples of media persuasion. He wants them to discover the deeper ideas or generalizations related to the concept of "Persuasion." If he has not taken his own thinking to this level, then students will end their learning with simplistic answers.

For example, a simple response to the question, "How do the media affect public opinion?" might be "By using propaganda techniques to sway thinking." After discussing various propaganda techniques, the teacher continues to question, "Why do propaganda techniques work?" "Do all media use propaganda to sway public opinion in the same direction'?" "Does conflicting propaganda ensure that media is 'fair and balanced'?" "Is propaganda a positive, or a negative force, or both? Explain."

When students are given opportunities to deal with life-relevant questions, problems, and issues, they feel a need to know. They develop analytical and critical thinking skills as they research, question, dialogue, and defend positions. A particularly effective strategy asks students to take one position on an issue and then defend the polar position to gain insight into varying perspectives.

One of the problems with traditional content curriculum is that it often fails to make the significant connections to events and issues of the day. The textbook study can be dry, dull, and lack relevance for the student. The challenge for teachers is to help bring meaning to the students' learning.

One key to meaningfulness is to teach to the lessons that transfer through time, using events and content as examples rather than end products of the lessons. Another key is to help students find the connections between past and present events. A third key is to apply the teaching behaviors of a constructivist philosophy. Students who are motivated to take responsibility in the search for knowledge will see greater relevance in the content under study.

If there were one single factor that would revolutionize education and bring success for all children, I believe it would be the constructivist notion that students who are motivated to take responsibility for their learning will be successful learners. But to bring about this situation, we would need to change many traditional beliefs and practices in education:

- Teachers would need to forget the bell-shaped curve and believe that all children can and should be successful learners.
- The deficit model of grading developmental processes would have to go. The new paradigm would celebrate success as students move along the continuum in reading, writing, thinking, communicating, drawing, dramatizing, or any other developing process.
- The pursuit of trivia would be replaced by curricula that hold meaningfulness or importance for students.
- Teachers would need to continue the development of personal capacities in critical, conceptual, and creative thinking to challenge and motivate their students to even higher levels of knowing and performing.
- Curriculum and assessment would have to move from bits of study to coherent, in-depth, and conceptually integrated (interdisciplinary and intradisciplinary) units of study. Universal generalizations would be the focus for content instruction because they force the intellect to integrate conceptual and factual thinking.
- Teachers would intuitively know when to lead and when to follow in supporting each child's journey to self-responsibility.
- The current trend to have students (and teachers) self-reflect on their work according to defined criteria and standards would need to continue.

## Excellence in the Basic Skills for All

The most important job of the kindergarten, first-grade, and second-grade teachers is to ensure that every child can read, write, listen, speak, think, create, and compute. If the learning environment for these process skills is differentiated to meet different learning needs, and is positive and supportive, then the students will be successful. Academic progress helps engender a healthy esteem. It does little good to spend time on discrete self-esteem activities if the child feels like a failure every time he or she looks at a book. The time is better spent on building literacy and fostering individual creative expression. Children who are not academically successful in the primary grades usually fall farther and farther behind as they proceed through school. With a 30 percent drag at the elementary grade levels, it is no surprise that we have a 30 percent drop-out rate in high school nationwide.

Primary grade teachers, like their colleagues at other levels, have been affected by increasing curricular and societal demands. They feel (and sometimes are) compelled to teach every topic and every special program, from tarantulas to teeth. But the reality is that these teachers will not be able to meet the needs of all of their developing learners if they aren't freed from the overdemands on their classroom time. Add to the heavy curriculum the interruptions caused by intercom announcements and assemblies (a common problem in schools), and we have a serious time problem.

Students apply literacy skills in the context of content-based curricula. Teachers at the primary level should be allowed to teach to broad-based units of study in social studies and science and then apply the process skills they have been taught within the concept-based units. Art, music, and literature can fit into these units if they relate to the conceptual lens and unit title under study. Health can fit into science-based units, or may take a center focus for study. Mathematics has application across all fields of study. By teaching to broad units of study, teachers will have more time to meet the needs of individual students.

At the primary level, the teachers must directly teach students the process skills of reading, writing, and so on. *Teach directly* means focused daily instruction and opportunities for application, with the critical skills necessary for successful performance. Critical skills in reading aren't the hundreds of microskills that used to fill up the front of teachers' manuals, but they are the essential components for being able to decode words, read fluently, gain meaning, and construct knowledge. This instruction is time-consuming and challenging because of the beginning development of our youngest learners.

A final thought on reading instruction—I have observed that too many teachers in elementary and even primary grade levels are not able to listen to a child read and determine their "instructional" reading level. Furthermore, they often cannot describe the child's reading strengths and weaknesses. How can these teachers help individual children progress in reading if they cannot tell their reading level and strengths and weaknesses? A friend of mine has a son in fifth grade; this boy was lagging in reading. I suggested to her that she ask the teacher the child's instructional reading level, and what weaknesses he perceived. The teacher told her he didn't know the instructional reading level because there was no test for that, and that he didn't know what her son's reading problems were. It seems that would be an embarrassing admission for a teacher. We can't rely on reading specialists alone or special education assessments to carry the load for diagnosis. All teachers are teachers of reading development for the children in their classrooms. Where is the training breakdown for teachers like this?

# STIRRING THE HEART AND SOUL

Joanna was in the 11th grade. Her grandparents were survivors of the Holocaust. She wanted to share their story with her classmates as her English project, but knew that a simple retelling would not convey the depth of pain, degradation, and grief that spun their world in the concentration camps. Joanna spent hours talking with her grandparents, internalizing their thoughts, fears, anger, and hopes as they recounted the terrible years.

Joanna searched for the Holocaust videos that showed families being herded onto trains traveling to annihilation. She pieced film clips together to build a montage of images—fearful children clinging to mothers; husbands, wives, and babies crying as they were separated; faces of questioning, then pain; smoke paving a trail toward the heavens; and sunken eyes and gaunt bodies hanging onto fences like skeletons.

On the day of the class presentation, Joanna portrayed her grandmother as a young teenage girl, living through the Holocaust. As the video silently rolled through the stirring scenes, Joanna sat beside the monitor and poured out her grandparents' story of loss and grief, of pain and fear, of hatred and hope.

The students sat quietly, riveted on the emotional performance. Questions hung in the air: "How could humans treat other humans in this way?" "How do people find the strength to survive when their families are destroyed?" "Could this happen again?"

Joanna stirred her classmates. They felt personally involved in the human story. As a finale to the presentation, Joanna introduced her grandparents to the class. They shared how they had moved on to rebuild their lives and ended with a plea, "Never forget the lessons of the Holocaust. Be always on the lookout for man's inhumanity to man, whether it be on your own street or in a far corner of the world."

Joanna's presentation stimulated a general discussion of contemporary examples of people's inhumanity to one another. Students looked to the deeper reasons underlying the acts of inhumanity, such as fear, ignorance, and prejudice. They talked of the ramifications of inhumane acts and considered the question, "How 'civilized' are people?"

## Feeling Teachers for Feeling Students

Joanna's teacher encouraged his students to express their passion for the subject matter in their presentations. He modeled enthusiasm for thoughts, ideas, and knowledge. Whether the subject under discussion engendered empathy, anger, joy, or pride, the teacher demonstrated the role of emotion. Joanna could have told the students her grandparents' story as if she were reading an essay, but the students would not have been able to empathize with their pain. They soon would have forgotten the lessons. When feelings are tapped in a nonthreatening environment, learning can be enhanced.

Teachers as a group are caring individuals who reach out to each child, intent on fostering academic, social, and emotional development. They recognize that the child's personality is a fragile work in progress. They manage their own emotional lives privately and focus in school on supporting each child in myriad ways:

- *Modeling Values and Ethics.* Positive enthusiasm, empathy, reason, dialogue in conflict, honesty, and caring
- *Knowing and Connecting Interpersonally With Each Child.* Asking each one about their thoughts, activities, and opinions
- *Supporting Risk Taking.* Encouraging the children to try, even if they fail, and creating an environment of trust and belief in abilities
- *Building on Success.* Valuing quality effort and praising growth
- *Providing Clear Directions and Expectations.* Setting the stage for quality learning
- *Allowing and Planning for Different Patterns of Learning.* Getting out the magnifying glass to read the work of the gifted writer who discovered that by writing microscopically, one could get more thoughts on a page
- *Seeing the Giftedness in the Children Who Are Perceived to Be "Problem Children."* For instance, to focus on their strengths, the "verbal motormouth" can be a narrator, the "graffiti artist" can be an illustrator, the "takeover leader" can be a classroom helper, and the "social butterfly" can help shy students join the group.

When teachers delight in the uniqueness of children, they come to know each child well. They take time to find out a child's likes and dislikes, and his or her interests and questions. They look for the spark that each child brings and take opportunities to fan the ember into flame. They see in the shy boy a desire to lead and in the crude drawing of a little girl a unique expression of deep emotion. They mention their observations and provide opportunities, guidance, and encouragement as the children realize they have gifts to develop.

In secondary schools—where students shuffle from class to class in 50-minute intervals, and bells fragment subjects, discussions, thinking, and learning—teachers have little time to discover the unique gifts of students. With up to 150 students per day flowing in and out, the first day's greeting, "I want to get to know you," becomes a major task.

Some secondary schools have restructured the use of time, personnel, and curriculum to solve the problems of too much to teach, too little time, and too many lost teenagers. Schools-within-a-school divide the student population and assign them to a multidisciplinary team of teachers. They plan a curriculum that can be offered in longer blocks of time so that students do not have to change classes every hour. Each teacher takes responsibility for personally connecting with an assigned group of students so that each student has someone to turn to with questions or for help.

As teachers start to have more time with students in class, they become more aware of students who need help, and they draw on resources to assist. The school has open communication channels with community agencies and calls for their help when necessary. Parents are contacted when a child is having trouble in school, and joint efforts prevent growing despair.

In some schools, the same group of teachers keeps their assigned students for more than a year. This allows a greater bond of understanding and respect to develop between students and teachers. When they enter school in the fall, students pick up where they left off, and time is not lost while new teachers assess what the students know.

Many elementary schools are also keeping a group of students with one teacher for multiple years. This practice, called looping, provides greater security for the child and allows the teacher to know each child personally. A teacher may have first and second graders in his or her classroom. When the second graders move on after two years, the teacher loops back and picks up a new group of first graders to add to the returning second-year students.

Elementary teachers have always believed in nurturing the development of each child, but some feel that even a full year with a child does not provide enough time to find and foster his or her unique talents and abilities. These teachers also desire the extended years with a child to provide a smooth transition and ongoing development of their educational program.

Finally, keeping a group of students for multiple years allows students to know their teacher as a social being with dreams, interest, and talents. In a classroom that stirs the head, heart, and soul, the teacher interacts positively with students. This teacher is passionate about learning and conveys the excitement to students.

## Stimulating the Creative Spirit

When we talk of a passion for learning that stirs the heart and soul, we talk of a creative spirit—and of minds that are eager to create and deliver with enthusiasm. Just as we provide students with opportunities to dialogue for gaining insight into the meaning of content, so must we provide opportunities for students to create and evaluate through various forms of artistic expression.

Elliott Eisner (1994), in *The Educational Imagination,* discusses the idea of connoisseurship in the arts as "knowledgeable perception" and appreciation. Eisner emphasizes that perception and appreciation for a work of art require a "sensory memory" (p. 215). The connoisseur must draw from memory the sensory comparisons made over a range of experiences in a particular mode of expression. Connoisseurship, says Eisner, goes beyond mere recognition of artistic aspects to the perception of subtleties, complexities, and important aspects of a work.

The traditional educational emphases on linguistic and mathematical forms of representation and the generally weak teacher training in art instruction have shortchanged our students. How can we engender the developing qualities of a connoisseur in our children? How can we help them appreciate the subtle stories in their own work? How can we help them use the arts as a form of unique personal expression and as a way of viewing, representing, and thinking?

In *Arts and the Creation of Mind,* Eisner (2002) tells us that the arts contribute to education by "refining the senses and enlarging the imagination" (p. 4). By heightening sensory perceptions, the arts "awaken us to the world around" (p. 10). Engagement of the imagination liberates us to creatively explore new possibilities, and develops "the disposition to tolerate ambiguity . . . as we develop individual autonomy through the creative process" (p. 10).

In *Multiple Intelligences: New Horizons,* Howard Gardner (2006) provides a valuable service in reminding us to draw on the multiple intelligences of children. Spatial intelligence, expressed in part through the arts, is one form of intelligence described by Gardner. But simply providing more standardized art activities— colored cutout bunnies with cotton ball tails or paper snowflakes to frame the bulletin board—won't develop the arts intelligence to the level of subtle nuance and expression.

When students use the skills of connoisseurship to assess the work in their creative products—whether it be a piece of pottery, a dance, a visual display, or a musical presentation—they expand their intelligence by integrating technical, sensory, emotional, and interpretive ways of knowing. This unique and complex response values and supports the developing mind.

Students who learn how to express their unique thoughts and ideas through multiple modalities and disciplinary perspectives have broadened opportunities for taking personal responsibility in learning. They are not dependent on the linguistic road to independence.

# LOVING TO LEARN

## The Passionate Learner

Passion—boundless enthusiasm, zeal, interest, excitement—is the antithesis of boredom. The passionate learner is every teacher's dream. But in a room of 30, we are likely to find only a handful of these enthusiasts. What does the passionate learner look like? How can we help all children find interest and excitement in learning?

Passionate learners share their interest and enthusiasm in a variety of ways. You may see a beaming face and glistening eyes as the student proudly holds up his or her work to be admired. You notice intent concentration as a problem is solved, or a piece of work is crafted to quality. Excited talk fills the room as thoughts and ideas are shared between team members making new discoveries. Or you see the introspective child, off in a corner, engrossed in a book on rocks and minerals—a future geologist.

What do these students have in common that qualify them as passionate learners?

- *A Love of Learning.* A realization that information brings interesting ideas and that new information can be connected to prior information to solve problems and make discoveries

- *Inquisitive Minds.* Questioning attitudes that seek to know answers
- *Self-Worth.* Students who care about themselves and value their own thoughts and ideas

How easy our job would be if all students maintained these qualities throughout their school years. But the reality is that many students fail to hold these attributes for a host of reasons. Perhaps their response to a threatening environment, at home or in school, is to shut down and withdraw. Perhaps they have never discovered the joy in learning.

Teaching is an art of individual prescription. Even though we may at times teach the group, we must know every child and his or her educational needs as an individual. We cannot assume that every child will naturally be a passionate learner, with an inquisitive mind and a healthy self-ethos.

We spend so much time in school focusing on the content we teach. A few students voraciously absorb the information. They have the attributes of the passionate learner. Some students dutifully memorize the required content and enter class with their pencils poised, ready to go for the silver or bronze. And about a third of the class sit back in their chairs with a glazed look in their eyes, trying to figure out the easiest way to pass the test with the least amount of effort. Finally, we have the bottom two seat-warmers who find school so excruciatingly painful that they count the days to the time they can legally leave school.

Could we reach more of our children if we assessed the learning environment for its ability to nurture passionate learners? Are there things going on in classrooms that destroy the passion that young children bring to school? I will share some ideas in this regard, but I encourage every teacher to evaluate his or her own classroom and come up with a "Passion for Learning Index." First, list all of the attributes of the learning environment in your classroom that nurture the passionate learner. Then, in a second column, list all of the attributes that hinder the passionate learner.

For each item in the nurture column, assign plus points from 1 to 100 and minus points to items in the hinder column. The points are your subjective judgment as to the negative or positive impact value of each item. The higher the point value, the greater the positive or negative impact. Total points should not exceed 350 in either column. Table 8.1 provides a sample listing to stimulate thought.

Once the points are assigned to the nurture or hinder items, the Passion for Learning Index can be determined by subtracting the negative points from the positive. In the example provided in Table 8.1, the index is +110. This result is your assessment of how well you nurture the critical qualities found in passionate learners. The higher your score and the closer you come to 350, the more enthusiasm you should see for learning. The teacher who completed Table 8.1 needs to address some critical aspects to raise the score. This Passion for Learning Index can also be determined for your school as a whole by doing the exercise as a total staff.

**Table 8.1**     The Passion for Learning Index

| Nurtures | | Hinders | |
|---|---|---|---|
| +60 | Teacher as facilitator of learning | −50 | Occasional sarcasm directed at disruptive students |
| +50 | Support for risk taking | −80 | Deficit model for assessing process development, as in writing |
| +70 | Open dialogue; thinking focus | −30 | Too open; unclear structure for the constructivist philosophy |
| +80 | Cooperative learning | −20 | Letter grade and time-driven evaluations |
| +90 | Valuing all students; interpersonal connecting | −60 | Performances usually written or spoken rather than allowing other modalities such as art, drama, or music |
| +350 | Total | −240 | Total |

Now comes the important step: What are you going to do about your negative scores? The answer: Develop your action plan, implement your strategies for change, and monitor the results by watching those passionate learners come to life!

## A Challenge to Teachers and Parents

Most children are naturally inquisitive. You can see it in their eyes at an early age. They study their environment. You notice the thoughtfulness as they see a real kitten for the first time. Their interest is sparked, and they toddle on chubby little legs after the vanishing ball of fur—eager to grab the strange little creature and examine it more closely.

The responsibility to nurture curiosity is a challenging task. It means being patient with the pesky questions that always seem too complicated to answer: "Where do babies come from?" "Why are leaves green?" "Where did my grandpa go?"

It means expanding the experience base of the child—reading books together, traveling, hiking on nature trails, talking, sharing, laughing, playing, using all of the senses to interact with the environment and to construct conceptual perspectives.

It means positively affirming children's ideas and efforts as they explore new territory. It means realizing that children are composed of many parts—minds, hearts, emotions, and bodies—all developing toward an integrated whole. It means continually stirring the head, heart, and soul and loving all children so that they love themselves.

## SUMMARY

Teachers and parents are partners. They share the job of nurturing the head, heart, and soul of a child. In their own ways, they contribute to the development of self-esteem, confidence, and the important belief in self. They look for the child's strengths and gifts and build on each successful try. They ensure competence in the basic skills of schooling and provide experiences that continually expand what the child knows and what the child can do.

Teachers design the environment for learning. Control-oriented structures are being replaced by busy, purposeful settings where students take increasing responsibility for constructing knowledge.

New skills beckon teachers to workshops and conferences. They realize that preparing students for the future is as complex as the future itself. Teachers of today must use higher-level thinking, processing vast amounts of information related to the students they teach, the abstract and essential learnings of content, and the most effective instructional strategies for each situation. A teacher's organized mind brings clarity to complexity and focus to an educational vision.

Children who love to learn do so with their minds, hearts, and souls. Teachers who have a passion for teaching and learning and a keen interest in the development of each child engage students in wanting to know—to explore questions and issues that extend from their world.

Loving to learn is a gift. In some, it is a natural quest of an inquisitive mind. In others, it is an undiscovered well, capped with untapped talent. Creating a love of learning means discovering a wellspring of talent, supporting the flow of energy, and celebrating success along the way.

I invite you to share the gift and the secret of loving to learn—stirring the head, heart, and soul.

# Resource A

# Alternative Unit Formats

# ALTERNATIVE UNIT FORMAT I

**Course: Unit Title** _____

**Instructor** _____

**Length of Unit** _____

**Conceptual Lens**

| Key Concepts and Subconcepts | Enduring Understandings (Generalizations) and Guiding Questions | Critical Content/ Key Topics | Learning Experiences and Resources | Assessments |
|---|---|---|---|---|
| | | | | |

# ALTERNATIVE UNIT FORMAT II

**Subject** _____

**Instructor** _____

**Length of Unit** _____

**Unit Planner**

Unit Title:


Conceptual Lens:


Critical Content (Key Topics):


Critical Concepts:


Generalizations (Enduring Understandings):


Guiding Questions:


Suggested Learning Experiences (Infuse Skills):


Performance Task(s):


Other Assessments:


Resources and Tools:

# Resource B

# Key Concepts in Different Disciplines

*A Guide to Curriculum Planning in Art Education* (Wisconsin Department of Public Education, 1995) presents a nice summary of key concepts in the visual arts. Though it is an older copyright, the timeless quality of the concepts make it a viable reference even today. If we look at a concept as being timeless, universal, abstract, and represented by different examples sharing common attributes, then we can consider elements and principles of design and the elements and principles of artistic conception as being concepts representing the various levels of generality, abstractness, and complexity.

The macroconcepts of artistic conception provide a set of conceptual lenses for evaluating the quality of artistic content and form. The Wisconsin Department of Public Education art guide (1995) suggests some of these broad concepts that are key characteristics of art evaluation:

- *Authenticity.* The degree to which the work of art is an authentic statement springing from the combined knowledge, skills, experiences, and attitudes of the artist
- *Integrity.* The internal consistency of the artwork that expresses the artist's recognized style or "voice"
- *Innovation.* In studio arts, the degree to which the work differs from work done by other artists or from earlier works by the same artist
- *Insight.* A quality in a work of art that causes people to realize something about the world or themselves that had previously gone unnoticed

The principles and elements of design are the perceptual tools shaping the visual forms of artistic expression (Wisconsin Department of Public Education, 1995, p. 95). The Wisconsin guide details some of the most common principles— the broader concepts associated with the form given to artistic content:

| | |
|---|---|
| Unity | Variety |
| Balance | Harmony |
| Repetition | Contrast |
| Gradation | Dominance |

The elements of design are the specific discipline-based concepts that provide the language for discussing art. The following are some of the most common elements:

| | |
|---|---|
| Line | Shape |
| Form | Color |

| Pattern | Texture |
|---|---|
| Direction | Value |

Christina Fitzgerald, a teacher from Palmdale School District in Palmdale, California, offers the macro- and microconcepts for drama shown in Table B.1. Each macroconcept can serve as an integrating or conceptual lens on the more specific microconcepts. The microconcepts provide the language and content for exploring and evaluating the macroconcepts.

**Table B.1**  Drama Concepts

| | | Macroconcepts | | |
|---|---|---|---|---|
| Character | Movement | Voice | Theme | Design |
| | | Microconcepts | | |
| Physical | Body position | Tone | Culture | Style |
| Personality | Action/reaction | Pitch | Conflict | Meaning |
| Background | Purpose | Size | Time | Mood |
| Relationship | Order | Quality | Perspective | Structure |
| Conflict | Influence | Dialect | Beliefs/values | Function |
| Motivation | Angle | Patterns | Choices | Expression |
| Change/growth | Line | Expression | Influence | Feeling |
| Obstacle | Balance | Articulation | Diversity | Symbol |
| Wants/needs | Timing | Pronunciation | Identity | Realism |
| Habits | Space | Beat/pause | Power | Selective realism |
| Feeling/emotion | Logic | Breathing | Destruction | Setting |
| Type/role | Physical expression | Diction | Innocence | Costume |
| Purpose | Direction | Emphasis | Isolation | Lighting |

SOURCE: Christina Fitzgerald, Palmdale High School, Palmdale, California. Used with permission.

Music also has macro- and microconcepts to structure the discipline. The set of concepts shown in Table B.2 was drawn from the music curriculum at Meridian School District No. 2 , Meridian, Idaho. The microconcepts supply the language for experiencing and evaluating the macrolevel ideas.

**Table B.2** Music Concepts

| Macroconcepts | | |
|---|---|---|
| Aesthetics | Expression | Performance |
| Microconcepts | | |
| Rhythm | Rhythm | Rhythm |
| Melody | Melody | Melody |
| Harmony | Harmony | Harmony |
| Timbre | Timbre | Timbre |
| Form | Form | Form |
| Dynamics | Dynamics | Dynamics |
| Articulation | Articulation | Articulation |
| Tempo | Tempo | Tempo |
| Text | Text | Text |
| Mood | Mood | Mood |
| Culture | Culture | Culture |

SOURCE: Meridian Joint School District No. 2, Meridian, Idaho. Used with permission.

Health concepts from the Meridian School District No. 2 curriculum shown in Table B.3 show some of the many health concepts that support the macroconcepts of physical, mental or emotional, and social health.

**Table B.3** Health Concepts

| Macroconcepts | | |
|---|---|---|
| Physical wellness | Mental/emotion wellness | Social health |
| Microconcepts | | |
| Disease/disorder | Relationships | Relationships |
| Nutrition | Feelings | Communication |
| Exercise | Behaviors | Family/community |
| Safety | Rights | Coping skills |
| Choices | Responsibilities | Needs |
| Responsibility | Stress | Interdependence |
| Abuse/neglect | Coping skills | Conflict resolution |
| Change/growth | Self-esteem | Rights/responsibilities |

| | | |
|---|---|---|
| Sexuality | Anxiety | Support resources |
| Safety | Needs | Lifestyles |
| Life cycle | Conflict resolution | |
| | Choices | |
| | Symptoms/signs | |
| | Lifestyle | |
| | Anger management | |

SOURCE: Adapted from Health Curriculum, Meridian Joint School District No. 2, Meridian, Idaho. Used with permission.

NOTE: The Health Committee in the Meridian School District No. 2, in Meridian, Idaho, used these concepts to structure its curriculum.

The physical education concepts shown in Table B.4 are a combination of suggestions from Elizabeth Shawver and Michelle Verdon from Davenport Public Schools, Davenport, Iowa; and the Physical Education Curriculum Committee from the Meridian Public Schools, Meridian, Idaho. Can you reorganize these concepts under the appropriate macroconcept headings?

**Table B.4**  Physical Education Concepts

| | | |
|---|---|---|
| Space | Speed | Motion |
| Movement | Strength | Range |
| Angle | Endurance | Force/power |
| Action/reaction | Patterns | Behaviors |
| Energy | Cooperation | Weight transfer |
| Flexibility | Conflict | Growth/development |
| Physical fitness | Motor fitness | Locomotion |
| Balance | Teamwork | Cooperation |

SOURCE: Adapted from Elizabeth Shawver and Michelle Verdon, Davenport Public Schools, Davenport, Iowa, and the Physical Education Curriculum Committee, Meridian Public Schools, Meridian, Idaho. Used with permission.

The National Research Council (1996) suggests 10 integrating or macroconcepts as conceptual lenses for the content of science (see Table B.5). These are called *integrating concepts* because they can be applied across the life, earth, and physical science disciplines, and because they lead to the broadest conceptual ideas for explaining our lives and universe. In other words, the macroconcepts can be applied across all of the microconcepts. The microconcepts are a random set of concepts drawn from the national science standards (National Research Council, 1996). Notice that these microconcepts could be structured further according to their levels of generality, complexity, and abstractness.

The National Council for the Social Studies (1994) uses a set of eight conceptual themes that are actually a set of macroconcepts for the different disciplines of social studies (see Table B.6). Each set of macroconcepts emphasizes a different discipline of the social studies.

**Table B.5**  Science Concepts

| Macroconcepts | | | | |
|---|---|---|---|---|
| Systems order | Evidence models | Change constancy | Evolution equilibrium | Form function |
| Microconcepts | | | | |
| Environment | Properties | Matter | Balance | Living things |
| Entropy | Conductivity | Energy | Heredity | Natural/constructed |
| Relative distance | Similarities/differences | Transfer | Ecosystem | Organism |
| Population | Fission/fusion | Waves | Habitat | Cells |
| Patterns | Cycles | Motion | Position | Organs |
| Behavior | Waves | Force/power | Regulation | Diversity |
| Transfer | Traits | Conservation | Survival | Density |
| Interaction | Erosion | Mutation | Behavior | Conduction |
| Reproduction | Weathering | Adaptation | Natural selection | Convection |
| Niche | Fossils | Disorder | Extinction | Bonding |

SOURCE: Macroconcepts drawn from the *National Science Education Standards*. Washington, DC: National Academy Press.

**Table B.6**  Social Studies Concepts

| Macroconcepts | | | |
|---|---|---|---|
| Culture | Time, continuity, change | People, places, environments | Individual development and identity |
| Individuals, groups, institutions | Power, authority, governance | Production, distribution, consumption | Civic ideals |
| Microconcepts | | | |
| Culture | Role/status | Leadership | Freedom |
| Similarities/differences | Patterns | Government | Equality |
| Perspective | Conflict/cooperation | Limits | Citizenship |
| Behavior | Traditions | Transportation | Policy |
| Identity | Laws/rules | Communication | Supply/demand |
| Needs/wants | Interdependence | Groups/institutions | Incentives |
| Time | Common good | Origin | System |
| Change/continuity | Rights/responsibilities | Ethics/values and beliefs | Barter |
| Location/place | Environment | Customs | Exchange |
| Space/regions | Power | Influence | Markets |
| Resources | Order | Justice | Consumption |

SOURCE: Macroconcepts drawn from the *Curriculum Standards for Social Studies*. National Council for Social Studies Standards.

# Resource C

# What Work Requires of Schools

## RESOURCES: IDENTIFIES, ORGANIZES, AND ALLOCATES RESOURCES

1. *Time.* Selects goal-relevant activities, ranks them, allocates time, and prepares and follows schedules

2. *Money.* Uses or prepares budgets, makes forecasts, keeps records, and makes adjustments to meet objectives

3. *Material and Facilities.* Acquires, stores, allocates, and uses materials or space efficiently

4. *Human Resources.* Assesses skills and distributes work accordingly, evaluates performance, and provides feedback.

## INFORMATION: ACQUIRES AND USES INFORMATION

1. Acquires and evaluates information

2. Organizes and maintains information

3. Interprets and communicates information

4. Uses computers to process information

## INTERPERSONAL: WORKS WITH OTHERS

1. *Participates as Member of a Team.* Contributes to group effort

2. *Teaches Others New Skills*

3. *Serves Clients and Customers.* Works to satisfy customers' expectations

4. *Exercises Leadership.* Communicates ideas to justify position; persuades and convinces others; responsibly challenges existing procedures and policies

5. *Negotiates.* Works toward agreements involving exchange of resources, resolves divergent interests

6. *Works With Diversity.* Works well with men and women from diverse backgrounds

## SYSTEMS: UNDERSTANDS COMPLEX INTERRELATIONSHIPS

1. *Understands Systems.* Knows how social, organizational, and technological systems work and operates effectively in them

2. *Monitors and Corrects Performance.* Distinguishes trends, predicts impacts on system operations, diagnoses deviations in systems' performance, and corrects malfunctions

3. *Improves or Designs Systems.* Suggests modifications to existing systems and develops new or alternative systems to improve performance.

## TECHNOLOGY: WORKS WITH
## A VARIETY OF TECHNOLOGIES

1. *Selects Technology.* Chooses procedures, tools, or equipment, including computers and related technologies

2. *Applies Technology to Task.* Understands overall intent and proper procedures for setup and operation of equipment

3. *Maintains and Troubleshoots Equipment.* Prevents, identifies, or solves problems with equipment, including computers and other technologies

SOURCE: SCANS (1991).

# Resource D

# Sample Unit Planner

**Unit Title:** "North America"

**Conceptual Lens:** "Interactions *and* Diffusion"

**Course:** World Geography

**Teacher:** Kelly Coats

**Approximate Time Frame:** 5 weeks

## ENDURING UNDERSTANDINGS AND GUIDING QUESTIONS

| Enduring Understandings | Guiding Questions (C = Conceptual; F = Factual; P = Provocative) |
|---|---|
| 1. Human migration creates population patterns that shape the character of a place or region (e.g., urban to rural migration patterns). | 1a. What are the physical features and environmental conditions that influence migration? (C) |
| | 1b. What were the causes of the massive migration of people from east to west in the United States during the 1800s? (F) |
| | 1c. What are the push–pull factors that led to the urban to rural migration patterns in both Canada and the United States? (F) |
| | 1d. In what areas do most people in Canada live? In the United States? (F) |
| | 1e. How does human migration shape the character of a place or region? (C) |

*(Continued)*

(Continued)

| Enduring Understandings | Guiding Questions (C = Conceptual; F = Factual; P = Provocative) |
|---|---|
| 2. Migration, trade, and wars lead to the diffusion of language, religion, customs, and ideas. | 2a. What is the impact of cultural diffusion on the physical and human features of a region? (C) |
| | 2b. How did the early Spanish, French, and English explorers influence the culture of North America? (F) |
| | 2c. How have recent immigrants to the United States influenced the population patterns, culture, and economics of different regions? (C) |
| | 2d. Does cultural diffusion enhance or hinder the advancement of a society? (P) |
| 3. Human modifications of the physical environment in one place often lead to changes in other places. | 3a. How have humans adapted and changed the environment to meet their needs? (C) |
| | 3b. How can humans determine when they have "stressed" the environment? (C) |
| | 3c. What types of pollution are found in North America, and how are they affecting the environment? (F) |
| | 3d. Should all nations be concerned about environmental pollution? (F) |
| 4. Technology can be used to modify the physical environment but may cause negative environmental effects. | 4a. Why are more of the metropolitan areas of the United States and Canada beginning to experience smog? (F) |
| | 4b. What challenges do industrial cities face as the economies of these cities become more dependent on high technology? |
| | 4c. What three main innovations have had the most impact on the environments of Canada and the United States? (F) |
| | 4d. How can a nation progress economically and still preserve the environment? (P) |
| 5. A country's standard of living is related to its accessibility to natural and material resources. | 5a. Why is it important to understand and use natural resources responsibly? (C) |
| | 5b. Why are nations with abundant natural resources within their borders at an advantage in the world politically, economically, and socially? (C) |
| | 5c. Should nations with greater natural resources be required to share with less-fortunate nations? (P) |
| | 5d. What are the natural resources that have helped the United States and Canada become two of the most powerful nations in the world? (F) |

| Enduring Understandings | Guiding Questions (C = Conceptual; F = Factual; P = Provocative) |
|---|---|
| 6. Natural disasters such as hurricanes, tornadoes, floods, and earthquakes can significantly damage environmental and human systems. | 6a. What were the physical and human geographic costs of hurricanes Katrina and Rita on the United States in 2005? (F)<br><br>6b. Why has it been so difficult to reestablish the culture of New Orleans after the hurricane? (F)<br><br>6c. How can people minimize the potential for damage from hurricanes, floods, or earthquakes?(C) |
| 7. As nations realize the material benefits, they shape economies and governmental policies to promote trade relationships and networks. | *(Questions for 7 and 8 not shown here)* |
| 8. Economic activities can be classified by the degree of dependence on the natural resources of a region, as primary, secondary, tertiary, or quaternary. | |

# CRITICAL CONTENT

Students will know . . .

1. How geographic contexts and cultural diffusion in North America influenced events in the past and helped shape the present

2. How the character of the United States and Canada are related to their political, economic, social, and cultural characteristics

3. How the political, economic, social, and demographic data of the United States reflects its level of development and standards of living

4. How maps, graphs, and other geographic tools convey the size and patterns of spatial distribution in North America

5. The interrelationships among physical and human processes that shape the geographic characteristics of places in the United States such as connections among economic development, urbanization, population growth, and environmental change

6. Ways that humans depend on, modify, and adapt the physical environment and the positive and negative consequences

7. The effects of environmental conditions at different scales of impact

8. The unifying geographic characteristics of the concept of "Region" as an area of the Earth's surface

## KEY SKILLS

Students will be able to . . .

1. Use historical, geographic, and statistical information from a variety of sources such as databases, field interviews, media services, and questionnaires to answer geographic questions and to infer geographic relationships

2. Analyze and evaluate the validity and utility of multiple sources of geographic information such as primary and secondary sources, aerial photographs, and maps

3. Construct and interpret maps to answer geographic questions, infer geographic relationships, and analyze geographic change

4. Apply basic statistical concepts and analytical methods such as computer-based spreadsheets and statistical software to analyze geographic data

5. Design and draw appropriate maps and other graphics such as sketch maps, diagrams, tables, and graphs to present geographic information including geographic features, geographic distributions, and geographic relationships

6. Apply appropriate vocabulary, geographic models, generalizations, theories, and skills to present geographic information

## SAMPLE PERFORMANCE TASKS

1. You are a cultural anthropologist who has been commissioned by the National Historical Society to investigate and report on the effects of cultural diffusion on a region of the United States. After selecting a geographical region, use statistical information and census data to determine the cultural groups currently living in the area. Draw a map of the region and locate the settlements of the various cultural groups. Research primary and secondary documents using the Internet and a variety of other sources and create a table that compares the different groups on traditional elements of culture such as language, arts, food, clothing, and celebrations. Look for evidence of cultural diffusion among the various cultural groups in the present day society. Prepare a three-page written report describing your inferences and supporting rationale on how the cultural diffusion occurred in the region. Include your table of comparisons and cite your references.

2. Global warming is a controversial issue. You will be assigned a position and will debate the opposing view to the one you are assigned. The two positions are as follows:

   a. Global warming is a reality with serious environmental and human costs.

   b. Global warming is not a reality, but rather a hysterical response to normal fluctuations in weather patterns over long periods of time.

You will work with team members to research your position and prepare for a debate on the issue. Your team is to identify the geographic and scientific resources to help carry out your research, and the topics you need to address. Divide the research responsibilities among group members. Collectively organize your research and outline your points in preparation for the debate. Defend your position by providing researched evidence. Use longitudinal weather trend data, scientific studies, empirical evidence, and analyses by noted scientists to support your position.

Debate your points of view in front of a subcommittee of the Environmental Protection Agency (EPA) and end your debate by discussing these questions with the EPA subcommittee:

- When a debate concerning matters of survival is stalemated, what is an acceptable course of action?
- Whose responsibility is it to act on the problem?

**Scoring guides** will be developed by the teacher for these performance tasks.

# OTHER FORMS OF EVIDENCE

- Quizzes
- Critical content tests
- Regional maps showing locations of settlements

# LEARNING EXPERIENCES

1. Cultural diffusion is the spread of such things as customs, ideas, products, and language to other regions through trade, migration, and wars. The United States has spurred cultural diffusion throughout the world.

   - In your cooperative group, brainstorm products or concepts that have been diffused around the world, starting in the United States (e.g., Starbucks, McDonald's, music, clothing). In your group, discuss how these items got from the United States to other countries.

- Now brainstorm items that other countries and cultures have spread from other countries into the United States.
- Create a Venn diagram with another group that shows specific products or concepts that have been spread from the United States to other countries and the specific products or concepts that have been diffused into the United States. In the overlap, put the common categories of diffusion (e.g., language and music).

2. Create a population density map of the United States and Canada. Overlay the population density map on a topographical map showing the landforms and resources. Write a three-paragraph summary describing the relationship between the density of the population in various areas and the geographical features.

SOURCE: Kelly Coats, Channelview Independent School District, Channelview, Texas. Used by permission.

# Glossary

**Benchmark.** An agreed-on developmental milepost to reach required academic standards.

**Career and technical education.** The current trend to infuse stronger academic content and skills into career and technical education programs to prepare students for higher education as well as for the workplace.

**Concept.** Mental construct that frames a set of examples sharing common attributes; timeless, universal, and abstract (to varying degrees). Examples: cycles, diversity, and interdependence.

**Conceptual lens.** A concept serving as a conceptual focus for a topic-based study. Pulls thinking to the conceptual level, and integrates thinking between the factual and conceptual levels.

**Constructivist.** A philosophy and methodology for teaching and learning that highlights the student construction of knowledge on a path to learner autonomy.

**Cooperative learning.** A teaching strategy that groups students in pairs or teams to problem solve, discover, and discuss ideas or investigate topics of interest. Maximizes the use of language and the intellect.

**Curriculum.** The content, concepts, generalizations, and skills that requires the learner to construct knowledge, understanding, attitudes, values, and skills through a complex interplay of mind, materials, and social interactions.

**Curriculum framework.** A planning guide for educators. States subject area content and process outcomes in general terms.

**Developmentally appropriate.** The match between the learning task and the student's cognitive, social, or physical ability to perform the task successfully.

**Integration.** A cognitive process. Uses a conceptual lens to integrate thinking between the factual and conceptual levels.

**Interdisciplinary.** A variety of disciplines sharing a common focus for study. Must be integrated through the use of a conceptual lens.

**Intradisciplinary.** A single discipline study. Must be integrated through the use of a conceptual lens.

**Multidisciplinary.** A variety of disciplines coordinated to a topic of study that lacks a conceptual focus.

**Objective.** A specific statement of what the students need to know, with specific content or skill focus. Measurable, usually by paper-and-pencil test.

**Performance assessment.** A complex demonstration of content knowledge and performance assessed according to a standard and a set of criteria. Shows what students know, understand, and can do.

**Performance indicator.** An observable behavior that reflects a point on a skill or knowledge continuum.

**Process skill.** An internal student ability that develops in sophistication over time. Examples are reading, writing, speaking, thinking, drawing, singing, and dramatizing.

**Scoring guide.** A multilevel set of criteria to show or measure development in assessing work or performance toward a standard.

**Standard.** An agreed-on definition of quality performance.

**Systems thinking.** A framework for looking at interrelationships and patterns of change over time (Senge, 1999, 2006). Critical for successful school restructuring.

**Topical theme.** A unit title that does not include a concept. Example: "The Amazon Rainforest."

**Tripartite model of curriculum design.** A balanced approach to concepts, critical content, and developmental processes in teaching and assessment.

**Universal generalization.** Two or more concepts stated as a relationship. Enduring understandings; the "big ideas" related to the critical concepts and topics of a subject. Generalizations transfer through time, across cultures, and across supporting examples: "Representative governments rely on citizen participation," "Living organisms adapt to changing environments."

# References

Arizona Department of Education. (2007). *Career and technology education*. Phoenix, AZ: Author.

Banks, J. A. (1991). *Teaching strategies for ethnic studies*. Boston: Allyn & Bacon.

Bloom, B., Englehart, M. Furst, E., Hill, W., & Krathwohl, D. (1956). *Taxonomy of educational objectives: The classification of educational goals. Handbook I: Cognitive domain*. New York, Toronto: Longmans, Green.

Bracey, G. (2005). *The 15th Bracey report on the condition of public education*. Bloomington, IN: Phi Delta Kappan.

Brooks, J. G., & Brooks, M. G. (1993). *The case for constructivist classrooms*. Alexandria, VA: Association for Supervision and Curriculum Development.

Buzan, T. (2002). *Mind maps for kids*: *Max your memory and concentration*. New York: Penguin.

Caine, R. N., & Caine, G. (1991). *Teaching and the human brain*. Alexandria, VA: Association for Supervision and Curriculum Development.

Caine, R. N., Caine, G., McClintic, C., & Klimek, K. (2005). *12 Brain/mind learning principles in action*: *The fieldbook for making connections, teaching, and the human brain*. Thousand Oaks, CA: Corwin Press.

Center for Immigration Studies. (2001). Immigrants in the United States—2000: A snapshot of America's foreign-born population. http://www.cis.org/articles/2001/back101.html

DuFour, R., Eaker, R., & DuFour, R. (Eds.). (2005). *On common ground*: *The power of professional learning communities*. Bloomington, IN: The Solution Tree.

Eisner, E. W. (1994). *The educational imagination*. New York: Macmillan.

Eisner, E. W. (2002). *The arts and the creation of mind*. New Haven and London: Yale University Press.

Erickson, H. L. (1995). *Stirring the Head, Heart, and Soul: Redefining Curriculum and Instruction*. Thousand Oaks, CA: Cowin Press.

Erickson, H. L. (2007). *Concept-based curriculum and instruction for the thinking classroom*. Thousand Oaks, CA: SAGE.

Gardner, H. (1999). *The disciplined mind.* New York: Simon & Schuster.

Gardner, H. (2006). *Multiple intelligences: New horizons.* New York: Basic Books.

Greider, W. (1997). *One world, ready or not: The manic logic of global capitalism.* New York: Simon & Schuster.

Hayes-Jacobs, H. (1997). *Mapping the big picture: Integrating curriculum and assessment K–12.* Alexandria, VA: Association for Supervision and Curriculum Development.

Hayes-Jacobs, H. (Ed.). (2004). *Getting results with curriculum mapping.* Alexandria, VA: Association for Supervision and Curriculum Development.

International Baccalaureate Organization. (2007). *A basis for practice: The middle years programme.* Geneva: Author. www.ibo.org

Johnson, D. W., Johnson, R. T., & Holubec, E. J. (1993). *Cooperation in the classroom* (6th ed.). Edina, MN: Interaction Book Company.

Johnson, D. W., Johnson, R. T., & Stanne, M. B. (2000, May). *Cooperative learning methods: A meta-analysis.* Minneapolis, MN: University of Minnesota. http://www.co-operation.org/pages/cl-methods.html

Kroll, M., & Paziotopoulos, A. (1995). *Literature circles: Practical strategies for responding to literature.* Darien, IL: Author.

National Assessment of Educational Progress (NAEP). (2005, July). *NAEP 2004 trends in academic progress: Three decades of student performance in reading and mathematics.* Pub. #NCES 2005463. Washington, DC: National Center for Education Statistics.

National Center on Education and the Economy (NCEE). (2007). *Tough choices or tough times: The report of the new commission on the skills of the American workforce.* San Francisco: Jossey-Bass Publishers.

National Council for the Social Studies (NCSS). (1994). *National standards for the social studies.* Washington, DC: Author.

National Council of Teachers of Mathematics. (2000). *Principles and standards for teaching mathematics.* Reston, VA: Author.

National Research Council. (1996). *National science education standards.* Washington, DC: National Academy Press.

Northwest Educational Regional Laboratory. (2000). K–3 Developmental Continuum for Reading. Portland, OR: Author.

Partnership for 21st Century Skills. (2002). *Learning for the 21st century: A report and mile guide for 21st century skills.* Tucson, AZ: Author. http://www.21stcenturyskills.org/index.php?option=com_content&task=view&id=29&Itemid=42

Paul, R. W., & Elder, L. (2006). *Critical thinking: Tools for taking charge of your learning and your life.* Boston: Pearson Prentice-Hall.

Plentiful, productive—and illegal. (2006, April 2). *New York Times.* http://graphics.nytimes.com/images/2006/04/02/weekinreview/02broder_graph.gif

Popham, W. J. (2006). *Assessment for educational leaders.* Boston: Pearson Education, Inc.

Rothstein, R., & Jacobsen, R. (2006). The goals of education. *Phi Delta Kappan,* December, 264–72.

Ruffing, K. (n.d.). The history of career clusters. http://www.careertech.org/uploaded_files/The_History_of_Career_Clusters_by_Katherine_Ruffing.doc, or at National Association of State Directors of Career Technical Education Consortium, Career Clusters, http://www.careertech.org/show/publications

Schmidt, W. H., McKnight, C. C., & Raizen, S. (1997). *A splintered vision: An investigation of U.S. science and mathematics education*. U.S. National Research Center for the Third International Mathematics and Science Study (TIMSS). Dordrecht/Boston/London: Kluwer Academic Publishers.

Secretary's Commission on Achieving Necessary Skills (SCANS). (1991). *What work requires of schools: A SCANS report for America 2000*. Washington, DC: U.S. Department of Labor, Secretary's Commission on Achieving Necessary Skills.

Senge, P.M.(1990) *The fifth discipline: The art and practice of the learning organization*. London: Century.

Senge, P. M. (1999). *The dance of change: The challenge of sustaining momentum in learning organizations*. New York: Doubleday.

Senge, P. M. (2006). *The fifth discipline: The art and practice of the learning organization* (5th ed.). New York: Doubleday.

Silberman, M. (1996). *Active learning: 101 strategies to teach any subject*. Boston: Allyn & Bacon.

Sousa, D. A. (2006). *How the brain learns* (3rd ed.). Thousand Oaks, CA: Corwin Press.

Taba, H. (1966). *Teaching strategies and cognitive functioning in elementary school children*. Cooperative research project. Washington, DC: Office of Education, U.S. Department of Health, Education, and Welfare.

Tomlinson, C. A., & Eidson, C. C. (2003a). *Differentiation in practice: A resource guide for differentiating curriculum, Grades K–5*. Alexandria. VA: Association for Supervision and Curriculum Development.

Tomlinson, C. A., & Eidson, C. C. (2003b). *Differentiation in practice: A resource guide for differentiating curriculum, Grades 5–9*. Alexandria. VA: Association for Supervision and Curriculum Development.

Tomlinson, C. A., & Strickland, C. A. (2005). *Differentiation in practice: A resource guide for differentiating curriculum, Grades 9–12*. Alexandria. VA: Association for Supervision and Curriculum Development.

Thurow, L. (1993). *Head to head: The coming economic battle among Japan, Europe, and America*. New York: Warner.

Thurow, L. (1999). *Building wealth: New rules for individuals, companies and countries in a knowledge-based economy*. New York: HarperCollins.

United Nations International Children's Emergency Fund (UNICEF). (1999). *United Nations convention on the rights of children* [Online]. www.unicef.org/publications/files/pub_sowc00_en.pdf

United Nations International Children's Emergency Fund (UNICEF). (2005). *Child poverty in rich countries*. Prepared by the Innocenti Research Centre in Florence, Italy [Online]. http://www.unicef-icdc.org/publications/index.html http://www.unicefirc.org/cgi-bin/unicef/Lunga.sql?ProductID=376

U.S. infant survival rates lower than most developed nations. (2006, May 9). *Medical News Today*. http://www.medicalnewstoday.com/articles/43094.php

Vaughn, J. L., & Estes, T. H. (1986). *Reading and reasoning beyond the primary grades*. Boston: Allyn & Bacon.

Wiggins, G. (1998). *Educative assessment: Designing assessments to inform and improve student performance*. San Francisco: Jossey-Bass.

Wiggins, G., & McTighe, J. (1999). *Understanding by design*. Alexandria, VA: Association for Supervision and Curriculum Development.

Wiggins, G., & McTighe, J. (2005). *Understanding by design* (expanded 2nd ed.). Alexandria, VA: Association for Supervision and Curriculum Development.

Wineburg, S. (1999). Historical thinking and other unnatural acts. *Phi Delta Kappan, 80*(7), 488–99.

Wineburg, S. (2001). *Historical thinking and other unnatural acts*. Philadelphia: Temple University Press.

Wisconsin Department of Public Education. (1995). *A guide to curriculum planning in art education* (2nd ed.). Milwaukee: Author.

# Index

Page references followed by *fig* indicate illustrated figures or photographs; followed by *t* indicate a table.

CORWIN
PRESS

The Corwin Press logo—a raven striding across an open book—represents the union of courage and learning. Corwin Press is committed to improving education for all learners by publishing books and other professional development resources for those serving the field of PreK–12 education. By providing practical, hands-on materials, Corwin Press continues to carry out the promise of its motto: **"Helping Educators Do Their Work Better."**

Made in the USA
Lexington, KY
07 May 2013